The BIG PENCIL PASTIMES® BOOK of Crosswords

James F. Minter

B

Bristol Park Books

First Bristol Park Books edition published in 2006.
Abridged from The New Mammoth ® Book of Crossword Puzzles.

Bristol Park Books, Inc.
450 Raritan Center Parkway
Edison, NJ 08837

Bristol Park Books is a registered trademark of Bristol Park Books, Inc.

Pencil Pastimes ® is a registered trademark of Bristol Park Books, Inc.

Published by arrangement with Crosstown Publications.

ISBN: 0-88486-379-4

Printed in the United States of America.

CONTENTS

PUZZLES

ACROSS

1. Coral or Red
4. Tie
8. — Valley, California
12. Used to be
13. Apiece
14. Biblical garden
15. Viper
16. Yellow vegetable: 2 wds.
18. Taunt
20. Mild oath
21. Steak order
23. Smooth, shiny paint
27. Rattling noise
30. Govern
31. Floor covering
32. Racing boat
35. Compass point
36. Border on
38. Tow truck
40. Next to
43. British streetcar
44. Depend (on)
46. Tip over
49. Certain legumes: 2 wds.
53. Majors or Marvin
54. — out, supplemented
55. Hint
56. Mine output
57. Actor Hackman
58. Take care of
59. Bob the head

DOWN

1. Hit sharply
2. Relieve
3. Spear-shaped vegetable
4. Arid regions
5. Unrefined
6. Scored in tennis
7. At what location?
8. What bees collect
9. Fuss
10. The "P" in RPM
11. Blyth or Miller
17. Light brown
19. Was seated
22. Snaky fish
24. Gourd fruit
25. Otherwise
26. Evil look
27. Crustacean
28. Oil from petroleum
29. Tier
33. Scrap: archaic
34. Read
37. Harangue
39. Bottle top
41. Society girl, for short
42. Choose
45. Ivy-League school
47. Roman emperor
48. Act
49. Table part
50. Presidential nickname
51. Males
52. Convent dweller

ACROSS

1. Links sport
5. Chief executive: abbr.
9. Serviceman's address: abbr.
12. Wicked
13. Graceful rhythm
14. Immediately
15. Jules Verne captain
16. Make brave
18. Psychic wound
20. Eros
21. Make a grating sound
23. Stage items
26. Dampness
30. Fencing sword
31. "Ode on a Grecian —"
32. Cave-dwelling dwarf
34. Suffix meaning "full of"
35. Secure
37. Attempt
39. Fill with joy
41. Ages
42. Baby's word
44. Imp
48. Two or more naval squadrons
51. A Great Lake
52. Note of debt: abbr.
53. Set; put
54. Detective, — Wolfe
55. Certain health pros: abbr.
56. Prefix meaning "within"
57. Adolescent

DOWN

1. Polite fellow
2. Above
3. Peru's capital
4. Baking items
5. Enjoyment
6. Edge of cup
7. Napoleon's island of exile
8. Type of jazz dance, the —
9. New Soviet leader
10. Author of "The Purloined Letter"
11. Possess
17. Folk knowledge
19. Man's nickname
22. Inclined (to)
24. Mexican monetary unit
25. Clairvoyant
26. Terpsichore, for one
27. Spoken
28. Vile
29. Legendary land: 2 wds.
33. Singer Horne
36. State: French
38. Agreement
40. Writer Zola
43. Actor Arkin
45. Algonquian Indian
46. Yorkshire river
47. Former Spanish kingdom
48. Kind of pine
49. Actor Chaney
50. Jar cover

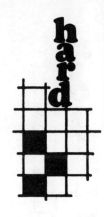

2

ACROSS

1. Jar cover
4. Male singer
9. Rap
12. Native mineral
13. Roused from sleep
14. Woman's name
15. Fuel
16. Kitten's cry
17. Burrowing creatures
19. Looks at
21. Opposite of highest
22. Pointed weapon
24. Dwells
25. Harbor
26. Walking sticks
27. Informal greeting
29. Social insect
30. Armored vehicles
31. Naughty
32. Compass point: abbr.
33. Toils
34. Summon
35. Birthday event
36. Light boat
37. Flight of steps
39. Wind instrument
40. Squander
41. In favor of
42. Show drowsiness
45. Likely
46. Slipknot loop
48. Breeze
49. Golf mound
50. Lock of hair
51. Foxy

DOWN

1. Piece of firewood
2. Man's name
3. Cake or pie
4. Lion trainer
5. Female sheep
6. At this time
7. All right, for short
8. Takes away
9. Ceramic pieces
10. Fruit drinks
11. Gone by
18. Is in debt
20. Dine
21. Chain parts
22. Reach across
23. Corn bread
24. Gangling
26. Horse-drawn vehicles
27. Ring of light
28. Not busy
30. Raging flood
31. Tropical fruit
33. Linger
34. Taxi
35. Glue's kin
36. Heals
37. Strike, as a fly
38. Bandage securer
39. Throw lightly
41. Enemy
43. Lubricate
44. In need of moisture
47. Rain — shine

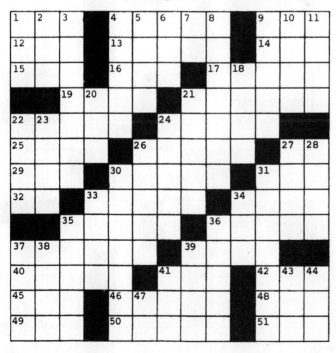

3

ACROSS

1. Thin nail
5. Certain radios, for short
8. Dissolve
12. Citrus fruit
13. Shack
14. Locality
15. Lyric poems
16. Fruit drink
17. Vocalize
18. Kind
20. Way of entry
22. Bob Hope specialty
23. Barnyard sound
24. Kitchen appliance
28. The — day, recently
32. Word with "port" and "mail"
33. House pet
35. Affirmative vote
36. Absorbent fabric
39. Discussed
42. Glutton
44. Rower's need
45. Roundabout way
48. Words of a song
52. Sour
53. In the past
55. First man
56. Cry of delight
57. Droop
58. Symbol of servitude
59. Bows drowsily
60. Secret agent
61. Large number

DOWN

1. Shapeless lump
2. Thumb a —, hitchhike
3. So be it
4. Map out; invent
5. Altered
6. Undeveloped plant
7. Hot vapor
8. Team's "good luck" animal
9. Great Lake
10. Optical glass
11. Labels
19. Wander idly
21. Dove sound
24. Flying mammal
25. Recline
26. Make a mistake
27. Fishing pole
29. Milliner's product
30. Scrutinize
31. Scarlet
34. Science of the earth
37. Greek island
38. One of us
40. Arm of the sea
41. Fine clothes
43. Lawn herbage
45. Daybreak
46. Reflected sound
47. Neck and neck
49. Object of worship
50. Bakery item
51. Diving duck
54. Ravine

ACROSS

1. Little child
4. Trousers
9. Marry
12. What we breathe
13. Black
14. Type of poem
15. Crowded mess
17. Woman's name, for short
19. Lunch or dinner
20. — by, adhered to
21. Ward off
23. Trudges
24. Kiln
25. Name
26. Pickup or flatbed: abbr.
28. Morsel
29. Window sections
30. Triumphant cry
31. — Dorado, legendary land
32. Baffling question
33. Wound mark
34. Pub game
35. — B. De Mille
36. King's son
38. Butter substitute
39. Dog's lead
40. Boulevards
43. Slippery fish
44. Enthusiastic
46. Forty winks
47. Hirt and Pacino
48. Long-legged bird
49. Make an effort

DOWN

1. Tic-—-toe, child's game
2. Lubricate
3. Brass instrument
4. Flower feature
5. Eve's son
6. Oslo's country: abbr.
7. "Volunteer State": abbr.
8. Emblems
9. Dictionary entries
10. Border
11. Act
16. Young adult, for short
18. Assistant
20. Change
21. Kimono
22. Wrongdoing
23. Cone-bearers
25. Flavor
26. Siamese
27. A Marx
29. Verandas
30. Charge —, credit arrangement
32. Skillets
33. Observed
34. Radio controls
35. Office worker
36. Urgent request
37. Film spool
38. Above
40. Before now
41. Corn unit
42. Mata Hari or 007
45. One — a time, singly

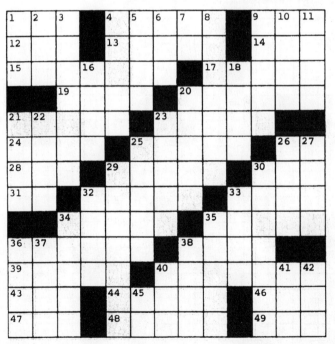

ACROSS

1. Coin opening
5. Linger
9. Statute
12. Musical sound
13. Never: 3 wds.
15. Cruising
16. Heavy weight
17. Invasion
18. Exist
19. Dress border
20. Birthday greetings
21. — off, diminish gradually
24. Knock sharply
25. Striped animal
26. Baseball club
27. — on, encourage
30. So be it!
31. Light brown
32. Urgent request
33. Sleeping place
34. Distant
35. Endures
36. Atlas item
37. Factions
38. Loafed; loitered
41. Conclude
42. Light-switch word
44. Close by
45. Miss Gabor
46. Adore
48. Assume command: 2 wds.
50. Fruit drinks
51. Lode load
52. In this place
53. Saucy

DOWN

1. Take a — at, attempt
2. Go slow, as a watch: 2 wds.
3. Dollar bill
4. Afternoon party
5. Irrigate
6. Tiny particle
7. Traveler's stop
8. At
9. Fibber
10. Among
11. Marries
14. Catch unawares
19. That woman
20. Mouser
22. Ripened
23. Writing tool
24. Sprinted
25. Restaurant bill
26. Prohibit
27. Otherwise
28. Recovers from: 2 wds.
29. Cooking fuel
31. Spigot
32. Cushion
34. Craze
35. Pot cover
36. Only
37. See 14-Down
38. Division word
39. Affectionate term
40. Huron or Erie
41. Always
43. Bird's home
45. Preholiday night
46. Baby's seat, sometimes
47. Lyric poem
49. Cry of surprise

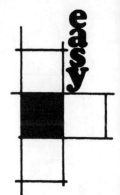

ACROSS

1. Swine
5. Golf score
8. Attire
12. Knowledge
13. Highest card
14. Declare
15. Mine entrance
16. Confused rush
18. Cans
19. — with, support
20. Born
21. Finale
22. Numerous
23. Elderly
24. Reposing
26. Stalks
27. Soaked
28. Also
29. Discolor
32. Bavarians
36. Clue
37. Real-estate map
38. Allow
39. Noah's boat
40. Three-petaled flower
41. Mast
42. Fence stake
44. Become weary
45. Paradise
46. German article
47. Once more
48. Escritoire
49. CIA's predecessor: abbr.
50. Bunks

DOWN

1. Inferior racehorse
2. Antiseptic
3. Pulverizes
4. Cliques
5. *En* —, chess term
6. Behaving
7. Prepared
8. Interruption
9. Justly punish
10. Deliver from sin
11. Varieties, as of dogs
17. One of us
22. Manner
23. Tiny particle
25. Taunt
26. Type
28. Puzzling problems
29. Formed
30. Angry speech
31. Leg joints
32. Moves smoothly
33. Of high mountains
34. Approached
35. Scatters
37. Madrid museum
40. Exists
41. Pierce
43. Writing fluid

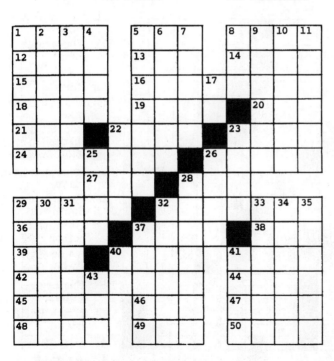

ACROSS

1. Educate
6. Turf
11. Spanish explorer
12. Improvise, as equipment: 2 wds.
13. Accede
14. Reflection
15. Plant problem
16. Grand —, Wyoming peak
18. Pastoral god
19. Thatching palm
21. Determined
22. Lively
23. Untamed
25. Hoarfrost
27. Beverage packaging: 2 wds.
29. Habit
33. Vega's constellation
35. Melba or Roger
36. Plus
39. Taxing group: abbr.
41. Convince
42. Witticism
43. Soda sipper
45. Word with "cake" or "down"
46. Unsuitable
48. Mother-of-pearl source
50. Italian port
51. Rustics
52. Neatness
53. Spirited mount

DOWN

1. Trumpet fanfare
2. Spanish articles
3. Help in wrongdoing
4. Geometric shapes
5. Member of Alice's tea party
6. Happy look
7. Edge
8. Wide open
9. Canister marking
10. "Pooped"
11. Baby's knitted shoe
13. Manual art
17. Of the ear
20. Picasso or Casals
22. Money of Acapulco
24. Non-professional
26. Silent
28. Pluck
30. Slight advantage
31. Popular synthetics
32. Free-for-all
34. Impressive displays
36. Friend, in the Southwest
37. Hermitlike person
38. Abide
40. Dutch shoe
43. Castor or Pollux
44. North Pacific island
47. U.S. author
49. A Grant

ACROSS

1. Affirmative vote
4. Additional
8. Bowling targets
12. Irk
13. Track-shaped
14. Castle, in chess
15. Viper
16. Recent
17. Spiteful
18. Biblical garden
20. Operatic solo
21. Bother
23. Flower
26. Roster
27. Derrick
28. Behold!
29. High card
30. Fame
31. Speak up at an auction
32. Myself
33. Coffee lightener
34. Rescue
35. Grove
37. Tourist's stop
38. Class; status
39. Jargon
40. Endure
42. Prohibit
43. Age
46. Drawn-out
47. Make a green salad
48. Sprint
49. Harness for oxen
50. Vow
51. Still

DOWN

1. Actress Gardner
2. Of course!
3. Cost; outlay
4. Legal tender
5. Baker's need
6. Uncooked
7. Overhead railway
8. Laud
9. Particles
10. Negative word
11. Wild blue yonder
17. Buddy
19. Freckle
20. Scare
21. Texas shrine
22. More congenial
23. Wide
24. Yellowish-green color
25. Cheryl Tiegs is one
27. Salesperson
30. Magnificent
31. Flashlight part
33. Alter
34. Shem, to Noah
36. Machine handle
37. Severe
39. Play's actors
40. Crafty
41. Also
42. Tropical snake
44. Regret
45. Picnic intruder
47. Fro's "companion"

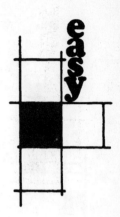

ACROSS

1. Court divider
4. Try; test
9. Crosscut item
12. Metallic rock
13. Rental document
14. Boxing great
15. Lagged behind
17. Book of maps
19. Beaver project
20. Cooking fat
21. Christmas greenery
24. Grew weaker
25. Fencing sword
26. Massachusetts city
27. Exist
29. Dusting cloth
30. Furry aquatic mammal
31. Skillet
32. Overhead railway
33. Secret agents
34. Curve; flex
35. Guide, as a car
36. Engagement symbols
37. Twirlers' sticks
39. Coniferous tree
40. Marry secretly
41. Causing to go
45. Snakelike fish
46. Garden tools
48. Female deer
49. Lawyer's charge
50. Manner
51. Cobbler's tool

DOWN

1. Negative word
2. Blunder
3. Hot or cold beverage
4. Calm, as fear
5. Appear to be
6. Depressed
7. While
8. Wishful person
9. Word with "potato" or "tossed"
10. Woe is me!
11. Opposite of foolish
16. Doing nothing
18. Abound; swarm
20. Strong winds
21. In this place
22. Iridescent gem
23. Table support
24. H₂O
26. Pigpens
27. Explosive sound
28. Terminates
30. Leadoff games of series
31. Ballpoint item
33. Cease
34. Robin or pigeon
35. Pilfered
36. Wash lightly
37. Meat
38. To the sheltered side
39. Sense
41. Firmament
42. Actress Lupino
43. Today
44. Become solid
47. Near

ACROSS

1. Fence opening
4. Bend forward
9. Light-switch word
12. Every one
13. Coronet
14. Fib
15. Harbor
17. Hunter's cabin
19. Ice-cream holder
20. Fill with cargo
21. Frighten
23. Writes down
26. Urban oasis
27. Undersea explorer
28. Exclamation
29. Finish
30. Conceals
31. Mongrel dog
32. Certainly not!
33. Buyer
34. Box
35. Wants
37. Drilled a hole in
38. Chickens
39. Cat's sound
40. Stood up
42. Enclosed field
45. Newsman Rather
46. Playground equipment
48. Foot part
49. Monkey
50. Meaning
51. Secret agent

DOWN

1. Cooking fuel
2. Pub drink
3. Poster
4. Rock
5. Grow weary
6. Cereal grain
7. Now — never
8. Castles
9. More aged
10. Fruit
11. Lawyer's charge
16. Kind of meat
18. Scent
20. Crowbar
21. Use up money
22. Light boat
23. Goes by bus
24. Drench
25. Fragment
27. Protective dams
30. Horse's gear
31. Root vegetables
33. Gifts for men
34. String
36. Gave light
37. Move slightly
39. Skillets
40. Woman's name
41. Knock
42. Brooch
43. Policeman: slang
44. Door unlocker
47. You and I

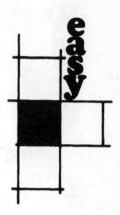

ACROSS

1. Checkers play
5. Dalmatian marking
9. Sacred; holy
11. Flower, rose of —
13. Irregular
14. Football "conference"
15. Dreadful
16. Jog
18. Pub quaff
19. Grid position
20. Decree
21. Perished
22. Rule
24. Blustery
25. Qualified voter
27. Miss Mercer of music
30. Connection
33. Finished
34. Sanctions
35. Small piece
37. Lair
38. Great in size
39. Lady: Italian
40. Part of U.S.A.
42. Bursts forth
44. Cloyingly sweet
45. Spending money in Pakistan
46. Begrudge
47. Fix

DOWN

1. Prospector's activity
2. Exaggerate
3. French exclamation of acclaim
4. Compass point
5. Close
6. Cushion
7. Predetermine
8. Rang, as a church bell
9. Any male: slang
10. Whole
11. Inoculation
12. Indigent
17. Western farms, often
20. Dropped
21. English actor, — Bogarde
23. Swerve
24. Courts
26. Be unsteady
27. — *operandi*, procedure
28. Fifth or Park
29. Not malignant
31. Closed
32. Kicked (a football)
34. "My Fair —," 1964 film
36. Food fish
38. Extremely
39. Deceive by trickery
41. Letter of the Hebrew alphabet
43. Island brew

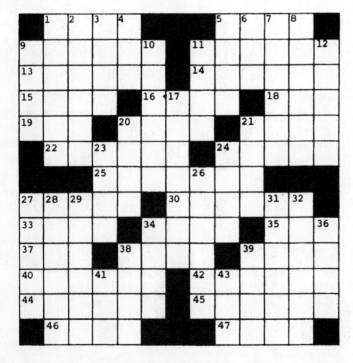

12

ACROSS

1. Applaud
5. Threaded nail
10. Cost
11. Swaps
13. Highway dividers
14. "Fink": slang
15. Droop
17. Had lunch
18. Strong cord
20. Haberdashery item
21. Robin's home
23. Gorilla or gibbon
24. Hit hard: slang
25. Uncommon
27. Skin openings
28. Sty sound
30. Discovered
31. Summit
32. Borsch vegetable
33. Sentry's command
34. Exist
35. Lumber cutters
39. Girl's name
40. Venetian-blind parts
42. Scary word
43. Household animal
44. Cargo unit
45. Fragrance
47. Cause to remember
49. Relocation aide
50. Challenges
51. Paradise

DOWN

1. Shipping container
2. Fishing cords
3. High card
4. Annoyance
5. "Hash mark"
6. Lifting device
7. Cost per unit
8. Asner or Wynn
9. Cowboy movie
10. Blueprint
12. Went by boat
16. Obtains
19. — hog, African wild hog
22. Have faith in
24. Boxing contests
26. Picnic pest
27. American poet
28. Exam marker
29. Akin
30. On one's —, standing
31. Fellow
32. Trademarks
34. Unattended
36. On top of
37. Adult females
38. Fly aloft
40. Mix
41. Identical
46. Fishing pole
48. Pa's mate

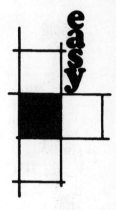

13

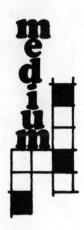

ACROSS

1. Keep out
4. Tidy
8. Bridge
12. Driving hazard
13. Competent
14. Window square
15. Winter month
17. "Say It — So"
18. Singles
19. Washes lightly
21. Tarots
23. Ms. Fonda
24. Pot covers
25. Clock sound
29. Lemon drink
30. "The Many — of Dobie Gillis"
31. Hawaiian dish
32. Scents
34. Ballpoints
35. Cry of woe
36. Exposes
37. Outcome
40. Hawaiian dance
41. Mr. Sevareid
42. Go too far
46. Baseball team
47. Be all —, listen eagerly
48. Have debts
49. Exam
50. Coin groove
51. Agent: abbr.

DOWN

1. Auction offer
2. High card
3. Taping machine
4. Titles
5. Wanes
6. Pub order
7. Patios
8. Small piano
9. Go by
10. Ms. Baxter
11. Meshed fabrics
16. Odds and —
20. Writing fluids
21. Applaud
22. Military assistant
23. Does the boogie-woogie
25. Salad ingredients
26. Telephone company employee
27. Ice-cream holder
28. "— Me Kate"
30. Brief period of quiet
33. Spigot
34. Friends
36. Explode, as a balloon
37. Lease
38. Cleveland's lake
39. Transgressions
40. Idol
43. Girl's nickname
44. Ram's mate
45. Vim and vigor

ACROSS

1. Golf score
4. Recumbent
9. College degrees: abbr.
12. Pub drink
13. Great privilege
14. Every one
15. Word describing a ballerina
17. Indian princess
19. Window glass
20. Fountain treat
21. Pure air: slang
23. Harold Robbins' "The —"
24. Place for a lily pad
25. Medium for "The Shadow"
26. Eastern State: abbr.
28. Conclusion
29. Pale purple
30. Nearest star
31. Direction: abbr.
32. Small mallet
33. Flat-bottomed boat
34. Orthopedists' concerns
35. Judgment
36. Actress Donahue
38. Western Indians
39. Roadhouse
40. Ineffectual
43. Guitarlike instrument
44. Nora's creator
46. Golfer's item
47. Sibling
48. Approaches
49. Maxim

DOWN

1. Chum
2. Miss MacGraw
3. Answer
4. Call
5. European capital
6. Individual
7. Discouraging word
8. Arbitrary
9. Small
10. Away from the wind
11. Arctic vehicle
16. Hourglass contents
18. Too
20. Decoration
21. Storefront sign
22. Tract
23. Bundles
25. Large stream
26. Plays on words
27. Poker stake
29. Cosmetic base
30. Daily PM occurrences
32. Extinct
33. Rind
34. Snacks
35. British guns
36. Flightless birds
37. Norse god
38. Consumer
40. Western country: abbr.
41. Ocean
42. Stitch
45. Exist

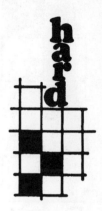

hard

ACROSS

1. Large monkey
4. Shovel's kin
9. Total (up)
12. Box for coal
13. Covered —, early American vehicle
14. — aside, save
15. Etch
17. Strong cord
19. Bowling area
20. Sign of faulty plumbing
21. Petty quarrels
23. Most difficult
26. Evergreen tree
27. Fence doors
28. "I pledge allegiance — the flag . . ."
29. Conclude
30. Employed
31. Raced
32. By
33. — up, conceal
34. In this place
35. Revolves
37. Plumbing needs
38. Picnic pests
39. Dog's treat
40. Wash lightly
42. Mailing fee
45. Noah's boat
46. Woman's garment
48. English beverage
49. Word of consent
50. Lugs
51. Affix (a time)

DOWN

1. "Honest —" Lincoln
2. Metal fastener
3. London's country
4. Graceful lake birds
5. Surface (a road)
6. Grow older
7. —, re, mi
8. Went into (a room)
9. The same
10. Newsman, — Rather
11. Permanent coloring
16. Fixed price
18. Lumps, as of tobacco
20. More tardy
21. Pointed weapon
22. Spotted horse or pony
23. Jack rabbits
24. Fixed look
25. Musical qualities
27. Donates
30. Most peppery
31. Tells again and again
33. Food tins
34. Gentle reminder
36. Holders for gasoline
37. Pillars
39. Drill (a hole) into
40. Beam of light
41. Dublin's country: abbr.
42. Peach stone
43. Golly!
44. Have a meal
47. Felling boxing blow: abbr.

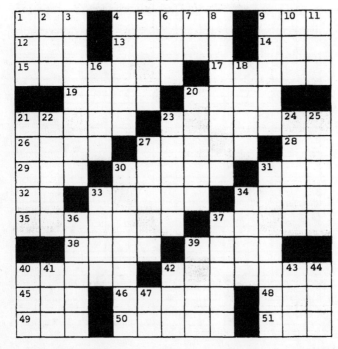

EASY

16

ACROSS

1. Ignited
4. Excuse
9. Gear tooth
12. "Apple cider" girl
13. — pole, Indian symbol
14. Fib
15. Chaps
17. Sacred song
19. Claws
20. Obligation
21. Foot digit
22. Heap
23. That man
25. Shellfish
27. Table-setting piece
29. Trouble
30. Dunne or Ryan
31. Scarlet
32. Memento
34. Frees (of)
35. Fourteenth letter
36. Beggar's request
37. Hairpiece
38. Prepare gifts
39. "Magic" drink
42. "E.T.," for example
44. Put in order
45. Bottle top
46. Goliath's foe
48. Exist
49. Ram's mate
50. Shuts noisily
51. Guided

DOWN

1. Raise
2. Notion
3. Exaggerated story: 2 wds.
4. Make amends (for)
5. Moos
6. Common contraction
7. Occur
8. Sudden urge
9. Potter's need
10. Lubricate
11. Jewel
16. Weaving machine
18. — on it!, hurry up!
20. Actress, — Keaton
22. Glances
23. Worked in the garden
24. Finishes
25. Baker's product
26. Property claim
27. Hobo
28. Fresh; new
30. Jamaica and Tahiti
33. Peel
34. Miss Hayworth
37. Sentence parts
38. Use a towel
39. Proper
40. Fairy-tale villain
41. Require
42. High card
43. Statute
44. Miss Gardner
47. Man's nickname

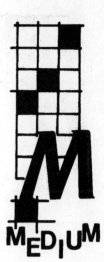

MEDIUM

HARD

ACROSS

1. Variety of dog
6. Frolics
11. "The — Queene"
12. Go away: archaic
14. Annuls
15. Town in southern California: 2 wds.
16. Jazzman Getz
17. Alexis or Feodor
19. Big-leaguer
20. Helios, to the Romans
21. "Way out yonder"
22. Ricochet
23. Metal spacer in printing
24. Backbone
25. Thread holder
27. Adhere (to)
28. Candied
29. Bookbinding leather
30. NHL milieu
31. Doting
32. FDR agency: abbr.
35. Palindromic first name
36. Legal document
37. Pillow cover
38. Guarantee
40. Dominion
42. Like better
43. Annoying sounds
44. Rhone tributary
45. Body-shop problem

DOWN

1. — Domingo
2. Ride a bike
3. Potential steel
4. Hold sign, in music
5. Piquant; eager
6. M*A*S*H character
7. Excessive
8. Wrong: prefix
9. Jack-o'-lantern
10. Trapping
11. Much ado
13. Figure of speech
18. Slump
21. African lily
22. Hebrew letter
23. Punch: slang
24. Decked out
25. Splinters
26. Cure-all
27. Dispute
28. Comprehend
29. Reine's spouse: French
31. Jacques, in an old song: French
32. Forerunner of bridge
33. Trims, as expenses
34. Singer Ed
36. English architect
37. Aerial maneuver
39. Sky sighting: abbr.
41. A Stooge

ACROSS

1. Armed conflict
4. Assist
8. Distance measures
12. Gorilla
13. Above
14. Shakespearean king
15. Cattle rush
17. In addition
18. Observed
19. Became aware of
21. Sandal or pump
23. Narrow leather strip
25. Armored vehicles
27. Commanded
31. Malt beverage
32. Speed
34. Hearing organ
35. Rearrange a covering artistically
37. Control a vehicle's move- ment
39. Wear away
41. Afresh
42. Fruits of the vine
45. Disembark
47. Rant
48. Certain inter- state carriers
52. Region
53. Mineral deposit
54. Dine
55. Man's name
56. Looks at
57. Cereal grass

DOWN

1. Used to be
2. Likely (to)
3. Argued logically
4. Expectation
5. Occurrence
6. Guided
7. Arrange ahead of time: hyph. wd.
8. Fitting on a shaft or pipe
9. Snakelike fishes
10. Repose
11. Walked (on)
16. Submissive
20. Terminated
21. Heavenly body
22. Patriot, Nathan —
24. Sprinkled, as a lawn
26. Stock market item
28. Transport animal for Santa
29. Roof edge
30. Sketched
33. Simon (called Peter), for example
36. Say again
38. Corporal or sergeant
40. Evade
42. Snatch
43. Uncommon
44. Assert
46. High cards
49. Cowboy, — Rogers
50. Beam of light
51. Female saint: abbr.

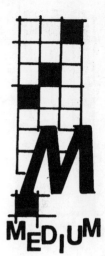

MEDIUM

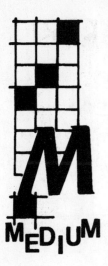

MEDIUM

ACROSS

1. Enjoy a meal
4. Salary
8. Oak or elm
12. Tell falsehoods
13. Attention-getting noise
14. Suspend
15. Liberty
17. The same
18. Victim
19. Shipped
20. Position
22. — Falls, honeymoon site
25. Mr. Reagan's title: abbr.
26. Mound
27. Nothing
28. That is: abbr.
29. Raise
32. Flickertail State: abbr.
33. Organ of hearing
35. Mineral sources
36. Sage
38. Train stop
40. Eyelid makeup
41. Flying animal
42. Football kick
43. 100 kopeks
45. Castle prison
48. Capri, for one
49. Chanted
50. Genetic material: abbr.
51. One who acts
52. Form of coal
53. Head: slang

DOWN

1. Pixie
2. Atmosphere
3. Indian tent
4. Walked in water
5. Sailor's shout
6. Precious stone
7. Alphabet letter
8. Object
9. Wickerwork palm
10. Within: prefix
11. Conceit
16. Rub out
17. Distributed, as playing cards
19. "— Marner," George Eliot book
20. Secret agents
21. Behave toward
22. British actor, David —
23. Wash with water
24. Birch tree
26. King of Judea
30. French river
31. "Dallas" family name
34. Mob
37. Apprentice doctor
39. Roofer
40. Sword thrust
42. Type of rock music
43. Free (of)
44. Group that performs for soldiers: abbr.
45. Twosome
46. Musician, Yoko —
47. Arrest
49. Columbia is its capital: abbr.

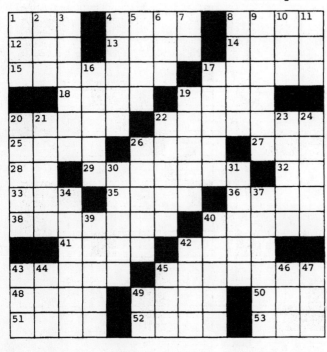

ACROSS

1. Astronaut's milieu
6. Brag
11. Edgar — Poe
12. Consented
14. Theatrical makeup
15. Dusted and vacuumed
17. Break a moral law
18. Scouts' walks
20. Baden-Baden, for one
21. Misled; deceived
23. Row of seats
24. Consumer
25. Hag
26. Routine tasks
29. Hunting dogs
30. Swift
31. Tree found at oases
32. Eager
33. Relief pitchers' warm-up area
36. Marsh
37. Haggard or Oberon
38. Large cask
40. Savile Row experts
42. Desire strongly
44. Blow softly, as a flute
45. Of the rise and fall of the sea
46. Facial features
47. Incantation

DOWN

1. Weakens
2. Tartan
3. Place in parallel rows
4. Metal container
5. Expressed eager interest
6. Broadway angel
7. Made eyes at
8. Greek god of war
9. Jacques Cousteau's milieu
10. Stress; strain
13. Be contingent (on)
16. Challenges
19. "Beware the — of March"
22. Sensational, as a headline
23. Bridge term
25. Gathers together
26. Skilled trade
27. Attack: 2 wds.
28. Judgment
29. Corridor
31. Handbags
33. "Uncle Miltie"
34. Elude
35. U.S. — Academy, Annapolis
37. Witticisms
39. Recount
41. Old card game
43. Rend

HARD

ACROSS

1. Sealed can
4. Tiffs
9. High mountain
12. Actress Balin
13. Holiday song
14. Victory sign
15. Carve (letters or designs) on
17. Representative
19. Mine product
20. Howard Cosell's field
21. Ledge
24. Railroad station
25. "Wishing" hole
26. Fluttered
27. Jolly sound
29. Noah's vessel
30. Gave a pink slip to
31. The present
32. Negative answer
33. Warning sound
34. Drag
35. Window parts
36. Movable barriers
37. Weapons for David
39. Firearm
40. Door joint
41. Female verse writer
45. Singer Turner
46. Bridle parts
48. Peggy or Michele
49. Actor Beatty
50. Frozen rain
51. A handful

DOWN

1. Shoelace
2. Tavern
3. Old horse
4. Woolen muffler
5. Surface a street
6. Exist
7. Toward
8. Struck sharply
9. Prevent
10. Fasting period
11. Domestic animals
16. Turn over and over
18. Well-behaved
20. "Lucky" number
21. Water bird
22. Gallant one
23. Large deer
24. Ventures
26. Telegrams
27. Golfer's target
28. Night birds
30. Places for rings
31. Cashew or pecan
33. Chanted
34. Breathe rapidly
35. Longed for
36. Visitor
37. Leg part
38. Enjoy
39. Departed
41. Crusty dessert
42. Tiny, playful fairy
43. Fix one's eyes upon
44. Stitch
47. Overhead train

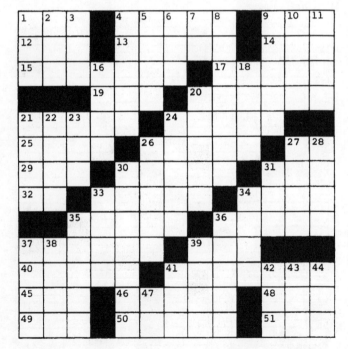

ACROSS

1. "You — There," TV oldie
4. Computer input
8. Popular side dish
12. Fishing pole
13. Subdivision of troops
14. Excavation
15. City in Texas
17. Holy book
18. Greek letter
19. Command
21. Foxy
23. Slow the progress of
27. Desist
30. Buddy
31. Prevaricate
32. Stylish: 4 wds.
35. Zodiac lion
36. Label
37. Identified
38. Mood
40. Fetch
41. Protective covering
43. Shade giver
47. Accumulate
50. Rope for raising a sail
52. Knox or Dix
53. Military assistant
54. Seedy fruit
55. Carry
56. Did garden work
57. Pipe joint

DOWN

1. Yemenite
2. Judicial garb
3. Revise (a text)
4. Scheduled
5. Pester
6. Row of seats
7. — odds, quarreling
8. Haberdashery purchase
9. Tennis stroke
10. Everyone
11. Like Willie Winkie
16. Lariat
17. Direct route
20. ⅛ ounce
22. Mailed messages
24. Astringent
25. Ceremony
26. Realty document
27. Sect
28. Fencing foil
29. Potent particle
30. Cribbage pin
33. Injure
34. Dapper
39. Adhesive
40. School mark
42. River of song
44. Kon-Tiki, for one
45. Pennsylvania port
46. Border
47. Matinee time: abbr.
48. Bovine bellow
49. Gallery display
51. Conducted
53. Cry of delight

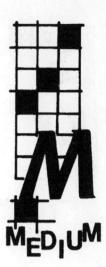

MEDIUM

ACROSS

1. Cilium
5. Psychic power
8. Employer
12. Spicy stew
13. By way of
14. Race track
15. Be unflappable: 2 wds.
17. Cuzco's land
18. Summit
19. Choose, in a way
21. Tractor-trailer
22. Fabrication
23. Millennia
25. Supporting
28. Fan
31. "Terrible" czar
32. Lake: poetic
33. Knack
36. Formed
38. Liberate
39. Despicable fellow
40. Glib
42. Cart
44. Presently
47. Dismounted
49. Bridge or pinochle: 2 wds.
51. Stupor
52. Rubber tree
53. Cruising
54. Retain
55. Cushion
56. Riverside

DOWN

1. Misplaced
2. Choir voice
3. Smack
4. Make — while the sun shines
5. Gave the slip
6. Fodder tower
7. Indulge
8. Jazz style
9. Go beyond the limits of
10. Hindu garment
11. Hit hard
16. Eve's son
20. Also
22. Passenger ship
24. Wanderer
25. Bridle part
26. Miss Gabor
27. Certain intermission: 2 wds.
29. Before: poetic
30. Crimson
34. Modern
35. China item
36. Notched
37. Round of applause
40. Group
41. Lily plant
43. Festive
44. Astronauts' organization
45. Portent
46. Frail
48. Spigot
50. Chatter

ACROSS

1. Frees from
5. Church seat
8. Twist
12. Operatic melody
13. Fruit drink
14. Region
15. Treaty
16. Pep
18. Explosive
19. Encountered
20. Sanctify; make holy
21. Mimicked
23. Affirmative answer
24. Mythical Greek giant
26. Chum
27. Water barrier
30. Sacred picture
31. That man
32. Lima is its capital
33. For each
34. Sack
35. Cut into cubes
36. Baseball stick
37. Prophet
38. Chars
41. Perform a tailoring task
42. Dine
45. Sponger; hanger-on
47. Auction
48. Eager
49. Angry
50. Largest continent
51. Scarlet and crimson
52. Snoop
53. Hamsters and parakeets

DOWN

1. Engrossed (in)
2. Formerly Persia
3. Tyrant; despot
4. Used a chair
5. Applied asphalt to (a road)
6. Prepare copy
7. Warning sign, "— paint"
8. Bouncing toys
9. Great Lake
10. Wimbledon necessity
11. 24-hour periods
17. Cain's victim
19. Adult males
22. Cooking utensil
23. Sweet potato
24. Gratuity
25. Frozen water
26. Swine
27. Diminish
28. Exist
29. Wet earth
31. Sombrero
32. Pastry
34. Lowest voice
35. Morning moisture
36. Fastening devices
37. Shabby; run-down
38. Mast
39. Roof edge
40. Very dry
41. Heavenly body
43. Dismounted
44. Afternoon events
46. Mischievous child
47. Plant fluid

EASY

25

EASY

ACROSS

1. Garfield, for one
4. Yellowish metal
9. Steal from
12. Be in debt
13. AM or FM set
14. "— Got a Secret"
15. White ant
17. Flat
19. Flower with thorns
20. Period before Christmas in the church calendar
21. Nasty odor
23. Less humid
24. "Star —," TV classic
25. More uncovered
26. Canada's continent: abbr.
28. Corn unit
29. Private teacher
30. Little lie
31. Belonging to me
32. Hurled
33. Cone-bearing tree
34. Basset or beagle
35. Not urban
36. Soup utensils
38. Tiny opening
39. "The Man Who — Be King," Kipling story
40. Frightened
43. Pacino and Hirt
44. Mistake
46. Word with "Stone" or "Space"
47. Golf peg
48. Tall marsh grasses
49. At present

DOWN

1. Folding bed
2. Wonder
3. Yorkie or Scottie
4. Cool; bracing
5. Appraise
6. Fruit drink
7. Yes: Spanish
8. Armed forces member
9. Nile, for one
10. Baking chamber
11. Band around the waist
16. Friar
18. At any time
20. Bow's partner
21. Stalk
22. Waiter's aid
23. Old-fashioned
25. Blazes
26. Sister ship of the Pinta
27. Cain's victim
29. Sound with lightning
30. Member of a hook-and-ladder's crew
32. Saw or rasp
33. Pleased sound of 1-Across
34. Dwelling
35. Lion's sounds
36. Hit (a fly)
37. Fishing rod
38. Trudge
40. Form of "to be"
41. Conceit
42. Morning moisture
45. "Do, —, mi . . ."

HARD

ACROSS

1. Explosive device
7. Character in "The Power and the Glory"
13. Los Angeles football player
14. On deck
15. Mouth: Latin
16. Cuddle
18. Interjection
19. Shoshonean
21. Actress Keaton
22. Thoreau's "majority"
23. Irish clan
25. Joanne —, actress
26. Moslem prince
27. Certain chords
29. Invidiousness
31. Article
32. London's Old —
33. Tableware
36. French etcher
39. Quince, for example
40. Norse sky god
42. Canonical hour
43. Land measure
44. Seasons
46. Cole or Turner
47. Avenue: abbr.
48. Hayworth's ex: 2 wds.
50. Starter's final word
51. Dainty
53. Expatriates
55. Joan, Peter, and others
56. "Hit the hay"

DOWN

1. "Swann's Way" author
2. Chilean island
3. Musical tone
4. Yellow-Pages features
5. Tear
6. Ancient Celtic priests
7. Tom Selleck role
8. Qualified
9. Caviar
10. That: French
11. Wry; para-doxical
12. Stick
17. Needlefish
20. Quintessence
22. It precedes "pi"
24. Sierra Nevada lake
26. Bring into agreement
28. Lair
30. Caesar's farewell
33. Muscular contractions
34. Bassanio's love
35. Blotches
36. German Reformation leader
37. Wild ass
38. Bristly
41. Type
44. Narrow opening
45. — -Coburg
48. Abby's sister
49. Young louse
52. Enlisted soldier, for short
54. Chinese distance unit

ACROSS

1. The "M" in M.V.P
5. Copycat
9. Hive insect
12. Christmas season
13. Use a pool's springboard
14. Footed vase
15. Halt!
16. Take note
17. Sample, as food
19. Help with the dishes
21. Sprite
23. Moved suddenly and quickly
27. Cautious
31. Depart
32. Metallic rock
33. — a chance!
35. Ball-point item
36. Smallest amount
39. Torture
42. Meddle (with)
44. Boot tip
45. Soon
47. Serpent
51. Goad (on)
54. Saucy
56. Recently purchased
57. Relieve (a pain)
58. Great Lake
59. Change the color of
60. "Peepers"
61. Entrance to a room

DOWN

1. Me
2. Not at home
3. Like "molasses in January"
4. Lukewarm
5. Stick (to)
6. Crusted pastry
7. Adam's mate
8. Funnyman Skelton
9. Yet
10. Pitching statistics: abbr.
11. Naval rank: abbr.
18. Golf gadget
20. Chum
22. Pleasure
24. Adhesive strip
25. Smooth; level
26. Fender mishap
27. Baltimore footballer
28. Region
29. 500 sheets of paper
30. Parking area
34. Small child
37. Bowling scores
38. Playing card
40. List of names
41. Husbands or fathers
43. Lassoed
46. Cruel Roman emperor
48. Plus
49. Composer of U.S. anthem
50. Female sheep
51. Get it?
52. Reimburse
53. Have no — for, dislike strongly
55. — Grande, U.S. border river

EASY

MEDIUM

ACROSS

1. Public vehicle
4. He and she
8. Bide one's time
12. Sixth sense, for short
13. Conceal
14. Nimbus
15. Business transactions
17. Halt
18. Poker stake
19. Bell's invention, for short
20. Twig
23. Think
24. Sixty minutes
25. Dividing line
29. Ancient
30. Drizzles
31. Shoe tip
32. Qualified
34. Soft drink
35. Think deeply
36. Radio part
37. Honking birds
39. Antlered animal
41. Coffee vessels
42. Connecticut capital
46. Location
47. Italian river
48. Court
49. Trial
50. Adolescent
51. Table support

DOWN

1. Rollaway item
2. Employ
3. Fitness center
4. Inanimate object
5. Clue
6. Border
7. Affirmative reply
8. Laundered
9. Robot
10. Common metal
11. Recording ribbon
16. Den
19. Felt-tip items
20. Brogan
21. Canvass
22. Fundamentals
23. Sand hill
25. Infant
26. Lubricant
27. Went by train
28. Calendar period
30. Ascend
33. Expansion insert
34. Ride the waves
36. Dakota Indian
37. Rush of wind
38. Sandusky's lake
39. Challenge
40. Sea eagle
42. Bonnet
43. Nocturnal bird
44. Fish eggs
45. House pet

ACROSS

1. Goal
4. Glowing coal
9. Soaked
12. Dove's cry
13. Very
14. Actor, — Wallach
15. Assign the care of
17. Male duck
19. Warmth
20. Halt
21. Pilfer
23. Follows closely, as a detective
26. Throw
27. Slide
28. Negative word
29. Towards
30. Afternoon show
33. Myself
34. A Reiner
36. Nutmeg spice
37. Harvest
39. Make ready
41. Cautions
42. Location
43. Flower holder
44. New England State
46. Skunk
49. Ancient
50. Join together
52. Couple
53. Stinging insect
54. Lassoes
55. Stitch

DOWN

1. Expert
2. Charged atom
3. May honoree
4. Peer
5. Have to
6. Morsel
7. — cetera, and so on
8. Regulations resulting in delay: 2 wds.
9. Gun or sword
10. Large deer
11. Bind
16. Domain
18. Fishing pole
20. Radiate
21. Keen; acute
22. Teacher
23. Pie serving
24. "An Unmarried —," 1978 film
25. Paces
27. Fixed look
31. Nonprofessional
32. Eradicate
35. Next to
38. Builds
40. Brooch
41. Charles, Prince of —
43. Cast a ballot
44. Unruly crowd
45. Malt beverage
46. Apple seed
47. Veneration
48. Haul
51. Certainly not!

EASY

ACROSS

1. Bath rug
4. Hopping insects
9. Strange
12. Fruit-juice drink
13. Wash lightly
14. Reimburse
15. Order
17. In that place
19. Common tree
20. Small rocks
21. Small spot
23. Cavities
24. Misplace
25. Burrowing animals
26. Exist
28. Picnic pest
29. H₂O
30. Naughty
31. — oneself, alone
32. Long walks
33. Hospital section
34. Motor inn
35. Flower with a velvety "face"
36. Circus comedians
38. Partner, in cowboy talk
39. Soup dipper
40. Put furniture into (a room)
43. High playing card
44. Woman's dirndl or hoop —
46. Fasten
47. Dover's State: abbr.
48. Oops!
49. Secret agent

DOWN

1. — Davis of music
2. Big fuss
3. — in a teapot, big to-do over nothing
4. Mr. Sinatra
5. Fishing cord
6. Finish
7. While
8. Colonist
9. Unlocks
10. Venture
11. Permanent colorings
16. "Three Blind —"
18. Does a garden chore
20. Shoe bottoms
21. Thick slice (of bacon)
22. Small horse
23. "Relative" of 34-Across
25. Manufactures
26. Taverns
27. Nelson —, Jeanette MacDonald's costar
29. One who testifies in court
30. Outlaws
32. Wolf's cry
33. Caution
34. Take part in a fashion show
35. Birthday celebration
36. Dressed (in)
37. Hankie trim
38. Cat's sound
40. Evergreen tree
41. Wee drink
42. You, there!
45. Felling boxing blow: abbr.

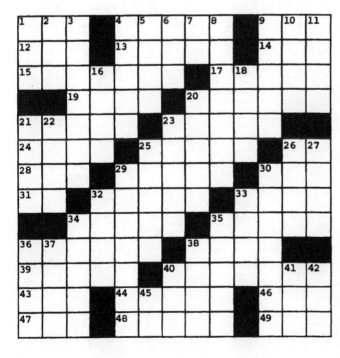

ACROSS

1. Curved line
4. Planted, as seeds
9. Struck
12. "Dear — ..."
13. In that place
14. High card
15. Lance
17. Snared
19. Rams' mates
21. Open-handed blow
22. Says again
25. Smooth
28. 13th letter
29. Odor
31. Intend (to)
32. Lincoln's nickname
34. Use a broom
36. Regret
37. Monk's room
39. Makes airtight
41. Chile's continent: abbr.
42. Joyce Kilmer poem
44. Behaved toward
46. Penny
48. Title
49. "Motor City"
52. Chairs
55. Actress Arden
56. Branch of peace
58. Dove's call
59. Small mass
60. Beg
61. Egg-layer

DOWN

1. Donkey
2. Mr. van Winkle
3. Crawl
4. Brooks
5. Sound of surprise
6. Soggy
7. Blunders
8. Business transactions
9. More cheerful
10. Frozen water
11. Comedian Knight
16. Fills with fear and wonder
18. Tropical tree
20. Cooks slowly
22. Respond (to)
23. Glowing coal
24. Frozen rain
26. Reason
27. Work dough
30. Discover
33. Chosen by vote
35. Delighted
38. Malicious glance
40. Identical
43. Prying person
45. Educate
47. Cash drawer
49. Lawn moisture
50. Actress Gabor
51. Knot together
53. Foot part
54. Male offspring
57. Richmond's State: abbr.

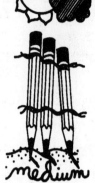

ACROSS

1. Concordat
5. Noisy impact
9. Pledge
12. Hibernia
13. Hack
14. Woodward role
15. Revised (a law)
17. Stormed
19. Furniture style
20. Sanctuaries
21. Synchronized
23. Generate
24. Olfactory detection
25. Picket
26. Stone or Space
29. Ring official, for short
30. Loses traction
31. Hope or Newhart
32. Gormandize
33. Uses a hand shuttle
34. Generous slice
35. Starts the bidding
37. Formal assemblies
38. Hank Aaron specialties
40. Crossbeams
41. Buoy up
42. Periodic wind of India
45. Give the green light to
46. Sign
48. Adjust, as an engine
49. Pasture sound
50. — up, corners the market
51. Imitated

DOWN

1. Legume
2. Goal
3. Soup choice: 3 wds.
4. Railroad car
5. Skier's stopping maneuver
6. Shaver
7. Hatchet
8. Optical illusions
9. Hearty first course: 2 wds.
10. "Hot spot"
11. Marries
16. Family man
18. Hail!: Latin
20. Succors
21. Fairly flew
22. Conception
23. Heckles
25. Programs for action
27. Ibex
28. Declines
30. Record players
34. Snooze break, south of the border
36. Fido or Spot
37. Racket
38. Steering device
39. Bread spread
40. Freight weights
42. Sea gull
43. Song from "A Chorus Line"
44. Actor Beatty
47. "What's in it for —?"

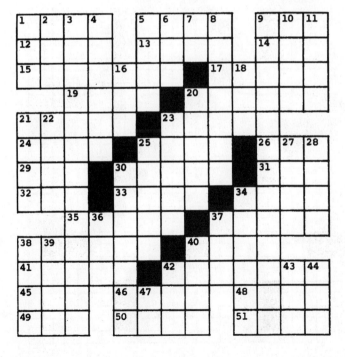

ACROSS

1. Load
5. Old Testament prophet
9. Steal from
12. Strong metal
13. Accompanied by
14. Adam's mate
15. Thaw
16. Tardy
17. Ocean
18. Large bundles
20. Overhead railway
21. Writing fluid
22. Military forces not on active duty
26. Guided
29. Golf mound
30. Consumed
33. Operatic solo
35. Poet's "before"
37. Nevada city
38. Outmoded
40. Anger
42. Insecticide: abbr.
43. Trembled, as from cold
46. Lyric poem
48. In the direction of
49. Light-giving devices
53. Kith and —
54. Indicate dislike of a play
57. Horn sound
58. Pestiferous rodent
59. Reverberate
60. In addition
61. Jolson and Capone
62. Marsh grass
63. Profound

DOWN

1. Arm or leg
2. Region
3. Child's plaything
4. Come in
5. Cobbler's tool
6. Actress, — Farrow
7. Furry aquatic animal
8. Lay aside
9. Refused to yield to
10. Baking chamber
11. Bird's bill
19. Arrange, as hair
23. Use one's eyes
24. Uncanny
25. Hearing organ
26. Race-track circuit
27. Epoch
28. Disagrees
31. Terminate
32. Negative word
34. Volcanic lava
36. Blunder
39. Choice word
41. Snakelike fish
44. With one —, unanimously
45. Obsolete
46. Gumbo vegetable
47. Clock face
50. Burrowing mammal
51. Sit (for an artist)
52. Pace
55. The woman
56. Turf

ACROSS

1. Soothing ointment
5. Not on
8. Plant stalk
12. Phrase of understanding: 2 wds.
13. Word from a ghost
14. Strenuous walk
15. Florida swamp region: 2 wds.
18. Lock opener
19. Flooded with water
20. Item for an acrobat
23. Ruffle
25. Lean and strong
26. Squints (at)
27. Noon to midnight: abbr.
29. "Roses — red"
30. Cures
31. Falsehood
32. One of us
33. Fatigued
34. Drying oven
35. Sends, as a letter
36. Helped
37. Aromas
39. Ancient
40. Alaskan peak: 2 wds.
46. Concerning: 2 wds.
47. Yours and mine
48. Superior: 2 wds.
49. Look after
50. Hot beverage
51. Pea jackets

DOWN

1. Small piece
2. Fire residue
3. Actor Marvin
4. Mildly
5. Follow orders
6. In favor of
7. Mist
8. Ladies' shoulder wraps
9. Of ocean movements
10. — out; uses frugally
11. Netlike cloth
16. Pet doctor, for short
17. Dens
20. Enjoyed the pool
21. Whitewall
22. Wrath
23. Phobias
24. Depend (on)
26. Ring, as a bell
27. Heap
28. Repair
30. Robbery: slang
31. Cover
33. Cautioned
34. Abduct
35. Grieve (for)
36. Famous boxer
37. Leave out
38. Finished
39. Gumbo vegetable
41. Witty remark
42. Actor's signal
43. Card game
44. Finish
45. Of course!

ACROSS

1. Magnitude
5. Likely
8. Naval officers: abbr.
12. Bird: Latin
13. Born
14. Dilapidation
15. High degree
16. Cross
18. Foment
20. Alternate, as crops
21. Kiln-dried barley
23. "— us go then, you and I" (T.S. Eliot)
24. Amusing
28. Storage structure
31. Greek letter
32. Berlin's river
34. Rower
35. Land of the Incas
37. Charm
39. As well as
41. Mentioned before
42. Praised
45. Minor parish officer
49. Land sought by Pizarro: 2 wds.
51. Trot or pace
52. Seaport in Yemen
53. Gossett or Ferrigno
54. Tabriz's country
55. Venture
56. Nevertheless
57. Pod vegetable

DOWN

1. Hindu garment
2. Mr. Lendl
3. Metallic element
4. Aleut
5. Gazelle, for one
6. Through
7. Lacrimal secretion
8. Sharp mountain crests
9. Continuance in time
10. Fine spray
11. Cut
17. Book: abbr.
19. Sailors
22. Vaudeville acts
24. Knowing: slang
25. Western Indian tribe
26. Raider
27. Begin: 2 wds.
29. Insect secretion
30. Raw mineral
33. Great Lake
36. Not finished
38. Slow musical passage
40. German article
42. Conduct
43. Alan or Robert
44. — City, California
46. Closed, as a theater
47. One with a forked tongue
48. Sicilian sight
50. Female of 5-Down

hard

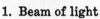

ACROSS

1. Beam of light
4. Flower part
8. Kill
12. Summer fruit drink
13. Quality of sound
14. Cod or Good Hope
15. Billfolds
17. Window sections
18. Falsehoods
19. Hourglass contents
20. Bend with age
22. Placards
25. "Our —," T. Wilder play
26. Isn't able
27. Female deer
28. Exclamation of pain
29. Move unsteadily
32. "Let it —," Beatles tune
33. Church bench
35. Sources of metal
36. Was in debt
38. Sloped
40. Tumbler
41. Peruse, as a book
42. Observed
43. Erie or Suez
45. Wall material
48. Word with "head" or "coat"
49. Precious
50. Epoch
51. Four-posters
52. Chats: slang
53. Lair

DOWN

1. Uncooked
2. Woman's name
3. Lemon-colored
4. Precipitous
5. Little children
6. Navy officer: abbr.
7. Myself
8. Meager
9. Came to earth
10. Simian
11. Absolutely!
16. Big cats
17. Sticky stuff
19. Melodies
20. Halts
21. Bather's need
22. Called on a P.A. system
23. Loose outer garments
24. Plants; sows
26. Was concerned
30. Use an adding machine
31. Actors' parts
34. Cautioned
37. Desired
39. Approaches
40. Cogwheels
42. Strike sharply
43. Corn spike
44. Hail!
45. Tiny vegetable
46. Before: poet.
47. Raced
49. Physician: abbr.

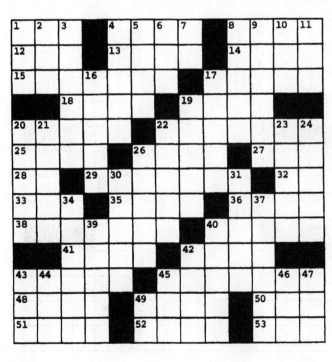

ACROSS

1. Entire amount
4. Carry (off)
8. Dietary fiber source
12. Regret (an action)
13. Spicy stew
14. Transportation for Huck Finn
15. Dine
16. Father: slang
17. Unquestioning belief
18. Capital of Texas
20. — up, finish
21. "The Lost —"
23. Musical tone
25. Elegance; style
28. As well as
29. Primary color
30. Sheer linen
31. Place; set
32. Female horse
33. High card
34. By way of
35. Punctuation mark
36. "—, the People . . ."
37. Congressional building
39. Stockings
40. Nestle (together), as from the cold
44. Art-supply store item
46. Evergreen
47. Fishing pole
48. Seep (out)
49. Prohibits
50. Mine product
51. Red vegetable
52. On —, nervous
53. Ink's "partner"

DOWN

1. Surface measure
2. Hawaiian feast
3. Allows
4. Office machine
5. Solitary
6. Tear
7. — and fro
8. Trademark
9. Sudden attack
10. Tea time: abbr.
11. — degree, extreme
17. Discover
19. Romulus, to Remus
20. Proceeded
22. Hawaiian island
23. Duration
24. Thought; concept
25. Defect
26. Shoestring
27. Wonder and respect
29. Zodiac symbol
31. Speak (up)
32. Form; shape
34. Flower holder
35. Path
37. Halley's, for one
38. Inanimate object
39. Mist
41. Fall
42. Traditional knowledge
43. First garden
44. Watch-chain ornament
45. Fish eggs
46. Passing craze
49. Exist

ACROSS

1. Valerie Harper role in a TV oldie
6. — Barton, Red Cross founder
11. Combined, as resources
12. Carpentry tools
14. Applied a cosmetic
15. 30: French
16. Gumbo vegetable
17. Ozzie's son
19. Bond
20. Greek letter
21. Mr. Walesa
22. Barrel
23. Long-running TV show
24. Baltimore team
25. Muscles
27. Obtuse
28. Stir vigorously
29. Yawl or yacht
30. A Kennedy
31. Average standard
32. National network: abbr.
35. Not in
36. Glance
37. Dice
38. Radiant
40. Sir Galahad's mother
42. Actress Ritter
43. Was showery
44. Musical chord
45. Church council

DOWN

1. Chess pieces
2. Siren
3. Gymnast Korbut
4. Scottish river
5. Phone-book entry
6. Ensnare
7. Lie in wait
8. Grow older
9. Some cars and homes
10. Dali and Goya
11. Shore (up)
13. Endeavors (to)
18. I: German
21. Grassy yard
22. Paint layer
23. Simple
24. Stuff
25. Cogitated
26. Overaggressive salesman
27. "Humdingers": slang
28. Certain Slav
29. Word of scorn
31. Wanderer
32. Cotton fabric
33. Prepared a fillet
34. Hastened
36. Buddhist monk
37. Abel's brother
39. Inventor Whitney
41. Deposit

hard

ACROSS

1. Blemish
5. Use a broom
10. Pebble
11. Canoe oar
13. Huron and Superior
14. Lyric poem
15. Chopping tool
17. Mature
18. Captured
20. Health resort
21. Nuisance
23. Marry
24. Movie bigwig
25. Unlock
27. Adolescents
28. Highway dividers
30. Plank
31. West Point student
32. Chimney deposit
33. Fragrance
34. Crafty
35. Long detailed narrative
39. High mountain
40. — away, hide
42. "Roll": slang
43. Allow
44. Consume
45. Speechify
47. Legislative body
49. Female horses
50. Rounded roofs
51. Concludes

DOWN

1. Word with "fright" or "name"
2. Jabs
3. Dollar bill
4. Exam
5. Verbal
6. Walked in shallow water
7. Paradise
8. Actor Asner
9. Wall coating material
10. Smack
12. Increase in size
16. Corn spikes
19. Inspires fear and reverence in
22. Paint tester
24. Chairs
26. Favorite animal
27. Also
28. Soup dippers
29. Accepted formally
30. Cub Scout members
31. Furnace fuel
32. Blackboards
34. Declare
36. Oscar or Tony
37. Portals
38. Fruit drinks
40. Sewing line
41. Residence
46. Sprinted
48. Not on your life!

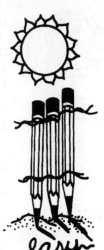

easy

ACROSS

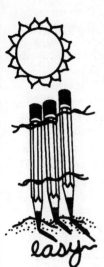

1. Skirt's edge
4. Vegetable dish
9. Dog's foot
12. Man's name
13. Foe
14. Lincoln or Vigoda
15. Doctor's client
17. More pleasant
19. Release (a fastening)
20. Football lineman
21. Old-fashioned; trite
23. At —, occasionally
24. Fills with wonder
25. Damp
26. The capital, for short: abbr.
28. Nourished
29. Quinine water
30. Something sticky: slang
31. Mr. Asner
32. Ruled, as paper
33. Snow vehicle
34. Shoestrings
35. Stop
36. Lively
38. Ran, as dyes
39. Rental contract
40. Clothes to be washed
43. Organ of hearing
44. Not here
46. Organ of sight
47. Notices, as of sales
48. "No Parking" and "Stop," for two
49. Snare for fish

DOWN

1. Sophisticated: slang
2. Period of time
3. Ripened
4. Shabby or run-down
5. The "A" in A.D.
6. Allow
7. Before noon: abbr.
8. Vigorous
9. Wolf groups
10. Adam's son
11. Existed
16. Country hotels
18. Frosted
20. Shy
21. Coffeehouse
22. Was in debt
23. Melodies
25. Bee's product
26. Carries out
27. Spy's cipher
29. Traffic summonses
30. Make happy
32. Girl
33. Observed
34. Fibbers
35. Information for a sleuth
36. Pesky insect
37. Peruse
38. Farm building
40. Lower limb
41. Type of bread
42. Still
45. Word of greeting

ACROSS

1. Skillet
4. Withstand
8. Immense
12. Japanese vegetable
13. Marine eagle
14. Iroquoian
15. Posies
17. Gershwin/Kahn song: 1929
18. Warm seasons: French
19. Gnaws
21. Nasser's successor
23. Aleutian island
24. Rara —
25. Visceral
29. Miss Ullmann
30. Actor Jannings and others
31. Argentite or bauxite
32. Toothless
34. The Charles' pet
35. Podded shrub
36. Clarified butters
37. Dwarfed tree
40. 21-Across was one
41. Tract
42. Horse feeders: 2 wds.
46. Ponce de —
47. Foillike sword
48. Forty winks
49. Charged atoms
50. Photocopy, for short
51. Thirsty

DOWN

1. Play on words
2. Commotion
3. Downward plunge: 2 wds.
4. Sire
5. Time spans
6. Whichever
7. Put down new roots
8. Velvety cloth
9. Like the Gobi
10. Magnitude
11. Oolong and pekoe
16. Between zetas and thetas
20. Paths: abbr.
21. Vendition
22. Zealous
23. "West Side Story" character
25. Envisions
26. Bridle part
27. "Laugh-In" alumnus Johnson
28. Pastures
30. Volcanic peak
33. Hebrew months
34. Moby Dick's pursuer
36. Welcome
37. Isle near Java
38. Mountain: prefix
39. TV-tube element
40. On the Banda
43. Elective: abbr.
44. Needlefish
45. CIA employee, perhaps

hard

ACROSS

1. Choir gown
5. Distress call
8. Totals (up)
12. Do as told
13. Pecan is one
14. Befit
15. Shoe bottom
16. Had a snack
17. Big truck, for short
18. Opposite of "buyer"
20. In poker, one who ups the ante
22. Guam and Wake
24. Property documents
27. Annoys
31. Your and my
32. "To fetch — poor dog a bone"
33. Butterfly snare
34. Gate-—, one who attends a party without an invitation
37. Warbucks of comics
39. Naval destroyer
41. Bed linens
44. Seem (to be)
48. Jimmy — Carter
49. Corn spike
51. Crippled
52. Wicked
53. Box top
54. Level
55. Ball-point items
56. Go by plane
57. Mailed

DOWN

1. Singer, Diana —
2. Double-reed instrument
3. Telephone inventor
4. It moves during winking or blinking
5. Fierce growl
6. Umpire's call
7. More strict
8. Help
9. Membership fees
10. Ten cents
11. Mix
19. Curvy letter
21. "Help Wanted" listings
23. Copycats
24. A Disney dwarf
25. Italy's continent: abbr.
26. Pitching statistics: abbr.
28. Finish
29. Mr. Skelton
30. Pigpen
32. Feminine pronoun
35. Expands
36. Chapeau
37. Short swim
38. Winesaps, for example
40. Robust
41. Ooze
42. Own
43. Ireland, to a poet
45. Roof part
46. Prayer ending
47. Landlord's income
50. Be on the sick list

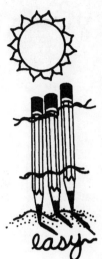

easy

43

ACROSS

1. Actress Turner
5. Health resort
8. Cookie sheets
12. Mine products
13. Relatives
14. Radiate
15. Banqueting
17. Short skirt, for short
18. Spud: dial.
19. Enticer
21. Turf
23. Singer Falana
24. Chases
28. Dakota Indian
31. Patriotic monogram
32. Bridge position
34. Compass point
35. Midler or Davis
37. Ironed
39. Bakery treat
41. Peeve
42. Suitcases
45. Raises
49. Adam's son
50. Recreation area
52. Blackthorn fruit
53. Hearing organ
54. Ballerina's skirt
55. Incline (toward)
56. Gaze at
57. Coin groove

DOWN

1. Barn section
2. Region
3. Orderly
4. Estimate; evaluate
5. "Hit the slopes"
6. Milk measure
7. Cherub
8. Synagogue
9. Mimics
10. Baseball team
11. Mix
16. Pants
20. Maternal
22. — volente: God willing
24. Alehouse
25. Employ
26. Chatter: 2 wds.
27. Dine late
29. Single
30. Actor Beatty
33. Three: comb. form
36. Followed: slang
38. Wraparounds
40. Plains Indians' tents
42. Very large
43. Competent
44. Amuse greatly: slang
46. Ump's call
47. "Wizard of Oz" dog
48. Soot
51. "You — My Sunshine"

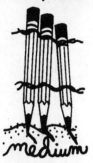

medium

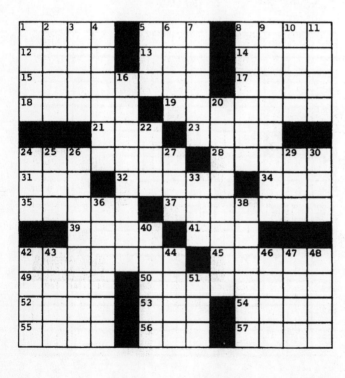

ACROSS

1. Location
5. "— Loves You," Beatles hit
8. Trade
12. Strong metal
13. Is able to
14. Group of three
15. Lease
16. Ancient
17. Go by horseback
18. Emerald —, Ireland
20. Doctrine
21. Frightened
24. Pull along
25. More tardy
26. Frail
27. Egotist's word
29. Epoch
30. Shrimplike creature
32. Bear's foot
33. You and I
34. Rip
35. Glove material
37. Contradict
38. Victor
39. Sow, as seeds
41. Appointment
42. Disembark
43. Fuel
44. The Orient
48. Formerly
49. Mr. Carney
50. Peddle
51. Moose
52. Golly!: slang
53. New Haven university

DOWN

1. Knight's title
2. Anger
3. 2,000 pounds
4. Whole
5. Nag
6. Robust
7. Finish
8. Thin mark
9. Twist
10. Assistant
11. Verse writer
19. Snake
20. Rapid —, subway system
21. Cabbage salad
22. Confine
23. Had lunch
24. Morning moisture
26. Armed conflict
27. Manufactured
28. Pitcher
31. Beam of light
32. Writing tool
34. Gentle
36. Nervous
37. Waltz or polka
38. Squander
39. Walk heavily
40. Path
41. Challenge
43. Joke
45. Ocean
46. Sickly
47. Brewed drink

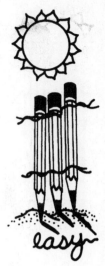

easy

ACROSS

1. Pea casing
4. Step
9. — in, confine
12. Logging tool
13. Use one of the senses
14. Grow older
15. Cage-sport position
17. Appoint
19. Journalize
20. Communion table
21. Covered with ooze
23. Lumpish mass
26. Steve of comedy, and family
29. Patriot, Thomas —
30. Beerlike brew
31. Raleigh's State: abbr.
32. Greek letter
33. Formerly named
34. Bee bite
36. Most towering
38. Musical quality
39. Rhyme
40. Copperfield of fiction
42. Poker stakes
46. Certain record-player
48. Raid
49. Shipment from Duluth
50. Schedule
52. Greek letter
53. Golfing norm
54. Stories
55. Turf

DOWN

1. Walk the floor
2. Work animals
3. Fender mishap
4. Fine grade of silver
5. Asphalt
6. While
7. Rome's country
8. Relax
9. Thin, thin mark
10. Urge (on)
11. Husbands or fathers
16. Trial
18. Long, heroic tale
20. Morning hours: abbr.
22. Abbreviation in a business name
24. Individuals
25. Red as a —
26. Nautical pole
27. Choir voice
28. Santa's steeds
29. Throbs
32. Deface
35. Close
36. Knight of TV
37. Fasting season
39. Stringed instrument
41. Part of a 3-piece suit
43. Dances, Ann Miller style
44. Reverberate
45. Slip sideways
46. Soak
47. —-la-la
48. Broke a fast
51. Actor Pacino

ACROSS

1. Currency
5. Soufflé item
8. Norway's capital
12. Region
13. Card game
14. Large number
15. Former President of Mexico
16. Isolation
18. Spicy meat
20. Type of sleeve
21. Lease
23. Bird's beak
24. Innkeeper
28. Soaks (flax)
31. Pub drink
32. Provided with oaks
34. Brazilian seaport, for short
35. Brief swims
37. Supports
39. Exclamation of triumph
41. Large bulrush
42. Diver's sound
45. Boston basketball player
49. Large animal
51. Verdi opera
52. Fragrant flower
53. Perceive
54. Horse's gait
55. Female sheep
56. Kennedy or Knight
57. Snakelike fish

DOWN

1. Ill-mannered fellows
2. Operatic melody
3. Sea mammal
4. Risk
5. Scene of "Hamlet"
6. Sticky substance: slang
7. Precious metal
8. Stableman
9. Sleeps
10. Mother of Castor and Pollux
11. — Wister, novelist
17. Charged atom
19. Dissolve
22. English river
24. Boy
25. — Baba and the Forty Thieves
26. Native to Katmandu
27. Subtracted
29. Bond
30. Distress signal
33. Give (out) sparingly
36. Forms
38. Tell
40. Shade tree
42. Withered: poetic
43. Farm tool
44. Archaic verb
46. Grow weary
47. Golden calf, for one
48. Certain pets
50. Born

HARD

ACROSS

1. Skelton or Buttons
4. Installs in office
9. Understand?
12. Dander
13. Jeweler's weight
14. Deli purchase
15. Symphony group
17. Lifetime
18. Highway section
19. Addition to a contract
21. Cognizant
23. Game of chance
25. Cavil
26. Walks in water
27. Optic organ
28. City of white cliffs
29. Paper sack
32. Vocal sounds
33. Soft-drink ingredient
34. Belongings
37. Might
38. Icy downpour
39. Shopping center
40. Was in session
41. Goal
46. ". . . but few — chosen"
47. Course of travel
48. Nothing
49. Okay!
50. Deep thinkers
51. Precious thing

DOWN

1. Cruise port, for short
2. Blunder
3. Proclaim
4. Drama setting
5. Facility
6. Skill
7. Coal distillate
8. Engine device
9. Color gradation
10. Impatient to get going
11. Abrasive powder
16. Stringed instrument
20. The I in T.G.I.F.
21. Perfect serve in tennis
22. Method
23. Washes
24. Pindar output
26. Habit
28. Jekyll and Zhivago
29. Tenpins game
30. Tankard serving
31. Needlefish
32. Kickoff gadget
33. Young donkey
34. Literary composition
35. Railroad signal
36. Gala parties
37. Strides
39. Dole (out)
42. Large snake
43. Jail: slang
44. Contend
45. Graceful tree

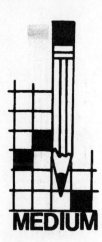

MEDIUM

ACROSS

1. Butter square
4. Did the crawl
8. Thick slice
12. Oklahoma city
13. Telegram
14. Story
15. Most drawn out, as a speech
17. Ventured
18. Confederate general
19. Building addition
20. Swindle
23. Roams
26. Grasp
27. Zoo compartments
28. Surprised cry
29. Noah's vessel
30. Rescues
31. Sheep's bleat
32. "The Price — Right," TV show
33. Surfaces a street
34. Corn hull
35. Akin (to)
37. Mucilage
38. Colored part of the eye
39. Limousine
40. Arouse
42. Birthday cake decorations
46. Not closed
47. "Lights out" bugle call
48. Acorn bearer
49. Map direction
50. Follow orders
51. Twisted, as a smile

DOWN

1. Buddy
2. Fuss
3. Sun-browned
4. Sugary
5. Judicious
6. Linkletter or Carney
7. One of us
8. Tolerates
9. Sweater size
10. Foamy brew
11. Bunk or cot
16. Happy
17. Has supper
19. Salary
20. Rocker, for one
21. Derby runner
22. Antlered animal
23. Gestured good-bye
24. Sunday dinner entree
25. Tremble
27. Bears' homes
30. Glossy fabric
31. School vehicle
33. Mom or Dad
34. Difficult
36. Enjoys
37. Garden flower
39. Batman's cloak
40. Exclamation of wonder
41. Gibbon
42. Taxi
43. Deep in pitch
44. Lend an —, listen
45. Firmament
47. — and fro

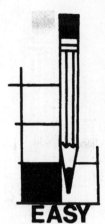

EASY

49

ACROSS

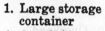

1. Large storage container
4. Capri, for example
8. Not covered
12. Actress Lupino
13. College official
14. Spoken
15. Table of —, book guide
17. Chain part
18. Facilitate
19. Annoying ones
20. Mexican food item
23. Ilk
24. Rainbow goddess
25. Release: 2 wds.
29. Five-dollar bill: slang
30. Free-for-all
31. Young Sawyer
32. Classic musical film by Disney
34. An astringent
35. Goddess of discord
36. Exquisite
38. Sat for a painting
40. Identical
41. Tiny particle
42. Mighty
46. Dorothy's dog in "The Wizard of Oz"
47. Dash; verve
48. Consumed
49. Listen to
50. Playthings
51. Edgar, to his friends

DOWN

1. Anglican parish priest: abbr.
2. Commotion
3. Shade of brown
4. Perfect model
5. Without meaning
6. Tardy
7. Printers' measures
8. Spanish dance
9. Greek philosopher
10. Rave
11. The "E" in B.P.O.E.
16. Social events
19. Native of Warsaw
20. Slight quarrel
21. Operatic solo
22. St. Paul is its capital
23. Move secretly: 2 wds.
26. Actor Wallach
27. Body's opposite
28. T.V. award
30. Female servant
33. Vibration
34. Declare firmly
37. Prophetic signs
38. Walkway
39. Sioux
40. Fly alone
42. Guppy or hamster
43. Strike out, in baseball
44. Shoshonean Indian
45. Conducted

ACROSS

1. Decay
4. Blemish
7. "Rings on — fingers"
10. Spring bloom
12. Doorway sign
14. Before: poetic
15. Borscht vegetable
16. Arizona city
17. Assist
18. Fearful reverence
20. Wed secretly
22. Lucifer
24. Embroider
25. Freedom
27. Otherwise
31. Pub order
32. Whitman and Frost
35. OPEC concern
36. Precious metal
38. Seamen
40. Donkey
43. Account entries
44. Send (money) in payment
46. Table support
47. Get — of, do away with
48. Extinct bird
50. First man
54. Gorilla
55. Always
56. Openwork fabric
57. Corral
58. Annapolis graduate:abbr.
59. However

DOWN

1. Chest bone
2. Mine output
3. Cause of extra innings
4. Souvenir
5. Logging tool
6. Ascends
7. Stack
8. Lake or canal
9. Stoplight color
11. Declare
13. Legend
19. Twist out of shape
21. Part of I.O.U.
22. Fodder tower
23. Brother of Cain
25. Loiter
26. Absolutely!
28. Weaving frame
29. "Dear —," letter opening
30. Overhead trains
33. Suit-makers
34. Location
37. Flood control
39. Lawful
41. Faction
42. Kitchen range
44. Ready to eat, as fruit
45. Home of 50-Across
47. Knock sharply
49. Cozy room
51. Week segment
52. Expert pilot
53. Player at Shea Stadium

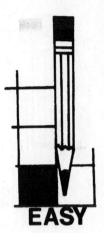

EASY

ACROSS

1. Corrugate
6. *Parfum*, e.g.
11. Thirty-first President
12. Judge's office
14. Suave
15. Mollusk
16. Diving bird
17. Pasture calls
19. "Gob"
20. "Legal beagle": abbr.
21. Decree
22. Entry permit
23. Enjoy
24. Taboos: hyph. wd. (slang)
25. Frighten
27. Condescend
28. Task
29. Adorn, in a way
30. Tree part
31. Stable baby
32. "— do I love thee?"
35. Commit a gaffe
36. Nanny's buggy
37. Greek letter
38. Asian peninsula
40. Titania's spouse
42. Tension cause, sometimes
43. Arrested
44. Word for a fog or a forest
45. Designer creation

DOWN

1. Painter, Jean Camille —
2. Automaton
3. Masculine name
4. Troops
5. Hypothesis
6. Scamper
7. Low islands
8. Print measures
9. Gauzy fabric
10. Betrayal
11. Graceful dance
13. Tapestry
18. Wood
21. Cabbie's quest
22. Vacuum
23. Feminine nickname
24. Dickens character
25. Baked, as eggs
26. Buddy
27. Rose's milieu
28. Golf shoe feature
29. Indian region
31. Construct
32. Popular tea ingredients
33. Sioux Indians
34. Magician's prop
36. Vatican name
37. — Daniels, of H'wood fame
39. Container
41. Hindrance

ACROSS

1. Sty resident
4. TV headliner
8. Bargain event
12. Big fuss
13. Tailor's item
14. Dramatic work
15. Exhausted: hyph. wd.
17. Starchy cereal grain
18. Miscalculates
19. Flying toys
20. Surfeits
22. Facial feature
24. Quote
25. Male chickens
29. Fruit drink
30. Declaims wildly
31. Falsehood
32. Destroyers of wood
34. For fear that
35. Lyric poems
36. Caverns
37. Not fresh
40. Food fish
41. Feel a liking (for)
42. Tells
46. Pub brews
47. Wicked
48. Metallic rock
49. Tidy
50. Faucets
51. Uncooked

DOWN

1. Cushion
2. Marriage vow: 2 wds.
3. "Eager beaver": hyph. wd.
4. Mixes
5. Sailors
6. Mimic
7. Traffic light color
8. Run
9. Dismounted
10. Edging fabric
11. Potato buds
16. Linden or ginkgo
19. Meringue candy
20. Begone, cat!
21. Military assistant
22. Small inlets
23. Garden tools
25. Cost per unit
26. Common staircase alternative
27. Get up
28. Adjusts, as a clock
30. Go by bus
33. Annoy harmfully
34. Actress Turner
36. Ringlets
37. Look over hastily
38. Story
39. Length x width
40. Stumble (over)
42. Tennis need
43. Actress Gardner
44. Historic period
45. Stitch

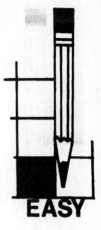

EASY

HARD

ACROSS

1. "— the cuff," extemporane- ously
4. Sir: Swahili
9. Crow's relative
12. Caviar, for ex- ample
13. Eagle's nest
14. A primate
15. Brush part
17. Wash lightly
19. Virtuous
20. Plundered
21. Type of poly- phonic compo- sition
23. Hindu social class
24. Legal claim
25. Hot drink
26. Exist
28. Virginia, — Dominion
29. Drive back
30. Ineffectual ob- ject
31. Correspon- dent's after- thought: abbr.
32. Ancient Asians
33. Outer layer
34. Cold drinks
35. Untidy
36. Hans Brinker
38. Hue
39. Machine for shaping metal
40. "Waiting rooms" for baseball players
43. Consumed
44. Face part
46. Decay
47. A Kennedy
48. Cry out loudly
49. Lad

DOWN

1. Globe
2. In favor of
3. Pretended
4. Drum major's rod
5. Fuse by heat- ing
6. Metric unit
7. Ulster: abbr.
8. Kind of spray container
9. Italian poet
10. Church projec- tion
11. Noxious plant
16. In a short time
18. Greek letter
20. Tatted fabrics
21. Sound of a horse's hoof
22. Troubles
23. Contends (with) success- fully
25. Fragrant wood
26. Sweet rolls
27. Whirlpool
29. Buys back
30. Agitate
32. Wool destroyer
33. Nevada city
34. Surfeited
35. Great power
36. Venetian blind item
37. — Smith, singer
38. Ballerina's skirt
40. A pair
41. Also
42. Pigpen
45. Surprised cry

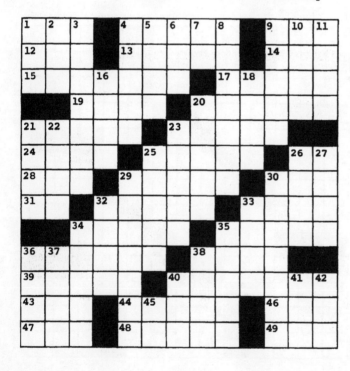

ACROSS

1. Faucet
4. Fragment
9. Sum (up)
12. Female sheep
13. Untied
14. Deposit
15. Even then
17. Call long-distance
19. Playing card
20. Reach across
21. Glowing particle
24. Seesaws, for short
27. Healthy
28. Goldilocks' "hosts"
29. Cry of surprise
30. Feminine name
31. Collapses
32. Actress Lyon
33. Mother
34. House's sides
35. Book leaf
36. Satisfies
38. Bet
39. Insects
40. Brooch
41. Squander
43. Most rapid
47. Fruit drink
48. Nephew's sister
50. Hive dweller
51. Deity
52. Guide
53. Actor Gazzara

DOWN

1. Hot beverage
2. Piercing tool
3. For each
4. Not busy
5. System of signals
6. Cowboy Rogers
7. While
8. Pungent vegetables
9. In solitude
10. Son of Jacob
11. Tint
16. Nobleman
18. Derby and beret
20. Closes tightly
21. Marsh
22. Bicycle part
23. Southern State: abbr.
24. Narrates
25. Baton —, Louisiana
26. Very thin
28. Large bundles
31. Attaches
32. Droop
34. Desire
35. Gasp
37. Relieved
38. Having more knowledge
40. Walk back and forth
41. Move from side to side
42. Fuss
43. Lawyer's charge
44. Recede
45. Glimpse
46. Two fives
49. That thing

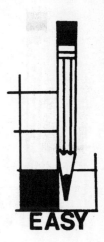

EASY

ACROSS

1. Church singing group
6. Pullman accommodation
11. Broadway musical
12. — in, landed, as a fish
14. Back section
15. Sweetener
17. Norfolk's State: abbr.
18. Auricle
19. Tightwad
20. Part of H.R.H.
21. Like
22. Factions
23. Gaunt
24. Enticed
26. Puts on the market
27. Devours
28. Channel changer
29. Browns by heat
31. Fun-house features
34. Lecture
35. Number of Rome's hills
36. Nearby
37. Burro
38. Juan Carlos' land
39. Contend
40. Tag player
41. Spherical
42. Bouquet beauty
43. "Wanted" poster offering
45. Revised copy
47. Leases
48. Curved roofs

DOWN

1. Wrinkle
2. Get wind of
3. Rowing blade
4. Basic verb
5. Dwells
6. Impulses
7. Bosc or Bartlett
8. For each
9. Overhead train
10. Divulge
11. Like the Wall of China
13. Reweaves
16. Secondhand
19. Catchers' gloves
20. Greeting for "Dolly"
22. Flash of light
23. Acquire knowledge
25. Breakfast and dinner
26. Fire-engine signal
28. "United we stand, — we fall"
29. Single step
30. Spring holiday
31. Intend
32. Jacks up
33. Spirited horse
35. "Taters"
38. Separate into categories
39. Cast a ballot
41. Scurried
42. Flange
44. All of us
46. Meet requirements

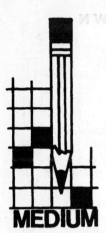

MEDIUM

ACROSS

1. Word with "check" or "verse"
6. French river
11. Pusillanimous
12. Non-citizens
14. Aloof
15. Small undulation
16. Equable
17. Roasting rod
19. Deadlock
20. Espouse
21. European capital
22. Tooth part
23. Item for Little Miss Muffet
24. Certain car windows
25. Sail extender
27. Traffic dividers
28. Book size
29. "Boom's" opposite: slang
30. Medical school subject: abbr.
31. Intimate
32. Warm Springs, for example
35. Body of water: French
36. Dianthus
37. Piercing wound
38. Pollen-bearing organ
40. Restrict inheritance of (property)
42. Having a "nosh"
43. Indeed!
44. Fish, in a way
45. Blisters

DOWN

1. Pronunciation symbol
2. Hebrew letter
3. County of England
4. Tennis need
5. Israeli parliament
6. Singer Lanza
7. Dismounted
8. "— off," cheat
9. Poseidon
10. Joins the armed services
11. Ship's complement
13. Oozes
18. Work at (a trade)
21. Buckeye State
22. Coin
23. Official order
24. Very great in size
25. Certain musical works
26. Mollify
27. Subjects of fish stories
28. — bottom, smuggler's item
29. Storage receptacle
31. Door joint
32. Vapid
33. Containers
34. With competence
36. Noted Quaker
37. "— Trek"
39. 1002, to Livy
41. Prefix meaning "new"

HARD

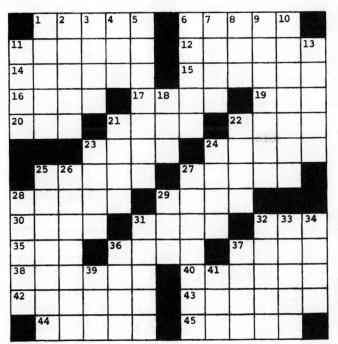

57

ACROSS

1. 50%
5. Foot lever
10. Edifice at Pisa, Italy
11. Gnarly trees
13. Speechify
14. Cut (off), as twigs
15. Mouser
17. Invite
18. Stumbles (over)
20. Cause of extra innings
21. Low, as a voice
23. Expert
24. Govern (over)
25. Delicate trim
27. Shows concern (for)
28. Blackboard material
30. Oven-cooked
31. Sparkle
32. Walking stick
33. Armored vehicle
34. Skillet
35. Morse code symbol
39. Gorilla
40. Hits hard
42. Perish
43. Precious stone
44. Possesses
45. Decorate
47. Military greeting
49. Painful spots
50. Famous
51. Understands

DOWN

1. Derby runner
2. No longer asleep
3. Permit
4. Worry (over)
5. The "P" in M.P.
6. Wed secretly
7. Short swims
8. Thoroughfare: abbr.
9. Professor's speech
10. Frog's kin
12. Went by ship
16. — off, begins a golf game
19. Grand Prix or Indy 500
22. Heavy board
24. Gathered, as leaves
26. Had lunch
27. Is able to
28. Forms
29. Football player
30. Shut (a door) noisily
31. Male-only social
32. Made happen
34. Dish
36. Worship
37. Paddock papas
38. Biddies
40. — off, isolate
41. Talk back to
46. Buck's mate
48. Behold!

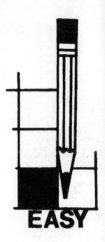

EASY

58

ACROSS

1. Paving substance
4. Liberate
8. Tepid
12. Lyric poem
13. Period of lessened activity
14. Great Lake port city
15. Feasible
17. Verdi opera
18. Broadway award
19. Favorable, as an opportunity
21. Gesture of indifference
23. Crave
24. Couple
25. Inclination
29. Joan of —
30. Vestige
31. Prohibit
32. Recover; get back
34. Cougar
35. Otherwise
36. Hive product
37. Snarl
40. Gelatin dish
41. Declare
42. Global area: 2 wds.
46. Center
47. Birthday greeting
48. Born
49. Half hitch, for one
50. Gaelic
51. Brownish color

DOWN

1. Summit
2. Commotion
3. Confine; limit
4. Toss
5. Precious gem
6. Building wing
7. Grace
8. Riches
9. Like a desert
10. Go by bus
11. Ornery
16. Tart
20. Start of many a fairy tale
21. Shadowbox
22. Rabbit
23. Make cloth
25. Attendance
26. Plentiful
27. Robert or Roberta
28. Serving piece
30. Cash drawer
33. Rue
34. Warsaw native
36. Throng
37. Small nail
38. Stratford's river
39. Roman emperor
40. Solar system number
43. Corn spike
44. Caspian, for one
45. Decade number

ACROSS

1. Young fellow
4. Bashful
7. Mist
10. Spoken
12. Actor, — Majors
13. Stuffing herb
14. Unadorned
15. Historic period
16. Become weary
17. Start
19. Portion
21. Turf
22. Asphaltlike substance
23. Jewel
26. Unused
28. Deserve; earn
32. Above
34. "Spare the — and spoil the child"
36. Cut into cubes
37. Engagements
39. Bite; pinch
41. It's mightier than the sword
42. Pale
44. Group of like things
46. Part of a place setting
48. Two-wheeled wagons
51. Two of a kind
52. By way of
54. Very dry
56. Matured
57. Make a mistake
58. Fishing rod
59. Guided
60. Like a beet
61. Cargo weight unit

DOWN

1. Throw lightly
2. Spirited steed
3. Challenge
4. Slim
5. Opposite of him
6. Leavening
7. Carnival
8. Fairy-tale monster
9. Command to Dobbin
11. Table supports
13. Gaped
18. Charged atom
20. Meat choice
23. Supreme Being
24. Actress, — Gabor
25. Encountered
27. Was victorious
29. Tear
30. Frozen water
31. Number of Commandments
33. Bounty
35. Throw away
38. "Used" a chair
40. Pod vegetable
43. At no time!
45. Snare
46. Book part
47. Fibbed
49. Jog
50. Grain storage tower
51. Buddy
53. Anger
55. Cozy room

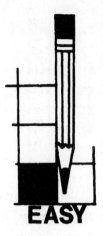

EASY

ACROSS

1. In favor of
4. Vitality
7. Wharves
9. Stories
11. Certainly
13. Buccaneer
14. Golfer's peg
15. The "W" in N.O.W.
17. Yellowish-brown
18. — upon, attack
20. Old horse
21. Coagulate
22. Engine
24. Craze
25. Cover with pitch
26. Plant fluid
27. Road chart
28. Locations
30. Buddy
31. Wicked deed
32. Take a chair
34. And not
35. Employer
37. Siesta
39. Mediterranean fruits
41. Squirm
43. Material for jeans
44. Underneath
45. Observe
46. Two fives

DOWN

1. Cone-bearing evergreens
2. Buy back
3. Metallic rock
4. Average
5. Overjoyed
6. Blossom part
7. Cherry seed
8. Stitch
9. Metal used in cans
10. Japanese coin
12. Contributor
13. Wooden pin
16. Disfigure
19. Add (up)
21. Stares open-mouthed
23. Faucet
24. Plump
26. Muscular strength
27. Of the sea
28. Knight's title
29. Not married
30. Fishing sticks
31. Female sibling, for short
33. Claw
34. Signal meaning "yes"
35. Skirt's edge
36. Chest bone
38. Church seat
40. Compete (for)
42. Obtain

Easy

Medium

ACROSS

1. Outdo
4. Do oneself —, do extremely well
9. Health farm
12. Exclamation of disgust
13. Slip of the memory
14. Pie plate
15. Stadium shout
16. Behave
17. Desk enhancer, often
19. Sea eagle
21. Style of beard
22. Portable boat
24. Billiards shot
25. Desertlike
26. Practice
27. Song, "Let It —"
29. Clock reading
30. Defect
31. Cushion
32. Cry of surprise
33. Bend
34. Sharp flavor
35. Crowd
36. Ski inn
37. Owned property
39. Do as told
40. Ground
41. Valise
42. Sphere
45. Be incorrect
46. Historical age
48. Bill's partner
49. Travel via 4-Down
50. Correct!
51. U.S. anthem writer

DOWN

1. N.L. athlete
2. In the past
3. Western capital
4. 747 or 707
5. Regatta is one
6. Make a choice
7. You and me
8. Bank-statement entry
9. Condition
10. Long (for)
11. Poker stake
18. Endure
20. Scepter
21. Grand old name of films
22. Johnny of songdom
23. Operatic solo
24. Shade of purple
26. Robust
27. Thrill: slang
28. Advantage
30. Moreover
31. Enclosure for race-horses
33. Baltimore athlete
34. Heavy weight
35. Part of H.S.T.
36. Ignite
37. Shoal
38. Jimmy — Carter
39. Engine worker: abbr.
41. Marsh
43. Caviar
44. Lad
47. 3.1416

ACROSS

1. Lodger
7. Account entry
13. Obliterate
14. Caribbean capital
15. Branch of service: abbr.
16. Jack Lemmon movie of 1980
18. Thoron's symbol
19. Apart: prefix
21. Join
22. Wicked
23. Reverberate
25. Compass point: abbr.
26. Ginza drink
27. Farm machine
29. Tammany official
31. Lawn moisture
32. Soup morsel
33. Gems
36. Swindler: 2 wds. (slang)
39. Dairy stock
40. Pronoun
42. Domesticate
43. Pronoun
44. Book parts
46. Feminine name
47. — Cajon, CA
48. Laments
50. Pierre's State: abbr.
51. One of the three Gorgons
53. Proust
55. American inventor
56. Husband or wife

DOWN

1. McGuffey's claim to fame
2. Certain work site
3. From
4. Picture border
5. Beige
6. Family name of comedy fame
7. Vertical troughs
8. Deserve
9. Feminine name
10. Prosecutor: abbr.
11. Mine's air shaft
12. In single file
17. Storage box
20. Trails closely
22. Eleuthera, et al.
24. Unfastens
26. Perfume
28. Sheep
30. GI's mailing address: abbr.
33. Plot
34. Labored untiringly
35. Medicine man
36. Beauty preparations
37. Entertains
38. Sewing need
41. Conceit
44. Mexican coin
45. Ginger cookie
48. Motor coach
49. Theater sign: abbr.
52. Charles' lady
54. Copper's symbol

Hard

Easy

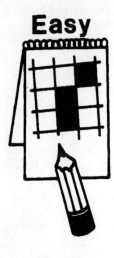

ACROSS

1. Hawaiian dance
5. Given without cost
9. Beer or ale
13. Flat-bottomed boat
17. Tiny particle
18. Incline
19. Fury
20. Corn bread
21. Chart
22. Looking (for)
24. Body support
25. Basic necessity
27. Fastening device
28. Lamented loudly
29. Cereal grain
30. Wharf
31. Harbor
32. Expressive shoulder movement
35. Twilight
36. Users of covered wagons
40. Burden
41. Military headquarters
42. Clock's time indicators
43. Storage tub
44. Picnic pest
45. Word with "drink" or "sell"
46. Needs
47. Type size
48. Busy insect
49. Refugee from Sodom
50. Hauling vehicles
51. Astronomical sight, — Way
52. Stout
53. Book parts
54. Cut (off) twigs
55. French cap
58. Metal threads
59. Jar cover
60. Feminine name
63. Praise
64. Sleeveless garments
65. Counterfeit
66. Scold continuously
67. Vase
68. Garden implements
69. Small coin
70. In this place
71. Etches
73. Assist
74. Used oars
75. Level
76. Small restaurant
77. Startling sound
78. Carves, as a roast
81. Decrease
82. Mail delivery charge
86. Broaden
87. Island near the Malay Peninsula
89. Fishing pole
90. So be it!
91. Gelatin shaper
92. Floor covering item
93. Ruler
94. Omelet recipe's instruction
95. Man's nickname
96. Looks at
97. Canary's "home"

DOWN

1. Overacting performers: slang
2. Mormon State
3. Easy pace
4. Exist
5. Navy
6. Raise (a family)
7. Organ of hearing
8. Mail order direction
9. Building material
10. — and file, ordinary people
11. Hen product
12. You and I
13. Pixie
14. Type of fuel
15. Formerly
16. Uncultivated plant
22. Male deer
23. Pawn: slang
24. Farm buildings
26. Noisy
28. Forests
30. Perform a household chore
31. Liquid measures
32. Thick slice
33. Sharpening stone
34. Fixed price per unit
35. Pixilated
36. Trousers
37. Wicked
38. Display stand
39. Remain
41. Infantryman's shoe
42. Jack rabbits
45. Venetian-blind part
46. Carries on (war)
47. Apple seed
50. Is concerned
51. Fashion
52. Gave a meal to
53. Tubes
54. Similar to
55. Color of an unclouded sky
56. Acquire by labor

57. Ladder part
58. Rouse from sleep
59. Lighting device
60. Afresh
61. Challenge
62. Matured
64. Caverns
65. Office storage cabinet
68. Black bird
69. Losses

70. Owl's sound
72. Modern; new
73. — on, persevere
74. Showy flower
76. Fudge, for example
77. Drills
78. Mop
79. Citrus fruit
80. Thought
81. Not tame

82. Native of Warsaw
83. Opera melody
84. Saucer-shaped bell
85. Border
87. Male heir
88. Bakery item
91. University degree: abbr.
93. Honored barrister: abbr.

Medium

ACROSS

1. Bus charge
5. Explosion
10. Ledge
15. At what time?
19. Skater's spinning leap
20. Of sound waves
21. Thick soup
22. Amusement park feature
23. Ice-hockey site
24. Sparkle
26. Concept
27. Oil source
28. Badger
29. Nothing
30. Potential
32. May's birthstone
34. Floats in the air
36. Khartoum's river
37. Keen enjoyment
38. Occasions
39. Striking difference
43. Pixies
45. More attractive
46. Zodiacal sign
47. Boxing decision: abbr.
48. Housetop
49. Gaels
50. Dollar components
51. Ordinance
52. Debt chit
53. Bright retort
54. Veranda
55. Dinner dish
57. Jazz combo
59. Hard to chew
60. Type of engine
61. Game on horseback
62. Pickling solution
63. Tree trunk
64. Counsel
67. Impact of a blow
68. Rephrased
72. Race course
73. Stretch of land
74. Goliath was one
75. Lode deposit
76. Beach acquisition
77. Fissure
78. Cheerful
79. Albacore
80. Top off a cake
81. Damp
82. "The — Family Robinson"
83. Identifying tag
84. Halloween outfits
86. Composure
87. Hot-dog holder
88. Mount Blanc's range
89. Standard measure
90. Food stores
93. Indian village
96. Sixth sense, for short
97. "Miffed"
98. Caldron
99. Indigo plant
100. Emotional outlet: 2 wds.
105. Shortening
106. Kingly title
107. Unevenly notched
108. Bay window
109. Reclined
110. Let it stand, to a printer
111. Insurgent
112. Cowboy, out West
113. Unit of force

DOWN

1. Broad humor
2. Maxim
3. Tryst
4. Wapiti
5. Igneous rock
6. Clear-headed
7. Mine passage
8. Transgression
9. Kindergartner
10. Divides into shares
11. Peanut shells
12. Memorable period
13. "— freedom ring"
14. Sensibilities
15. Author
16. "Hole up"
17. Biblical garden
18. Orderly
25. Imply
28. Musical clef
31. Choir voice
33. Shoal
34. Cleverly amusing
35. Singer Ed
36. Toward the Arctic
38. Veil fabric
39. Easy job: slang
40. Book of maps
41. Do a figure-eight
42. Drying cloth
43. Pennsylvania port
44. Diving bird
45. Casals' instrument
46. Brink
49. Wire rope
50. Nobleman
53. Artist's garb
54. Main idea
55. Aviator
56. Wanton look
58. Homeric poem
59. Teamster's vehicle
60. Soft and fluffy
62. Modified leaf
63. Chili ingredients
64. Garret
65. Northern constellation
66. Wind indicators
67. Military VIPs: slang

68. Washer cycle
69. Baseball maneuver: 2 wds.
70. Sea eagle
71. Transaction
73. Gives it a whirl
74. Semblance
77. Bach or Beethoven
78. Hearty gulp
79. Lecture
81. Ponder (over)
82. Comedian Sales
83. Folk knowledge
85. Writing pad
86. Light color
87. Seldom
89. Gaggle members
90. Budged
91. Car wheel adjustment: hyph. wd.
92. Building block
93. Free ticket
94. Monad
95. Dublin's land
97. Lost one's footing
101. "You — There," TV oldie
102. Watch chain
103. Solemn promise
104. Brazilian macaw
105. Part of GOP

Medium

ACROSS

1. Through
4. Sketches
9. Mineral spring
12. Where — you?
13. Rent again
14. Ball point or quill
15. Rodeo whip material
17. Major part of the Earth's surface
19. "I goofed!"
20. Grain husk
21. Distortions
23. Extreme
26. Signs one's name to: slang
27. Not smooth
28. Perform
29. Female sibling, for short
30. Chili con —
31. That woman
32. Overhead railway
33. Unspoken
34. Chief
35. Dwells
37. Opera's Beverly
38. Singles
39. Swallow hastily
40. Loud warning signal
42. Like an uncovered bottle
45. Part of a play
46. Small, two-door car
48. Decay
49. Certainly!
50. Join
51. Secret agent

DOWN

1. Golfing norm
2. Memorable age
3. Shapes again, as pottery
4. Trickles
5. Warren Beatty film
6. Malt beverage
7. You and I
8. Warehouse function
9. Worn out
10. Pod vegetable
11. Actress Blyth
16. Moves like a rabbit
18. Bills and coins
20. Impact (of a blow)
21. More prudent
22. Infirm; weak
23. Actress Day
24. Perfect model
25. Measures of wood
27. Kentucky Derby and Preakness
30. Rhythmic flow of sound
31. Elves, to Santa
33. Prong
34. Knoll; mound
36. Classifies
37. First-rate!
39. Yawn
40. Utter
41. —-cream cone
42. Chop; clip
43. Soak
44. Pigpen
47. Attached to

Hard

ACROSS

1. Spar
5. Vigor
8. Past due
12. Dog of tropical America
13. Galley's "propeller"
14. Home of Iowa State
15. Musical ornament
16. Actors' aides
18. Friends: Spanish
20. Austria's capital
21. Stein
22. Mr.: German
23. Nietzschean hero
26. School subject: abbr.
30. Suffix meaning "native of"
31. A planet
33. Form of "to be"
34. Four-posters
36. Coal or oil
38. Chums
40. Actress Merkel
41. Bring into harmony with, — to
44. Wakes up
47. Jewelry items
49. Whitewall
50. Nothing: French
51. Dawn goddess
52. English private school
53. Shouts of approval: Spanish
54. Posed for an artist
55. Respite

DOWN

1. Spy, — Hari
2. An astringent
3. Economized
4. Language or dialect
5. Pea cases
6. Site of the anvil and hammer
7. Hinders
8. Modern devices
9. Prayer closing
10. Sea bird
11. She: Italian
17. Baronet's title
19. Grimm villain
22. Speedy mammals
23. Kin
24. Shoshonean Indian
25. Miss Dietrich and others
27. Hanger-on
28. Windshield wiper's path
29. Born
32. Unit of time
35. Rejects with contempt
37. Joiner; connector
39. Black cuckoo
41. Of aircraft
42. Follow: slang
43. Catalpa or ginkgo
44. Aide: abbr.
45. Aphrodite's son
46. Transmitted
48. Indian region

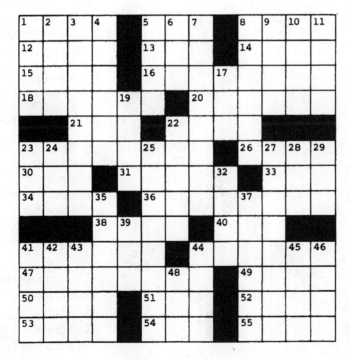

ACROSS

1. Fruit seed
4. Rope fiber
8. Large tank
11. Path
12. State positively
13. Wrath
14. Assistant
15. Fragile
17. Operate, as a car
19. Also
20. Equipment
22. Rambling flowers
26. Storage box
28. Poultry pen
31. Crude metal
32. Actress Lupino
33. Amass and hide away
35. Falsehood
36. Cozy room
37. Group of three
38. Tavern
39. Glossy fabric
42. Greatest amount
44. Actress Charisse
46. Respond to a stimulus
49. Certain author
54. Dreadful; terrible
55. Bustle
56. Dollar bills
57. Region
58. Church seat
59. Certain tide
60. Modern

DOWN

1. Couple
2. Highly provoked
3. Vex
4. Possessed
5. Abel's mother
6. Thaw
7. Former; previous
8. By way of
9. Actor Carney
10. Golf mound
11. Boy
16. Dove call
18. "To — his own"
21. Plant's underground part
23. Game for one
24. Ireland
25. Observed
26. Auction offers
27. Notion
29. Paddle
30. Very proper
34. Portal; entrance
40. Frozen water
41. Stocking material
43. Family car
45. Eat in style
47. Foreman's gang
48. "— for Two"
49. Short sleep
50. Lyric poem
51. Promise
52. Ocean
53. Recipe abbreviation

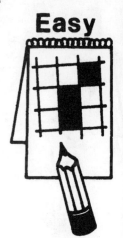

Easy

70

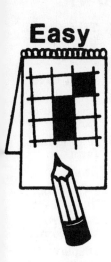

Easy

ACROSS

1. Cigar residue
4. WAVE's "sister"
8. Apple's center
12. Regret
13. Bob of comedy
14. Eager
15. Positioned in the middle
17. Darn, as socks
18. Perforation
19. Get-up-and-go
21. Sand bar
23. Bartlett or bosc
24. Noisy
25. Small cosmetic cases
29. Morning hours: abbr.
30. Phonies
31. Garden tool
32. Seesawed
34. Fender mishap
35. Pay attention to
36. "Love" flowers
37. Great excitement
40. Swift
41. Bellow
42. Earth, air, fire, and water
46. Print-shop supplies
47. Ooze
48. Guitarlike instrument, for short
49. Track event
50. Occupies a chair
51. Drag behind

DOWN

1. Curved line
2. "Sweet" girl of song
3. Chicken coop
4. Turtle's shield
5. Skin opening
6. Gorilla
7. Cashed in, as coupons
8. Photographer's need
9. Finished
10. Wedding band
11. Nelson —, of operetta fame
16. Frog's kin
20. Siestas
21. Louver board
22. There's no place like "it"
23. Nudged
25. Neglectful
26. Reddish-brown horse
27. Musical quality
28. Groups of games, as in tennis
30. Touch
33. Desire for water
34. Medicinal amount
36. Inclined walkways
37. Neat
38. Sharpen
39. Do an autumn lawn chore
40. 3 per yard
43. Waikiki wreath
44. Boxing decision: abbr.
45. Stitch

Hard

ACROSS

1. Correct
6. Roundabout ways
8. A Truman
9. Hilarious occurrence
11. Diplomacy
12. Thus
13. Rename
15. Recreational area
16. Small roll
17. Seine
19. Conjunction
20. Boxer, — Lesnevich
21. Scarlett —, GWTW heroine
23. Thoroughfare: abbr.
24. Liken
26. Raleigh's State: abbr.
27. Religious pamphlet
29. Rather than: poetic
30. Leader of the "Long March"
31. Continent: abbr.
32. Hole in one
33. Evergreens
34. "Loony"
36. Football position: abbr.
37. Hourglass filler
38. Former Oriole, — Powell
40. Community chest, for one
41. Estimating
43. Exploits

DOWN

1. Take a break
2. Pronoun
3. Depart
4. Great Lake
5. Prefix with "cycle" and "angle"
6. Ship's platform
7. Sward
8. — of Avon, Shakespeare
10. Popular sandwich filling
11. Display of temper
12. Whodunit character
14. Saint —, large canine
15. Adhesive
16. Derelict
18. Mexican snacks
20. Received
21. Galena, e.g.
22. That man
24. Measure of volume: abbr.
25. Amount to
28. Bedouin
30. Intellect
32. Quarrel
33. Pointed tooth
35. Jackal's kin
37. Exposes to daylight
39. Lout
40. Appropriate
42. Peach State: abbr.

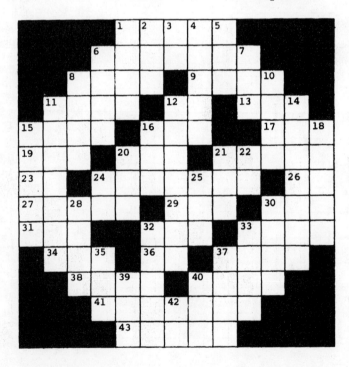

ACROSS

1. Binge
6. Cereal seed
11. Begin: 2 wds.
12. Dawdle
14. Uncommon
15. Story in a building
17. Roman 6
18. Inquire
19. Animal
20. Cushion
21. Perform
22. Wharves
23. Green gemstone
24. Printer's measure
25. By —, by memory alone
26. Candy ingredient
27. Girl
28. Current fashion
29. Guile
31. Sharp flavor
32. Type of radio: abbr.
34. Seek (for)
35. "Home on the —"
36. Hello!
37. Baby's age on his first birthday
38. Instruments for a jazz band
39. Golf score
40. At home
41. Cooking direction
42. Narrated
43. Go back again
45. Lifts
47. Wearing a judge's garment
48. White-sale item

DOWN

1. Spring or fall
2. Prepare (coffee)
3. Fish eggs
4. Alphabet letter
5. Results of causes
6. Sheen
7. Square or cube —
8. Atmosphere
9. That thing
10. Sagebrush State
11. Exchange
13. Jockey
16. Body of water
19. Increase
20. Book leaf
22. Current of air
23. Jurist
26. Ballads
27. Bowling alley
28. What polite people have
29. Group of singers
30. Marathoner
31. Small pie
32. Type of Swiss house
33. Robins and swans
35. Circular
38. Jack rabbit
39. Sit for a portrait
41. Prefix meaning "under"
42. Bind
44. As far as
46. Cry of surprise

Medium

73

Easy

ACROSS

1. Mama's mate
5. Laundry cycle
9. Full of pep
11. Romantic song
13. Cruise ship
14. Be ambitious (to get)
15. Apartment dweller
17. 100 years: abbr.
18. Employ
19. Golf mound
21. Reverence
23. Burn mark
25. Tree fluid
28. Fruit drinks
29. Youngster
30. Relieves (of)
31. Uncomfortably warm
32. Retained
33. Finish
34. Fishing pole
35. Permit
37. Grow older
39. Correct; improve
42. "I Love A —," song
45. Wear away
47. Overjoyed
48. Stitch again
49. Once more
50. Ended

DOWN

1. Chum
2. Dismounted
3. Evergreen tree
4. Pennsylvania and Park, for two
5. Used to be
6. Swiss peak
7. Bread serving
8. Jack rabbit
10. Historic periods
11. Baseball club
12. Cozy room
16. Settled in
19. Tell tales (on)
20. Vocalized pause
21. Excitement
22. Moistened
24. Policeman
25. Do wrong
26. Say further
27. End of a letter, sometimes: abbr.
28. Exclamation
30. Withdrew
32. Boxing decision: slang
34. Campaigned for office again
36. Always
37. Gorilla
38. Festive occasion
39. Taillight color
40. Average: hyph. wd.
41. First garden
43. It sounds like "eight"
44. "Grass sparkle"
46. Lamb's mother

ACROSS

1. Dyeing tank
4. Ship's pole
8. Salver
12. Rink surface
13. Choir voice
14. Sharpen
15. Metric measure
16. Film spool
17. Sums (up)
18. Dud: slang
20. Choice thing
22. Tennis-court divider
24. Incantations
28. Cut in two
32. Son of Abraham
33. G.I.'s address: abbr.
34. "— on your life!"
36. Depot: abbr.
37. Fishing net
40. Hire, as a bus
43. Closed cars
45. Historic period
46. Thaw
48. River at Lyon
52. North Sea feeder
55. Seine tributary
57. Vitality
58. At hand
59. Pindar output
60. Fictional Baba
61. Excavates
62. Bog fuel
63. "— freedom ring"

DOWN

1. Medicine bottle
2. Parcel of land
3. Abound
4. Eliot's Silas
5. Pub brew
6. Short distance
7. Thruway fees
8. English river
9. Pistol: slang
10. Also
11. Certainly!
19. Individual
21. News service: abbr.
23. Knockout count
25. Ultimate
26. Overdue
27. Wound mark
28. Back talk
29. Fencing foil
30. Empty
31. Disney dwarf
35. Film, "— Sting"
38. Nominators
39. Compass point
41. Take into custody
42. Rousing cheer
44. Sailboat
47. Neap or ebb
49. Race-track shape
50. View at Khartoum
51. Send forth
52. Grid player
53. Luau neckwear
54. Satchel
56. Masefield topic

Medium

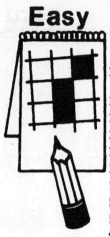
Easy

ACROSS

1. Failure: slang
5. Favorites
9. Adriatic or Bering
12. Valentine word
13. Spoken
14. Faucet
15. Cain's victim
16. Story
17. Function
18. Tepees
20. Slim
22. A few
24. Golf gadget
25. Actor Steiger
28. Box tops
30. Soon
33. Starts the day
35. Reveal secrets
37. Nothing more than
38. Trampled (on)
40. Determined
41. Terminate
43. Has debts
45. Contributing elements
48. Range; gamut
52. Behave
53. Apportion (out)
55. Eager
56. Dublin's country: abbr.
57. Biblical garden
58. Resounded, as bells
59. Guided the way
60. "Miffed"
61. Otherwise

DOWN

1. Tire mishap
2. Ear part
3. Microwave appliance
4. Animal hides
5. Kettle
6. Cleaned the blackboard
7. Lofty
8. Icy downpour
9. Scholars
10. Relieve (a pain)
11. One who mimics
19. One and only
21. Tidy
23. Light fog
25. Ewe's mate
26. Shipment from Duluth
27. Conducted (a band)
29. Pack away
31. Bullfight cheer
32. Profit
34. Transmitted
36. Citrus drinks
39. List of names
42. Rounded roofs
44. Frighten
45. Be unsuccessful
46. Land measure
47. Change the decor
49. Egg-shaped
50. Fasteners
51. Border
54. Compass point

ACROSS

1. Lofty peak
4. Handout
8. Queen of Carthage
12. Farm crop
13. Soviet range
14. Fe
15. Purpose
16. Wordiness
18. Of an imaginary line
20. Transgression
21. Footwear
22. For each
24. Hit sign: abbr.
26. Subjoined
30. Crowd-scene actor
34. Price: French
35. Noon, in old Rome
37. Front
38. Strained
40. Mingled
42. Woeful
44. Comic Caesar
45. "... from Ghent to —"
48. French king
50. Link
54. Safe
57. A Gabor
58. Bohea and souchong
59. Ancient Persian
60. Unit of resistance
61. Alcott and Lowell
62. Hewing tools
63. Sturdy tree

DOWN

1. Precinct
2. Bobcat
3. Foot: comb. form
4. Apartment type
5. Bobby of hockey
6. Cambodia's neighbor
7. Pitcher Dock
8. Fort in New Jersey
9. Blue flag
10. — death, kill: 2 wds.
11. Cameo stone
17. Concerning: 2 wds.
19. Vertices
23. Critic Reed
25. Leather for a whip
26. Pertinent
27. FDR program: abbr.
28. Slangy refusal
29. Across: prefix
31. Cowpoke's nickname
32. "Norma —," role for Field
33. Append
36. Freudian concepts
39. Mild oath
41. Pert girls
43. Tenet
45. Film canine
46. Ledger entry
47. Medical "photo": hyph. wd.
49. Wild goat
51. Dry: comb. form
52. Iris layer
53. Noted virologist
55. WWII agency: abbr.
56. Pindaric poem

Hard

ACROSS

1. Formerly
5. Bunker or Nob
9. Saluki, for one
12. Campus building
13. Region
14. Highway: abbr.
15. Bounce a basketball
17. Coil of yarn
19. Nobleman
20. Ms. Darcel
21. "Casablanca" cast member
23. Actress Day
24. News service: abbr.
25. Black or Valentine
27. Portable shelter
30. Carpentry tool
32. Room scheme
34. Cowboy Rogers
35. Yukon vehicle
37. Bridge expert
39. Approval
40. Postpone
42. Swiss capital
44. Decree
46. Russian river
47. Artist's stock
48. Israeli city: 2 wds.
51. Ski lodge
52. Practical joke
54. Arnaz of TV
55. Fooyung ingredient
56. Doorway sign
57. Poker stake

DOWN

1. Eccentric
2. Hide — hair
3. Town newsman, of yore
4. Set sail
5. Auditorium
6. Dander
7. The: French
8. Powerful beam
9. Author of "Sister Carrie"
10. Elevator magnate
11. Hereditary transmitter
16. Food staple
18. Make argyles
20. Benefactor
21. Girl of Dundee
22. Iridescent gem
23. Lure
26. Secretary of Treasury
28. Time for lunch
29. Youngster
31. Marriage rite
33. Insurgent
36. College VIP
38. The Sagebrush State
41. Supple
43. Bird of rhyme
44. Early Ron Howard role
45. Pealed
46. Barber's call
48. Asian language
49. Adherent: suffix
50. Contend
53. Draft animal

ACROSS

1. Mist
5. Sharp knock
8. Gifts to the poor
12. Biblical garden
13. Chill
14. Axe or saw
15. Engrossed
16. Coast
18. Realm
20. Abhorred
21. Poetic "before"
22. Highland group
24. Cotton bundle
26. Carelessly
30. Actor Wallach
31. Gander's mate
32. Cow's sound
33. Openhanded
35. Yield
36. Dispatch
37. Knight's title
38. Group of adjoining rooms
41. Conclude
44. With particulars: 2 wds.
47. Reflected sound
48. Heap
49. Feminine name
50. Handle roughly
51. Stalk
52. Cut (grass)
53. Actress Baxter

DOWN

1. Present
2. Genesis man
3. Dirigible airship
4. Complete
5. Ascend
6. High card
7. Vegetable morsel
8. Near: 2 wds.
9. Plunder
10. Additional
11. Snow vehicle
17. Form
19. Do's follower
22. Cumulus item
23. Young girl
24. Implore
25. Brewed drink
26. Before long
27. U.S. citizen
28. Turf
29. Garden tool
31. Welcome
34. Regard highly
35. Motion picture
37. Yes: Spanish
38. Drinks slowly
39. Single thing
40. Doing nothing
41. Defect
42. Avoid
43. Cavity
45. Intention
46. Marriage vow: 2 wds.

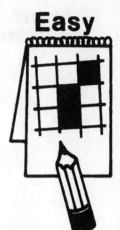

Easy

Hard

ACROSS

1. Breakfast item
6. Break open
11. Blanketlike cloaks
13. Large cactus
15. Live luxuriously: 5 wds.
17. Friend: French
18. Macaws
19. Fearful wonder
20. Lighting device
22. Regretful
23. Canadian Indian
24. Furtive person
26. Compete
27. Embers
28. Irritates
30. Actor Linden
31. La —, opera house
33. Yogis, e.g.
37. Trail secretly
38. Faction
39. — King Cole
40. Deal (with)
41. Dancer Kelly
42. Paddock parent
43. Wiles
44. Peace symbol
45. Stupid mistake: slang
46. Steeped beverage
47. Ear part
48. Soldier's gesture
49. Exclamation of wonder: 2 wds.
52. Part of Congress
54. Narrow opening
55. Army rank: abbr.
58. Talus
59. Fleshy fruit
60. Stop!
61. Legal document
62. Blueprint
63. Pile
64. Bushy clump
65. Pairs
66. Coral islands
68. Veteran: 2 wds.
70. Loses warmth
71. Climbing plant
72. Precipitous
74. Happy look
77. Tee- —, snicker
78. Flower part
82. Insincere talk
83. Dragged, formerly
85. Spanish coin
86. Public notices
87. Upbraided
89. AFL- —, labor union
90. Trifling amount: 4 wds.
93. Absence of noise
94. Uses a mountaineer's technique
95. Thick
96. Raises

DOWN

1. Everyone: 3 wds.
2. Prompt: 2 wds.
3. German expletive
4. Send
5. Roman garments
6. Goofy: slang
7. Grunts of disgust
8. Bitter herb
9. African desert
10. Garden tool
11. Rings
12. — Tuesday, last day before Lent
13. Sleeper's sound
14. Pointed archways
16. White iris
21. Processions
23. Foal
25. 1,000: prefix
27. Violin holder
29. Statute
30. — Park, FDR's home
31. Coast
32. Pirate: 2 wds.
33. Gold source
34. Concisely: 3 wds.
35. Printer's mark
36. Cubic meter
37. Get lost!
38. What sailors "sail": 2 wds.
41. Asian desert
42. Sunfish
44. Venetian official
45. Thai coin
47. Tardy
48. Commotion
50. Brewer's need
51. Spirit
52. Took care of: 2 wds.
53. Sign up
56. Aims
57. Bugle call
59. Trudge
60. Hooted
62. Weak; sickly
65. Man's nickname
66. Tennis triumph
67. Foot parts
69. Sword handle
72. Bible word
73. Wobble
74. Gobs
75. Prado's city
76. Shoe part
77. Author, Bret —
79. Wrinkle
80. Gazelles
81. Plunders
83. Therefore
84. Exclude; ban
87. Storage boxes
88. Fool
91. Female swan
92. Auditor: abbr.

SPECIAL CHALLENGER CROSSWORD

"SOBRIQUETS"

by JOHN GREENMAN

Here is a real toughie for you. We have omitted giving you such helps as "2 wds.," "hyph. wd.," and "slang"; but in the spirit of fair play, all abbreviations and foreign words are so indicated.

ACROSS

1. Lucy's ex
5. Turkish money
10. Imitative
15. Mount St. Helens' spill
19. Gretel's aversion
20. Awkward
21. Mississippi mouth
22. Role model
23. Georgia
25. Rhode Island
27. Necessitated
28. Darling dog et al.
30. Ordain
31. Dresden article
32. "Oysters — season"
33. Peking governess
34. Obis
38. Talent-show props
41. Saloon entertainer
44. Malayan sailboats
45. Send out an SOS, maybe
46. Mallard flocks
47. Boston, familiarly
49. Idumaea
50. California
52. CIA part-timer
53. *Pas "oui"*
54. Charon's fares
55. Muscle spasms
56. Rock star David
57. Cut through a yard
59. Woody Hayes, e.g.
61. Punctual
62. Singer-actor John
63. Fissure
64. Nappy fabric
65. Is prodigal
67. Attracts hacks
68. Drove by on the way back
71. Glee club section
72. D.C. quadrennium
73. Add more Styrofoam

74. Salt
75. Imitation morocco
76. Oregon
79. Cracker topper
80. Dutch oven, e.g.
81. Conic surface
82. Puccini's milieu
83. Forts' fronts
84. Hind and jenny
86. Boorish
87. Some poultry
88. Shiftless
89. Is, doubled?
90. Where one "Road" led
91. Xerxes' realm
94. David Low's "Colonel"
96. Beat
101. Hawaii
103. Delaware
105. Radial neighbor
106. Tyrrhenian Sea feeder
107. Nene, e.g.
108. Character in "Winnie Winkle"
109. Ballet feat
110. Chicago's — Tower
111. "Marvelous!"
112. Exploits

DOWN

1. Inside info
2. Smooth
3. Spot on the Exchange
4. Followers of Manco Capac
5. Fine cotton threads
6. Put underground
7. Take a vision test
8. Quick, in a way
9. Tommy's gun?
10. Handsome youth

11. Texas tree
12. Bits of *cartographie*
13. Depot: abbr.
14. Like patchwork quilts
15. Chinese fruit tree
16. Hebrew month
17. Suffrage
18. Safe at sea
24. Taxidermy needs
26. O'Casey and Connery
29. Light-bulb element
33. Directions: Scottish
34. Laid out
35. Fervidness
36. Oklahoma
37. Deli delight
38. Typifies chutzpah
39. Atlantic City data
40. Never: German
41. Steal eggs?
42. Missouri
43. Lily's descendant
45. Stir from bed
46. Refuse to move
48. Borscht need
50. Blame-takers
51. "Watergater" Maurice
52. Grammar topic
54. Uses binoculars?
56. Stollen
58. Squelched
59. Ring
60. Bribery
61. Ex-larvae
63. Sculpt
64. Dividing membranes
65. Deform
66. Asocial
67. "Lemons"
68. Nurtures
69. Sprat or Horner

82

70. Boutique purchase
72. Home of the brave
73. Paths: abbr.
76. Stabilizers
77. Composer Ned
78. Modern-day gym
79. Worker's comp?
81. 1976 Olympic charmer
83. Quite disgusting
85. Reason to say "Oops!"
86. Colonel Cronkites
87. Pool adjunct
89. Fix
90. Charlotte —, dessert
91. St. —, Minn.
92. *La femme*
93. Barrett or Jaffe
94. Rum cake
95. German coins: abbr.
96. Brace
97. Aleutian island
98. Greek crosses
99. Little follower?
100. *"Ditat —,"* Arizona's motto
102. Do macramé
104. Debtor's letters

DIAGRAMLESS

MEDIUM

This Diagramless is 15 boxes wide by 15 boxes deep.

ACROSS

1. Corn remnant
4. Niña or Pinta
8. City in Oklahoma
9. Detests
11. One who asks for a handout
13. Mini-pie
16. Whittle
17. By way of
18. Nibble
19. New growth, as on a twig
21. Vine berry
23. Electrical mishap
24. Scowl
25. October birthstone
26. Boutique
30. Not at home
31. Baseball deal
32. Be a copycat
33. Landlord's proof of ownership
35. Uncommon
36. Poe subject
38. "Hot under the collar"
40. Refuge
41. Long window curtain
42. Help with dishes
43. Urge (on)
44. Roster
45. Require
47. Personal affront
50. Passé
52. Caviar
53. Velvety growth on trees, rocks, etc.
54. Ram's dam

DOWN

1. Taxi
2. Keatslike poem
3. Highlander's instrument
4. Portion
5. Tortoise's racing companion
6. That thing
7. Favorite
10. Taste with relish
12. Fence door
14. Prison outbreaks
15. Make lace
18. Ingot
19. Protect from the sun
20. Golfing goal
21. Mucilage
22. Assess
23. Fifth tire
24. Thor or Odin
25. Speechify
27. Possess
28. Start the bidding
29. Desk-set item
31. Pitfall
34. Funeral song
36. Ecstasy; bliss
37. Fifth or Park: abbr.
39. Storm (about)
40. Give the villain his due
41. Lair
42. From hence Chicago gets its nickname
44. Stretches the truth
46. Grand Coulee or Hoover
48. Deep, as a voice
49. Golf gadget
51. In the direction of

DIAGRAMLESS

MEDIUM

**This Diagramless is 15 boxes wide by 15 boxes deep.
Starting box is on page 217**

ACROSS

1. — away, erode

5. Fiend of fairy tales

6. Children's TV host: 2 wds.

10. Group of three

12. Migratory worker of the 1930's

13. Woman's name

16. Charged particles

17. Ivan, Peter or Nicholas

18. Marx Brothers film: 2 wds.

20. Challenge

21. Calendar month: abbr.

22. Lower limb

23. Place

26. Compass direction: abbr.

29. Highway: abbr.

30. Scored on one shot, in tennis

32. Culinary herb

34. Product of tatting

38. Deep black

39. Cereal grain

40. Cupid

41. Gaggle members

42. Noblewoman

44. Civil disturbance

45. Golf-ball holders

DOWN

1. Part of a sentence

2. Self

3. Shoptalk; jargon

4. Smells offensive

6. Stately dance

7. "Bronx cheers": slang

8. Type of inlet

9. Sunday oration: abbr.

10. "— the season to be jolly ..."

11. Housetops

13. Total

14. Double

15. Land measure

19. Small barrel

24. Makes amends

25. Pieces of office furniture

26. America's symbolic Uncle

27. Cicatrix

28. Weird

31. Change the color of

33. Word with "electric" or "private"

34. Lake: French

35. I love: Latin

36. Place for a trial

37. Tennessee — Ford

41. Obtains

43. Pedal digit

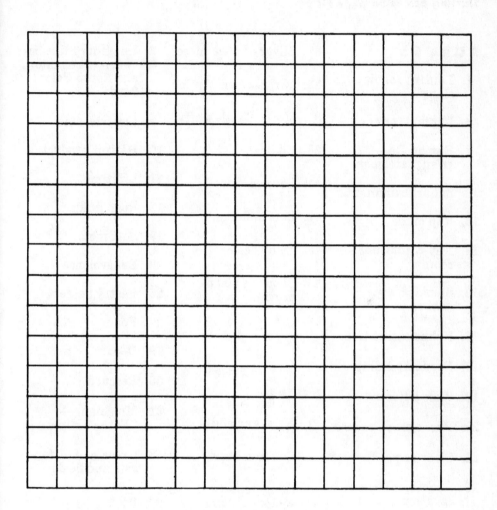

DIAGRAMLESS

HARD

This Diagramless is 17 boxes wide by 17 boxes deep.
Starting box is on page 217

ACROSS

1. Loutish fellow: slang
4. Laptev, for one
7. Eamon De —, Irish statesman
10. Sahara ruminants
13. Rub oil on
14. Any edible mushroom
15. Smokies, e.g.: abbr.
16. Public estimation
17. Feed-bag tidbit
18. Wise adviser
20. Phonograph record
21. Clear as profit
22. Archeological excavation
24. "Hill Street" role: slang
26. Wire spiral
28. Perfect examples
31. Sea eagle
32. Silver service piece
36. "Crackerjack" pilot
37. Morro Castle's city
38. Eddies
41. Leveled (off)
42. Lots and lots
43. "Stop" color
44. Shout of disapproval

DOWN

1. Maui garland
2. Coffee maker
3. Gangster's weapon: slang
4. Vaccine
5. Select group
6. Rise
7. Left quickly: slang
8. Imaginary line between the equator and South Pole: 2 wds.
9. Irretrievable
10. Detroit product
11. Lifetime
12. Road guide
19. Soft metal
23. Benevolence
25. Pastry dessert
27. Foam
29. Depart
30. Rescued
31. Musician, — "Fatha" Hines
33. Greek god of forests and fields
34. *Eins*
35. Little boy
38. Cry
39. Court
40. Altar response: 2 wds.

DIAGRAMLESS

EXPERT

This Diagramless is 17 boxes wide by 17 boxes deep.
Starting box is on page 217.

ACROSS

1. Cut corners
7. "Twelfth Night" lady
8. Safety device
13. Two-timer's offense
14. "Dallas" dowager
15. "Tizzy"
16. Herd of saddle horses
17. Garrulous gift
20. Thriller episode
23. Debussy subject
24. Cádiz cheer
25. Estuaries
26. Blossom for Whitman
29. Locale of Frogner Park
30. Triangle
31. Beyond: prefix
33. Teen's "terrific"
34. Vital statistic
35. *Douceurs*
38. Dry out and shrivel
40. Stapleton role
42. Bumpkin
43. Mother of Perseus
44. Inauguration ritual
45. Linker
46. Joke or choke
49. A cause of corruption
51. Continue a speech
52. Certain Alaskans
55. Insensate
58. Special vocabulary
59. Mt. Ida nymphs
62. Shaping machine
63. Trawler equipment
64. Bloch or Borgnine

DOWN

1. Sound from Niobe
2. Roman 151
3. Stacks the deck
4. A Karamazov brother
5. Hit off
6. "Cough up" a lot of dough: 4 wds.
8. Aitch preceder
9. Einstein's birthplace
10. Styptic
11. Heckle
12. Word to Abby
16. Frequented
17. *Or*
18. UFO occupant
19. Prom queen
21. Walkway
22. Jack-tar
27. Nipa palm
28. Bulk-mail items
32. Rival of Amneris
34. Crucial
36. One of a nautical trio
37. Sober
39. Crowd response
41. Close attention
46. Chutzpah
47. Other: Latin
48. Courteous bloke
50. German painter and engraver
53. Disgusted grunt
54. Oxford's tip
56. German possessive
57. Curse or scourge
60. French preposition
61. Sky speeder: abbr.

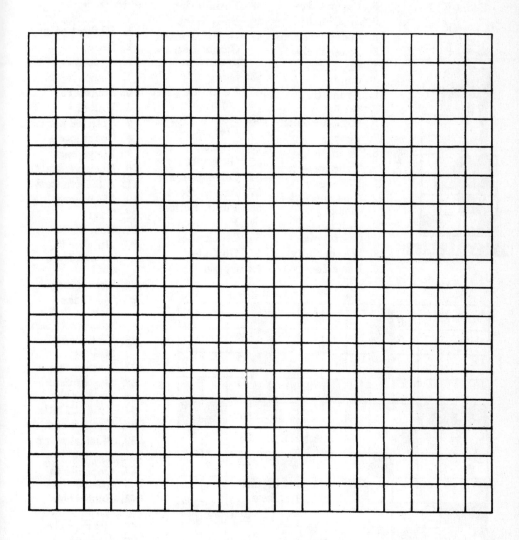

ACROSS

1. Mont Blanc and others
5. Party-giver
9. Small bed
12. Loden garment
13. Poker stake
14. Cry of triumph
15. Aromatic spice
16. High-schooler
17. Tear
18. Go in
20. Type measure
21. Fish eggs
22. Clearness of thought
26. — Angeles, California
29. Wander idly
30. Bee colony
33. Burden
35. Exclamation of disgust
37. Margarine
38. Foundation
40. Body joint
42. — Nol, former Cambodian premier
43. Offer
46. Feminine pronoun
48. Not on your life!
49. Station
53. Gain victory
54. Dismounted
57. Atmosphere
58. Public notices
59. Poi source
60. Thick slice
61. Golf peg
62. Space
63. Building wings

DOWN

1. Highest point
2. Lend
3. Agreement
4. Tough metal
5. Sombrero
6. United
7. Spirited horse
8. Court game
9. Large bag
10. Buckeye State
11. Adhesive item
19. Floor covering
23. Taxi
24. Gem State
25. Number needed for a duet
26. Toss lightly
27. "— Clear Day . . .": 2 wds.
28. "Whodunit" feature
31. Antique car
32. Day of the week: abbr.
34. Knight's title
36. Towel word
39. Musical work
41. Cushion
44. Opposite in nature
45. Rental contract
46. Hit sharply
47. Conceal
50. Tow
51. Spoken
52. Flaps
55. Anger
56. — tee, exactly: 2 wds.

medium

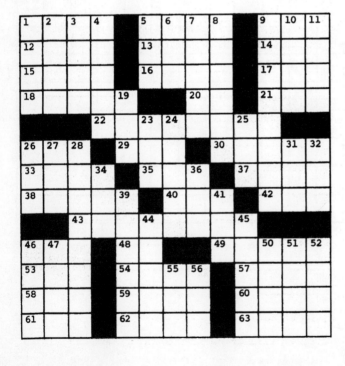

92

ACROSS

1. Mr. Hammarskjöld
4. Strikebreaker: slang
8. Fruit drinks
12. Turkish bigwig
13. Scarlett's home
14. Existed
15. Sweet dishes
17. Continent
18. Golf gadgets
19. Less restricted
20. Church officers
23. Legal equal
24. Retain
25. Immunizing fluids
27. Large truck
30. Curve
31. Cap's brim
32. Anger
33. Dry (wine): French
34. Pismires
35. Leg joint
36. Ali's milieu
38. Malt vinegar
40. Suppose
42. French designer
43. — Longa, ancient city
44. Abandoned
48. Adolescent
49. Charity
50. Boulevard: abbr.
51. Radio's "Vic and —"
52. Fail to hit
53. Kitten's sound

DOWN

1. Parental nickname
2. Grow older
3. Cooking fuel
4. Direct
5. Fondling
6. The "A" in B.A.
7. Low: French
8. Cognizant
9. Worthy
10. Lake or canal
11. Singe
16. Tread
19. Trepidation
20. — out, supplements
21. — majesty, treason
22. Told about
23. Dull remarks
26. Superlative suffix
28. District
29. —-do-well, lazy
31. Wind indicator
35. Author, Jean —
37. Foolish
39. Fertile loam
40. Feedbag contents
41. Entreaty
42. Lox shop, for short
44. Beaver's product
45. Highlander's cap
46. Cain's mother
47. Lawn moisture

hard

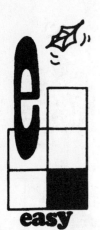

easy

ACROSS

1. Restaurant bill
4. Punish (a child)
9. "Tea for —"
12. Woman's name
13. Hauling vehicle
14. Use oars
15. Used for sheets
17. Bulb vegetable
19. Gorilla
20. Part of a movie ticket
21. Seagoing vessels
24. Most torrid
27. Apple center
28. Stories
29. Cry of triumph
30. Mine product
31. Employed
32. Water barrier
33. You and me
34. Peels
35. Ripped
36. Withdraws from business
38. Dips (doughnuts)
39. Marries
40. Score a victory
41. Get up
43. "Yes, We Have No —"
47. Is able to
48. Quiver
50. Petroleum
51. Organ of sight
52. Ocean movements
53. Ironic

DOWN

1. Knock
2. Fruit drink
3. Exclude
4. Exchanges
5. Wan
6. Epoch
7. Negative reply
8. Tangled; intricate
9. Clan
10. Court; seek as a mate
11. Have
16. Sleeveless garment
18. Pecans or filberts
20. Shoe bottoms
21. Scrub
22. Racing animal
23. Anger
24. Jack rabbits
25. "Jaws" star
26. Makes gentle
28. Wearies
31. Most difficult
32. Rickles or Ameche
34. Bakery items
35. Food fish
37. Strong cord
38. Eats the main meal
40. Rouse from sleep
41. High playing card
42. Mr. Milland
43. Wicked
44. At this time
45. Ventilate
46. Foxy
49. Hello!

ACROSS

1. Top of a wave
6. Diminish
11. Scabbard
12. Precepts
14. Walk off the job
15. Stout
17. Twice: prefix
18. Coffee-maker
19. Candid
20. Fleeting fashion
21. Electrical current: abbr.
22. Harmonize
23. Custody
24. It being the case that
26. Ridicules
27. Suitor
28. "— are born great . . ."
29. Cranky
31. "Ol' Blue Eyes"
34. "Hot lead"
35. Abstains from food
36. Vocalized pause
37. "— port in a storm"
38. Southpaw: slang
39. Winning serve
40. Football position: abbr.
41. Embankment
42. Utopia
43. Make fun of
45. Heroine of "Ivanhoe"
47. Exclude (from)
48. Trail of a hound

DOWN

1. Place of worship
2. Restraint for Dobbin
3. Devour
4. City map abbreviation
5. Author of "Walden"
6. Revise (a law)
7. Enjoy the sunshine
8. Hatchet
9. "La" follower
10. Set sail
11. Brave's wife
13. Sympathizes (with)
16. Forbids
19. Rover's tormentors
20. Surface of a cut gem
22. French port
23. Stupors
25. Dark wood
26. British field marshal, for short
28. The March girls
29. Variety of beet
30. Like Saturn
31. Umpire's call
32. Just off the press
33. Sphere of activity
35. Flu symptom
38. Mother of Helen of Troy
39. Arabian gulf
41. Women's —, social force
42. Ram's mate
44. Concerning
46. Military man in charge: abbr.

medium

ACROSS

1. African grass
5. Cereal grain
8. Lot
12. Viewed
13. Utmost
14. Big chunk of the world
15. Amy Lowell's expertise
17. Din
19. Jinx
20. Anger
21. Emulated Stanwyck or Streep
24. Carefree
27. Tam's lack
28. Flatfish
29. Sphere
31. Useful fold-away item
32. Opposite of "wanes"
33. Deface
34. Musical tone
35. Affirm
36. City near Phoenix
37. Bee's treat
39. Warning device
40. Pullet
41. Canine coat
42. Put back
45. Outside one's own country
49. One of the Ages
50. Conjunction
52. John Glenn's State
53. Depend (on)
54. Weeding aid
55. "The Eternal City"

DOWN

1. Viper
2. Delibes or Durocher
3. Charge
4. Nation's song
5. Cameo stone
6. Near
7. Suspense movie
8. Phase
9. Invite
10. Cause of extra innings
11. Break bread
16. Florid
18. Zodiac member
21. Basics
22. Sing like young Bing
23. Claim; right
24. Bulldog's kin
25. "Iliad" poet
26. Rub out
28. Port city of Georgia
30. Muffin choice
32. Necessity of life
36. Reflect
38. Considerable portion
39. Inferior: prefix
41. Lose color
42. Umbrella support
43. Epoch
44. Large amount
46. Cry of triumph
47. Objective
48. Buck's mate
51. *Nein*

ACROSS

1. Information
5. Nudge
9. Tree's fluid
12. Employs
13. Courtroom exhibit
15. Dance movement
16. Scarlet
17. Unusual
18. Toward
19. Evergreen
20. Detroit ballplayer
21. Of the fleet
24. Enthusiast
25. Repaired
26. Carton
27. Large
30. Capri, for one
31. Candle material
32. Actress Turner
33. Lay — law down
34. Boy
35. Flavorful
36. Gladness
37. Might
38. Mattress covering
41. Thirsty
42. At home
44. Surface (a road)
45. Service charge
46. Fury
48. Across the ocean
50. Musical work
51. Commandment number
52. Possesses
53. Red vegetable

DOWN

1. Fine powder
2. Amaze
3. Golf mound
4. Poisonous snake
5. Jeopardy
6. Above
7. Young goat
8. Actor Asner
9. Stocking mishap
10. Land measure
11. Look intently (at)
14. Poetic name for Ireland
19. Passing fashion
20. Levy
22. Wheel spindle
23. Alphabet letter
24. Cunning fellow
25. Be the right size
26. Wicked
27. Foundation
28. Secret plotting
29. Merry
31. Method
32. Statute
34. Biblical refugee
35. Plaything
36. Scoff
37. Printing machine
38. Blemish
39. "To — and to hold"
40. Level
41. College official
43. Cozy place
45. Not many
46. Steal
47. Mimic
49. Thus

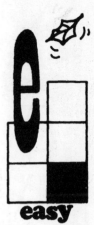

easy

97

ACROSS

1. High peak
4. Weeps aloud
8. Runway
12. Gorilla
13. Arrow poison
14. Needle case
15. Ambitious person
17. Model
18. Expends
19. Subjects
21. Goodfellow
23. Charles Lamb
24. Building wings
25. Salutation
29. Fourth caliph of Islam
30. Dams
31. Forest sight
32. Factory items
34. Impression
35. Mine products
36. Math functions
37. Volcanic "vent"
40. Printer's direction
41. Theater section
42. Good thing to take to a feast
46. Biblical brother
47. Weekday: abbr.
48. Enemy
49. Marries
50. Gaelic land
51. Affirmative

DOWN

1. Pagoda
2. Harvest goddess
3. "The —," Platonic dialogue
4. Warning device
5. South American Indians
6. Famous film rat
7. Pioneers
8. Iterate
9. Particle
10. Thalia, for one
11. Bakery sales
16. Egyptian goddess
20. Hurries
21. Paper quantity
22. Earthen pot
23. Indians
25. Create
26. "Put the finger on"
27. Sext's follower
28. Obtains
30. Lead-in
33. Tourist stops
34. Eat sparingly
36. Cubic meter
37. Talon
38. Kimono
39. Matured
40. Griffe
43. Greek letter
44. Digit
45. Eyes, to a Scot

hard

ACROSS

1. Brief snooze
4. Hit hard: slang
8. Display
12. Mine product
13. Desertlike
14. Solitary
15. Passbook entry
17. Went out with
18. Victory signal
19. Sufficiently cooked
20. Becomes wan
23. Fighter
26. Fragrance
27. Dull people
28. New Orleans' State: abbr.
29. Line of theater seats
30. Highway sections
31. Sack
32. Hesitater's syllable
33. Clear liquid
34. Spouse
35. Member of Congress
37. Lions' and horses' hair
38. Tied
39. Cushion
40. Prying bar
42. Be fond of: 2 wds.
46. Always
47. Delicate trimming
48. Female sheep
49. Sailors
50. Lyric poems
51. Finish

DOWN

1. Silent "yes"
2. "All men — created equal"
3. Brisk energy
4. Foundations
5. Cleveland's lake
6. Illuminated
7. Football play: abbr.
8. Inclines
9. Traveler's stop
10. First counting number
11. Marry
16. Above
17. — on, loves too much
19. Risk-taker
20. — over, studies closely
21. Worship
22. Not high
23. Silly mistake: slang
24. Fill with joy
25. Shows great anger
27. Conductor's wand
30. More recent
31. Prohibit
33. Falters
34. Manufactured
36. At no time
37. Former fillies
39. Walk back and forth
40. Allow
41. Actress Gabor
42. Ill-mannered fellow
43. Lawyer's charge
44. Possess
45. "Danger" color
47. Behold!

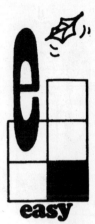

easy

ACROSS

1. Donkey
4. Slide
8. Petty quarrel
12. Pied Piper follower
13. Morse, for one
14. Cleveland's lake
15. Montgomery's State: abbr.
16. Declare openly
17. Rounded roof
18. "Scram!"
20. Metal container
21. Auto fuel
22. Water absorbers
26. Always
28. Ink stains
29. Elected prosecutor: abbr.
30. Golf score
31. Chairs
32. Outfit
33. Exists
34. Trades
35. Wagers
36. Basements
38. Friday's follower: abbr.
39. Have lunch
40. Denudes
43. "Shoo!"
45. Sound of laughter: hyph. wd.
47. Groove
48. Cover with asphalt
49. Fragrance
50. Poetic "before"
51. Mimics
52. Dogs and cats
53. Lawn moisture

DOWN

1. Kuwait native
2. Bargain event
3. Totter; reel
4. Reads briefly
5. Adore
6. Marriage vow: 2 wds.
7. Church seat
8. Closed cars
9. Fork tine
10. Ready, —, fire!
11. Golf mound
19. Canoe paddle
20. Folding beds
22. Smacks
23. Kettles
24. Prepare copy
25. Droops
26. Long narrative poem
27. Holder for cut flowers
28. Grizzly
31. Hit sharply
32. Went to bed
34. Blackboards
35. Keep out; exclude
37. Depart
38. TV headliners
40. Injection
41. Untainted
42. Hobo's meal
43. Health resort
44. Jockey's headwear
45. Short leap
46. Fruit drink

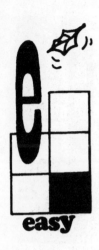

easy

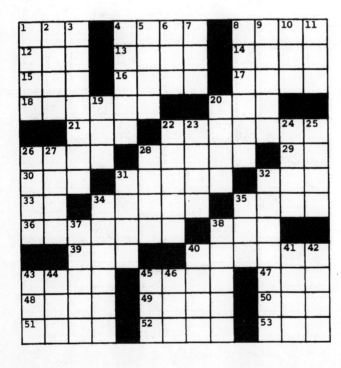

ACROSS

1. Concluding music section
5. Treated mercifully
11. Rabbit fur
12. Released conditionally
14. 1979 sci-fi film
15. Part of USNA
16. Wealthy, influential man
18. Otto — Bismarck
19. TV's "Mindy"
20. Chatters: slang
21. So long!: hyph. wd.
22. Theatrical wardrobe items
23. Tribal symbol
24. Eyetooth
27. City where El Greco painted
28. In conformity with
29. Wail
30. Reputation
31. City on the Aar
32. Draft agency: abbr.
35. Friend: French
36. Boisterous comedy
38. Contributes to a cause
40. Asian capital
41. Unyielding
42. Like helium or xenon
43. Twisted-horn antelopes
44. Tool

DOWN

1. Plant of the arum family
2. Sleep inducer
3. Japanese parliament
4. Pestiferous
5. Ship's radio operator: slang
6. Tailless rodents
7. Smell —, be suspicious: 2 wds.
8. Divining stick
9. Raise the spirits of
10. Reduced in rank
11. Arctic nomad
13. Live wire
17. Hockey goal
21. Phone fee
22. Toasting beverage
23. County division
24. U.N. member
25. Stylish: 3 wds.
26. In name only
27. Canvas cover, for short
29. Quadrupeds
31. Harmonize
32. Tendon
33. Disdain
34. Revue offering
36. Bandleader Kenton
37. Ethiopian lake
39. Physician's group: abbr.

hard

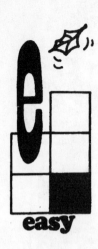

easy

ACROSS

1. Fence opening
4. Path or track
9. Recede, as the tide
12. Mimic
13. Kentucky Derby competitor
14. Very small
15. Arena for sports events
17. "Trick or —!"
19. Perform
20. Long-legged birds
21. Dangerous fish
24. Requirements
25. Fireman's need
26. — away, erodes
27. In this way
29. High mountain
30. Clenched hands
31. Cushion
32. Prefix meaning "down"
33. Gasps
34. Nevada city
35. Dog's sounds
36. Jungle cat
37. Hurricanes
39. Do wrong
40. Exchange
41. Drooping
45. Your and my
46. Not smooth
48. Payable
49. Marry
50. Article of bed linen
51. Picnic pest

DOWN

1. Car fuel
2. Likely (to)
3. Small vegetable
4. Through — and thin
5. Overwhelming defeat
6. Coat sleeve
7. Exists
8. Post office items
9. Pitchers
10. Bird's bill
11. Wagers
16. Challenge
18. Fishing poles
20. Chairs
21. Food fish
22. Cavity
23. Egyptian cobra
24. Homes for birds
26. Blinks
27. Sensible
28. Fragrance
30. Tillers of the soil
31. Margaret, to her friends
33. Cowboy's companion, for short
34. Sound (a bell)
35. Plank
36. Not loose
37. Pack (away)
38. Not false
39. Wise man
41. "A Boy Named —," silly song
42. Ms. Lupino
43. Convent dweller
44. Obtain
47. Cry of surprise

ACROSS

1. Commercials
4. Provide with workers
9. Stadium cheer
12. C.S.A. general
13. Caravan component
14. Ripen
15. Suppose
17. Friend of Felix
19. Dirty: French
20. Splendid
21. *Escargot*
23. Mel's place
24. Monk's hood
25. Walk daintily
26. "— Lucky," Grant film
28. Mornings: abbr.
29. Gamut
30. Payable
31. Pine Tree State: abbr.
32. Lecterns
33. Baseball's Rose
34. Tortellini, for example
35. Collar part
36. Baffles
38. Typewriter feature
39. Second-generation Japanese-American
40. Censure
43. "— a Wonderful Life," Capra film
44. Shadows: slang
46. Capek's "Robot" play
47. Trifle (with)
48. Related on one's mother's side
49. Greek letter

DOWN

1. Tall mountain
2. The: German
3. Teeter-totters
4. Oar
5. Docile
6. Soul: French
7. Iron's symbol
8. Ruffle
9. Blacksnake
10. Gelatinous substance
11. Music's Alpert
16. Jib or spanker
18. "Graf —," German battleship
20. Vocalizes
21. Confidence game: slang
22. City in Alaska
23. African language
25. Spars
26. Silent
27. Stagger
29. Lull
30. Regard as wretched
32. Knight's wife
33. Brace
34. Cat
35. Slip
36. Fit of pique
37. Yugoslav leader
38. Strike with force: slang
40. Narrow inlet
41. Not in
42. Angelico or Lippo Lippi
45. One

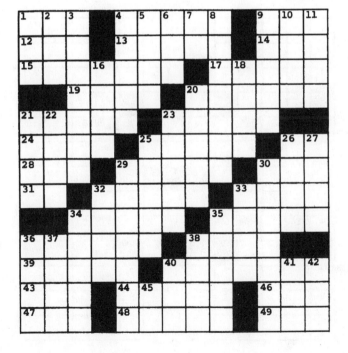

hard

ACROSS

1. Ski site
6. Faulty
11. Linger nearby
12. Slow, in music
13. Sport centers
15. Place for curtains
16. Saucy
17. Three: prefix
19. Eat a big meal
20. Conclusion
21. Sorrowful sounds
23. Poet's "ever"
24. Evergreen shrubs
27. "— Man River," Kern tune
28. Attending
29. Ranchers
34. School organization
36. Flies high
37. Charged atom
40. Ireland, formerly
42. Friend: French
43. Ten: prefix
44. Knocked sharply
46. Votes in
48. Canadian Indians
49. Partly frozen rain
50. Detests
51. Irritable

DOWN

1. Mold
2. Actress, Sophia —
3. Work too hard at
4. Caged (up)
5. Period of time
6. — Baba, Persian hero
7. Darn
8. West —, Caribbean islands
9. Rock
10. Planter
14. Portico
15. Breeze
18. Jogged
21. Dissolves
22. Lines of stitching
25. Mauna —, Hawaiian peak
26. Highway: abbr.
29. Floor covering
30. Frog's kin
31. On the —, in flight: slang
32. Great Lake
33. Female relatives
34. Roost
35. Coronet
38. Group of eight
39. Mean
41. Fencing sword
43. Printer's term
45. Curvy letter
47. D-Day craft

medium

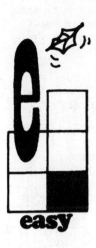
easy

ACROSS

1. Tuck's partner
4. Piece of china
9. School subject: abbr.
12. Exist
13. Work
14. Pro's opposite
15. Flapjack
17. Cook's garb
19. Ice-cream holder
20. Sailing
21. Playground equipment
23. Shone
26. Story
27. Wharves
28. Never!
29. Mornings: abbr.
30. "Goldilocks" characters
31. Summer drink
32. Myself
33. Tilt
34. Always
35. Defend
37. Nourishes
38. Copenhagen native
39. Potter's oven
40. Saber
42. Devour
45. That girl
46. Singer, — John
48. Hearing organ
49. Aye
50. Hazards
51. Health resort

DOWN

1. Siesta
2. Man's name
3. Writing needs
4. Jet
5. Erie or Tahoe
6. Lincoln's nickname
7. Toward
8. 3-Down parts
9. "Vamoose!" (slang)
10. Dove's call
11. Country restaurant
16. Cipher
18. Green vegetables
20. Watchful
21. Postage item
22. Less believable, as an excuse
23. Titan
24. Concluded
25. Busy folks
27. Tranquility
30. Small appliance
31. Boulevards
33. Polaris, for one
34. Congers
36. Scents
37. Helsinki natives
39. "Nut": slang
40. Timid
41. Tiny
42. Pennies: abbr.
43. Atlas chart
44. Historic period
47. Rockaway Beach's locale: abbr.

EASY

ACROSS

1. Canary food
5. Pack too full
9. Mail drop
13. Out of harm's way
17. Bear dwelling
18. Tie, as shoe strings
19. Conceal
20. Serving platter
21. Sales condition: 2 wds.
22. Catches up with
24. Uncommon
25. Set free
27. Female horse
28. Indian groups
30. Dark bread
31. Salary
32. Dance movement
33. Orchard
36. The thing here
37. Pupils
41. Ready for harvest

42. Uttered
43. Dagger wounds
44. Historical age
45. Frozen water
46. Tented area
47. Tremble
48. Hive insects
49. Author's alias: 2 wds.
51. Frighten
52. Morse system, and others
53. Dollar bill
54. Work very hard
55. Junior, to Dad
56. Injections
59. Sparkle
60. Give (a football) to a nearby teammate on a play: 2 wds.
64. Citrus fruit
65. Canoes or barges
66. Shoe bottom
67. By way of
68. Actress Gardner
69. Big-city blights
70. Beer ingredient
71. Gone by, as time
72. Sweat
74. Daring
75. Stops
76. Free ticket
77. Melody
78. Knight's title
79. Defrauds
82. Actress Hayworth
83. Try
87. Bellow
88. Even swap: 2 wds.
91. Close by
92. Otherwise
93. Advocate strongly
94. — chowder, menu listing
95. Threesome
96. Moistens
97. Minus
98. "— it up," overacts
99. Dispatched

DOWN

1. Disfiguring mark
2. Lessen (a pain)
3. Wickedness
4. Be worthy of
5. Shut (a door)
6. Talk wildly
7. High playing card
8. Imaginary sea creature
9. Divide among others
10. Prefer
11. Lyric poem
12. Lab glass: 2 wds.
13. Zebra marking
14. Desert wanderer
15. Travel cost
16. Potato buds
23. Labels
26. Sailor's "yes"
29. Cincinnati baseball team
31. Beat, as egg whites
32. Tent peg
33. Clutch tightly
34. Crop of China
35. Doing business
36. Domesticate
37. Gaze fixedly (at)
38. Require
39. Elm or oak
40. Talk back to
42. Identical
43. Close —, narrow escape
46. Food tins
47. Reads (a page) quickly
48. James —, Sean Connery role
50. Short letter
51. Long, narrow cuts
52. Ice-cream holder
54. Disgrace
55. Pepper's partner
56. Give a whack to
57. Bee's home
58. Actor Sharif

59. Goes bad, as milk
60. Contain
61. Football-shaped
62. Clenched hand
63. Greasy substances
65. Full of happiness
66. Store event
69. Petty quarrel
70. Large butterfly

71. Mothers and fathers
73. Extras, as tires
74. Cigar stub
75. Punch
77. Fatigues
78. Flower stalks
79. Ship's personnel
80. Cavity
81. Sunrise direction

82. Oil-drilling equipment
83. Eve's mate
84. Only
85. Ache
86. Jog
89. "Blessed — the peacemakers"
90. Montgomery's State: abbr.

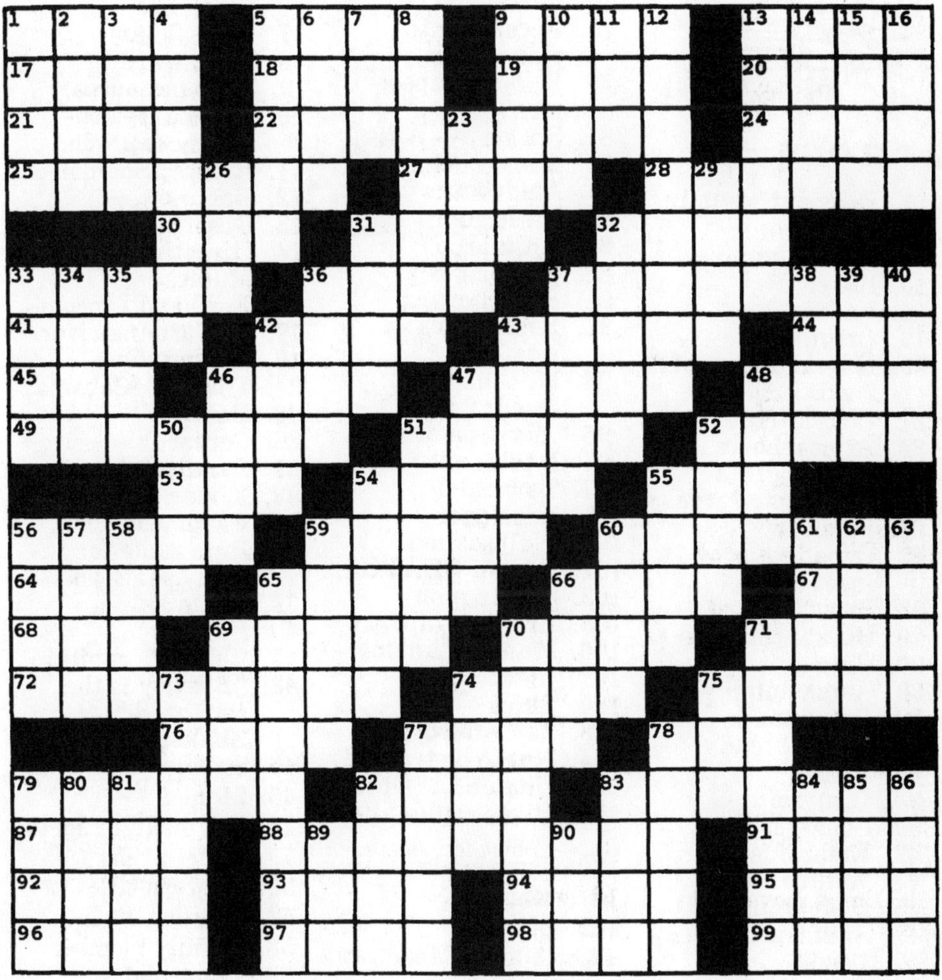

HARD

ACROSS

1. Easy out, usually: hyph. wd.
6. Ballet jump
10. Ravel
14. Vacant
19. Originated
20. Having a part of: 2 wds.
21. Citrus fruit
22. Atmospheres
23. Flower girl's offerings: 2 wds.
25. Small fry
27. Canadian province: abbr.
28. Snow leopard
29. Says incorrectly
30. Grime
32. Asian holiday
33. Relatives
34. Break bread
35. Tastes
38. Incursion
40. Songster Starr
42. Embroider
44. Wither
45. Hearty laugh
47. Sniffs out
49. Lead
51. Consolidate
52. Asian river
54. Vats
55. Pleasant
56. Sharp tools
57. Spanish name
59. Receipt, of sorts
60. Spires
62. Plovers
65. Le Carré character
66. Theater sign: abbr.
67. Depression
68. Diving bird
70. Certain bench
73. According to plan: 2 wds.
76. Pollster's specimen
81. Rocker, — Ant
83. Roman helmet
84. Anklebones
85. False god
86. A Child
88. Scottish cap
91. French river
92. Misbehaves: 2 wds.
94. Mohammed's steed: 2 wds.
95. Luzon peninsula
96. Iatric: abbr.
97. Taradiddle
99. Irish poet
100. Wall section
101. Part of SEATO
103. —-Magnon
105. Literary initials
106. Man's nickname
107. Cleft
110. Ships
113. Zesty flavors
115. Not to be trusted
116. City on the Ohio
118. River rapids: 2 wds.
120. Turn aside
121. Name
122. Mist
123. Audrey Meadows role
124. Yucatan Indians
125. Smelting materials
126. Was in debt
127. Changes course

DOWN

1. Greek island
2. Town in Maine
3. Government building: 2 wds.
4. Employ
5. Gourd
6. Small bus
7. Pass (a law)
8. Metalware
9. Type measures
10. Legendary conveyance: 2 wds.
11. Rivers: Spanish
12. Beguile
13. Gossips
14. Direction
15. Muffles
16. Ford and Lincoln
17. N. Carolina river
18. Affirmative
24. Town in Alabama
26. Barred
29. Collier
31. Candies
33. Kin's partner
36. Farm vehicle
37. Puts aside for future use: 2 wds.
39. Beam
40. Fabrics
41. Canada's capital
43. "Brevity is the soul of —": Shakespeare
45. Artillery
46. Monad
47. Payment, of sorts
48. Half: prefix
50. Eastern title
52. English river
53. Family member
56. Lengthwise
58. African lake

61. Golf VIP, for short
62. Hybrid brambles of the rose family
63. Hail!
64. Dine
67. Without restraint
69. Ski wax
70. "The — Game," B'way/screen hit
71. Elicits
72. Animation master: 2 wds.
74. Label
75. — *breve*

76. Channel island
77. Pertaining to a malt drink
78. Principled
79. Feminine name
80. Secluded valley
82. Scale tones
84. Malayan coins
87. — *Wiedersehen*
89. Aims
90. Crafts
91. Author Fleming
93. Actress, Molly —
95. Scout's award
98. Mustang
100. Kicked

102. Ghana's capital
104. Walking —, ecstatic: 2 wds.
106. Coarse fabric
108. Mote
109. Recaps, in London
111. Strikes
112. Little: suffix
113. Winter warm spell
114. Flatten (a fly)
116. Rotating piece
117. Yellow bugle
118. Pronoun
119. Wing

MEDIUM

ACROSS

1. A.M. TV show
6. Bouillon or consommé
11. Mail drop
15. Con game: slang
19. Eat into
20. D.J.'s milieu
21. Part of D.S.T.
22. Marco —
23. Furtherance
25. So be it!
26. Individuals
27. Appear
28. Discusses: slang
29. Myth
31. Manipulates
32. Bobble the ball
33. Shanties
34. Stack
35. Facility
37. Shout to a sled dog
38. Nonsense: slang
39. Book's insides
43. Pierce
46. Predicament
47. Give utterance to
48. Masefield topic
49. Attain
50. Unruffled
51. Score
52. Chair crossbar
53. Main; chief
54. Weaving device
55. Wears well
56. Ristorànte fare
57. Buck's mate
58. Darkness; gloom
59. Conduits
60. Fabled bird
61. Catch
63. Roués
64. Mini-novel
68. Anger
69. Twining plants
70. Mine find
71. Epoch
72. Mature person
75. Dice throw
76. Its symbol is Au
77. Transaction
78. Contend (with)
79. Selling "pitch": slang
80. Wine choice
81. Prize money
82. Sixth sense
83. Meager
84. Do as told
85. Free "ducats"
86. "Hot under the collar"
88. "Mimi" or "Mame"
89. Ilk
90. Bolger and Charles
91. Adjust an upright
92. Ivory source
93. Obtained
96. Honolulu's island
98. Deli purchase
101. Clamors
102. Sniff
103. Read hurriedly
104. Bauxite, etc.
105. Feat of skill: 3 wds.
108. Yarn fluff
109. Fissure
110. More along in years
111. Reed or pipe —
112. Chances
113. Satisfy fully
114. Full of marsh grasses
115. Grinding aid

DOWN

1. Tantalize
2. System
3. Capital of the First State
4. Eden dweller
5. Hankering
6. Slight breeze
7. Accesses to jets
8. Keats' expertise
9. Metal container
10. Crisis communication: 2 wds.
11. Journey segment
12. Mortar ingredient
13. Augury
14. Trend
15. Husband or wife
16. General agreement
17. Toward shelter
18. Velvety growth
24. Pie shell
30. Wapiti
33. Quiet!
34. — apart, criticize
36. Munched
37. Great amount
38. Prosper swiftly
39. Indianapolis team
40. Artist's stock
41. Encamp
42. Icelandic story
43. Baseball deal
44. Marsh bird
45. Grand Prix, etc.
46. — up, connect
47. Potter's wares
50. Essence
51. Records, in a way
52. Ruin's partner
54. Entice
55. Compare
56. Common fund
58. Trade center
59. Jury group
60. Highway
62. Khartoum's river
63. Beam bolt
64. Gulp down (food)
65. Wanton looks
66. Obliterate
67. Chaucer output
69. Person

70. Twine
72. Holes in one
73. Medicinal amount
74. Position of control:
    2 wds.
75. Bridge part
76. Percussive
77. Allergy source
79. Shears' kin
80. Evergreen
81. Menlo or Hyde

83. Demure
84. Check the perform-
    ance of (a ma-
    chine)
85. Sheriff's group
87. Jeers
88. — and substance
89. Miscellaneous
91. A sense
92. Worn-out
93. Swallow greedily

94. Movie award
95. Itty-bitty
96. Norse capital
97. Sour
99. Diva's solo
100. Remaining
101. Any man or boy:
     slang
102. Par
106. Corrida shout
107. Enemy

SPECIAL CHALLENGER CROSSWORD

"SITTING PRETTY"
by JOHN GREENMAN

Here is a real toughie for you. We have omitted giving you such helps as "2 wds.," "hyph. wd.," and "slang"; but in the spirit of fair play, all abbreviations and foreign words are so indicated.

ACROSS

1. Marx brother
6. Minor or Major
10. Zenana
15. Common interrogative
19. Hebrew scholar of yore
20. — -do-well
21. Scene of an 1836 siege
22. Loathe
23. Perch for Scarlett O'Hara
25. Convertible couches
27. Irritated
28. U.S. seaman-author
30. Infuses deeply
31. That: Spanish
32. Nomadic group
35. Female rabbit
36. Committee chief: abbr.
39. Orator's gift
42. Sycophant
44. Rents
49. Vivid display
50. Munich's river
52. Goodbye: Spanish
54. Dating from birth
55. Slip
56. J.F.K.'s favorite
59. Word with "graph" or "harp"
60. Function
62. Hoopla
63. Henry VII or VIII
65. Moisture
66. Hardships
68. Baseball teams
71. Saxophonist's "gizmo"
72. Large employer of auditors: abbr.
73. Depraved places
75. Simon and Sedaka
77. Enlarged: prefix
79. Dry, as champagne
81. Part of Q.E.D.
83. Miffed states
85. UFO shape
88. "— bin ein Berliner"
89. Hoodwinks
91. Brad
93. Mount —, highest Lepontine Alp
94. Horse with sprinklings of white
96. Dairymaid's need
100. A Merkel
101. Creator of Prufrock
103. U.S. manufacturer
104. German title
105. Skim swiftly along
106. Hysteria
108. Neutral and second
110. Mater —
111. Greek letters
112. Asian holiday
114. Dakota tribe
116. Pooh's friend
118. Pilot and helmsman
123. Pintail duck
125. Tropical vines
129. S-shaped seats
132. Sportscar feature
134. Partly open
135. Spa: British
136. Verb suffix
137. TV personality
138. In —, as a whole
139. Ruhr steel center
140. Coral formation
141. Touts

DOWN

1. Padlock hanger
2. Friend: French
3. "Razzed"
4. Block
5. Refuges
6. Sturm — Drang
7. Comedian Foxx
8. Psalm ender
9. "People — always what they seem"
10. Taken
11. Confederacy member: abbr.
12. Sitarist Shankar
13. Edit
14. Asian language
15. Stop!
16. Half of Zelle's assumed name
17. Memo abbreviation
18. Hardy character
24. Slowly, in music
26. Dress up showily
29. Producing a din
33. Pedestal part
34. Decree
36. Summit
37. Recruiter, often
38. Adjustable recliner
40. Deputy: abbr.
41. Mehta's aid
43. L'il Abner —
45. High bond rating
46. Item for a small apartment
47. The Pumpkin —, 1964 film
48. Slackens
51. French sculptor
53. Perennial plant
56. Proved wrong
57. Fifth canonical hour
58. Clerical tribunals
61. Tank

64. Memory
67. Vaccine
69. German article
70. Throw
74. Tasty
76. Cache
78. Bitter herb
79. Lorelei
80. School: French
82. Wire: abbr.
84. Located
86. Boredom
87. Deciphers
90. Marksman's sport

92. Body of folkways
95. Calendar abbreviation
97. *Dies —*
98. Phooey!
99. Yellow-and-black bird
102. Aquarium fish
105. Ostentatious
107. Bubble
109. Dark and dull
113. Low cards
115. River to the Pamlico Sound
117. One of three "weird sisters"

118. Law: abbr.
119. Iberian river: Portuguese
120. *Coup d'—*
121. Saarinen
122. Criteria: abbr.
124. Behold: Latin
126. Type of tide
127. Swiss river
128. Floors: abbr.
130. Before, to a bard
131. Eros, to Aphrodite
133. Le —, Tunisian site of Roman ruins

DIAGRAMLESS

MEDIUM

This Diagramless is 15 boxes wide by 15 boxes deep.

ACROSS

1. Board's partner
4. Eden resident
6. Triumphant cry
9. Fills with boredom
11. Pub beverages
12. Encamp
13. Reads (a page) hurriedly
14. Assesses
16. Parishioner's seat
19. Actress Moreno
20. TV show now on reruns
21. Manages with what's available: 2 wds.
24. Dismounted
25. Mourning —, cooing bird
26. Tortoise's racing rival
28. New York City athlete
29. Cherishes deeply
30. Impaired
32. Mimics

33. Evens (the score)
34. Marry
35. Arbor Day plantings
37. Shows concern
39. Throw
43. Dry, as the desert
44. Experienced sailors
46. Get-up-and-go
47. Plane section
48. Use a crowbar

DOWN

1. Go to — for, defend
2. Work on newspaper copy
3. Have the nerve to
5. Chess pieces
6. Poetic sigh
7. Biddy
8. Biblical beast
10. Bowling scores
11. Expert
13. Hide (money) in a secret place: slang

15. Snacked
16. Turned ashen in color
17. Take one's leave
18. Clever person
19. Talks deliriously
20. Domesticates
21. Relocated
22. Grand Coulee or Aswan
23. Speaks pompously
25. Information: slang
27. Cleveland's lake
29. Statute
31. Takes it easy
35. Journey
36. Blushing
37. Do better than
38. "When Irish Eyes — Smiling"
40. Cereal grain
41. Injury to one's pride
42. Move slightly
45. Cunning

This Diagram/box is 15 boxes wide

DIAGRAMLESS

MEDIUM

This Diagramless is 15 boxes wide by 15 boxes deep.
Starting box is on page 217

ACROSS

1. Queries

5. Store away

6. Where llamas are found

7. These have nibs

11. Word with "sauce" or "dish"

12. Racing tracks

14. Bitten, as by a bee

16. Dance: 2 wds.

17. Spigot

18. Ajar (as a door)

19. Put off to a future time

21. Actress West

24. Uncle's mate

25. Litter member

26. Speck

27. Explosive: abbr.

28. Upper body

30. Object of admiration

31. Pronoun

32. Shoe part

34. Incline

36. Approaches

37. Coop occupant

38. Small barracuda

39. Garden tool

41. Level

42. Heroic act

DOWN

1. Poisonous snake

2. Increase by stages: 2 wds.

3. Sacred Moslem text

4. Moved to-and-fro

7. Powerful

8. Happening

9. Short sleep

10. Moved easily

13. Go on a date: 2 wds.

14. Intervenes: 2 wds.

15. Sailor

16. Made yarn

18. Feed-bag morsel

20. Mink or muskrat

21. Unassuming

22. On

23. Slippery fellow

26. Bishop's headgear

28. Two thousand pounds

29. Singles

31. Northerner

33. Vital fluid

34. Recipe direction

35. Quit

40. Terminal point

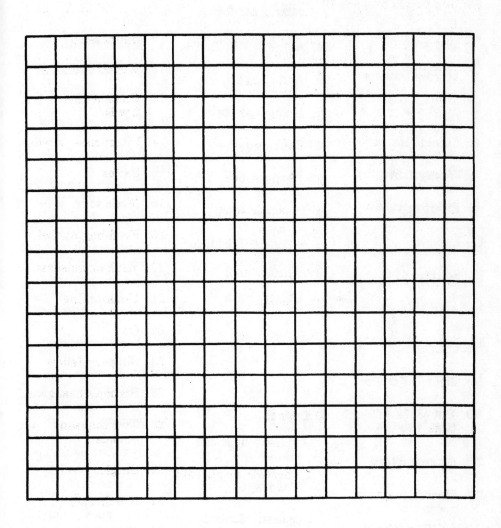

DIAGRAMLESS

HARD

This Diagramless is 15 boxes wide by 15 boxes deep.
Starting box is on page 217

"VERY STATELY"

ACROSS

1. Actress Dawber
4. Actor Lorre
6. Actress Harper
8. Woolly fabric
9. Bit of news
11. Labors
12. Sources of poi
14. Actor, Bruce —
15. Involved with
17. Smears with fat
18. Belonging to a remote period
20. Actress Arden
21. Wedding vow: 2 wds.
22. Burgundy and Bordeaux
25. Lucky number
27. Shoo!
28. Actress, Martha —
29. Actor Flynn
32. Moslem officials
34. Etna output
35. Entice
36. Duffy or O'Neal
38. Dissolve and wash away
39. Cereal grain

DOWN

1. Animal skins
2. Goddess of folly
3. Earn
4. Grow insipid
5. Actress Hayworth
6. Ore deposits
7. Supernatural; unearthly
8. Singer, Ernie —
10. Actress Freeman
11. Actor Stamp
13. Exerts much effort
14. Singer, Mac —
16. More mature
17. Actor Ayres
19. Hither's "partner"
23. Actor Holliman
24. Narrow piece of leather
25. Neglect
26. Brontë's Jane
30. Egg-shaped
31. At a subsequent time
32. Actress Faye
33. To a great degree
37. Actor, Aldo —

DIAGRAMLESS   EXPERT

**This Diagramless is 17 boxes wide by 17 boxes deep.
Starting box is on page 217**

ACROSS

1. Do an aerobic exercise
4. Escape: slang
7. Flooded
10. Inventor of calculus: 2 wds.
14. Luca — Robbia, sculptor
15. Hawaiian island
17. Parlor
18. Rictus
19. Caroled
21. 20th-century composer
23. Overalls part
26. Skin layer
29. Vaccines
30. — West, TV's Batman
32. Highway
33. Clock sound
36. Endangered goose
37. Alpine song
39. Privy to: 2 wds.
40. Acquire
41. West African country
42. Gudrun's husband

43. Betelgeuse, e.g.
46. Barrel strengthener
48. Drunkard
49. Sharpen
50. Certain Slav
52. Abundant
54. Cole slaw, for one
57. Sedate
59. Japanese port
60. Philanthropic inventor: 2 wds.
63. Tropical vine
64. Utter
65. Ottoman ruler

DOWN

1. Calendar abbreviation
2. Be in the red
3. Simpleton
4. Caps
5. Puzzled
6. Department-store locations
8. Hart
9. Sirens
11. Verbally

12. Food processor
13. Artless
16. Resistance to change
20. Makes tidy
22. New Orleans athletes
23. Thrill: slang
24. Think-tank product
25. Send into exile
27. Angry with: 2 wds.
28. Writer St. John and namesakes
31. Protégé's advisors
34. "Centennial State": abbr.
35. Fashion ribbing
38. Supports oneself: 2 wds.
44. Writer Loos
45. Take back
47. Sister of Clio
51. Tattles
53. Accurate, in a way: hyph. wd.
55. Zone
56. Properly
58. Yellowish-brown
61. Compass reading
62. Factory shift

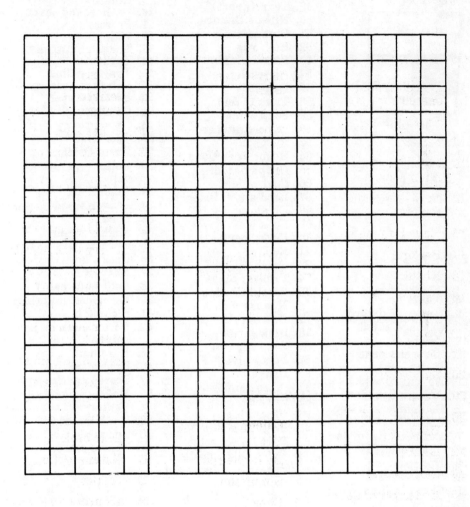

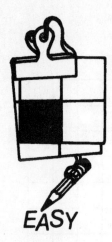

EASY

ACROSS

1. — chowder
5. Potato
9. Loafer or oxford
13. Cabbage salad
17. Cavity
18. Show concern
19. Wolf's cry
20. No longer wild
21. Actress Gardner
22. Boutonniere flower
24. Roomy bags
25. Put back, as funds
27. Chain section
28. Not speaking
29. "You — There"
30. Crop of China
31. Unpolluted
32. Glossy, as paper
35. Blink
36. Was sorry (for one's sins)
40. Happy as a —
41. Slam (a door)
42. Engagements
43. Mr. Charles of music
44. Big fuss

45. Enjoy the sun
46. One who takes long walks
47. Like the old owl
48. Hamilton bill
49. Tear (apart)
50. Nile or Danube
51. Curved roofs
52. Bath rug
53. Face wrinkles
54. Air cooler
55. Deluge
58. Tries to find
59. Soap shape
60. Expert pitcher
63. Rich soil
64. Hospital sections
65. Unfurnished
66. Coal weight
67. Lend an —, listen
68. Employs
69. Book leaf
70. Parka part
71. Replied
73. Specks
74. Frolics; plays
75. Beerlike brews
76. Not as much
77. Dove's call
78. Dismantles
81. Song for two
82. Party giver
86. Drags
87. Office employee
89. Payable
90. Otherwise
91. Body of a ship
92. Part for an actor
93. Fairy-tale monster
94. Real-estate document
95. And no other
96. Adjusts (a clock)
97. Nourish

DOWN

1. Burn the surface of
2. Valentine word
3. Woe is me!
4. Myself

5. Frighten
6. Use a peeling gadget
7. Spigoted coffeemaker
8. Card-player's action, at times
9. Glisten
10. —, line, and sinker
11. Possess
12. 12th letter
13. Taken unlawfully
14. Tardy
15. Prayer ending
16. Compass heading
22. Bottle stopper
23. Clock sound
24. Grows weary
26. Short nail
28. Extra-special
30. Roller —, skating palace
31. Actor Falk
32. Louver board
33. Load
34. Mighty metal
35. Hornet
36. Does a lawn chore
37. Neat; tidy
38. Relieve (a pain)
39. Permanent colorings
41. Fishing lure
42. Does a swan or jack-knife
45. Wire nail
46. Household tips
47. Scored a victory
50. Melon remnants
51. Venture
52. Dad's mate
53. Tempted
54. Travel cost
55. Insect on Fido
56. Bank deal
57. Rowing paddles
58. Jack rabbits
59. Suitcases
60. Tiny particle
61. Poultry cage
62. Concludes
64. Telegrams
65. Baseball equipment
68. Assists
69. Large pinup pictures
70. Owl's cry

72. Wept pitifully
73. Antlered animal
74. Optimistic, as a future
76. Number 7, to some
77. Apple centers

78. Wood shack
79. Story
80. Deceptive trick
81. Valley
82. Stop!
83. Border

84. Certain
85. Bird food
87. Energy source
88. Sock part
91. Westward —!
93. Preposition

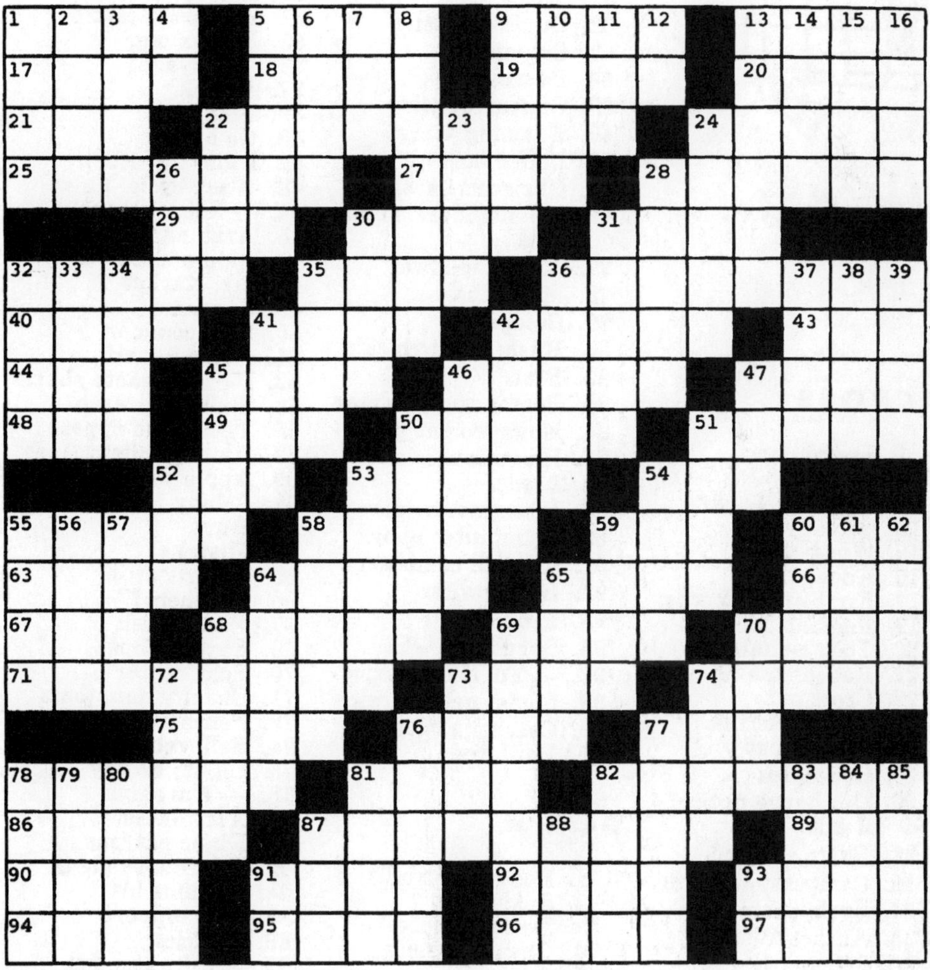

MEDIUM

ACROSS

1. Jewish law
6. Assist
10. Actress, — Lane
14. Solitary
15. Woodwind
16. Added to
17. First prize: 2 wds.
19. Football kick
20. Took a chair
21. Ranch sounds
22. Cross out
24. Storage boxes
25. Joshua's spy
26. Grownups
29. Discharge notice: 2 wds.
32. Extra reward
33. Campers' shelters
34. Lyric poem
35. Author Wiesel
36. Rib and tibia
37. Afrikaner
38. Bandleader: 2 wds.
40. Bike part
41. Years and years
42. TV's Karen —

44. Sacred book
47. Idaho's capital
48. Spoken aloud
49. Building material
54. Capture
55. "— Theme," from *Dr. Zhivago*
56. Former boy
57. Bluish-green
60. Cat: Spanish
61. Titles
62. Cupid's missile
63. Colonist
66. Decrease
68. Characteristic
69. Foaming wave
73. Coffee holders
74. Christmas song
76. — contendere, legal plea
77. "Egg" follower
78. Met solos
79. Companies
80. Bushes and vines
82. Best
83. Performer Newman
84. Engagement gift
85. Hawaiian drink: 2 wds.
87. Ice-cream holder
88. ⅟₆₀ minute: abbr.
91. English composer
92. Iron worker
95. Prophet
96. Songbird
97. — Fe, New Mexico
98. Soviet news service
99. Catch sight of
100. Bordered

DOWN

1. Restaurant bills
2. Spicy stew
3. Decisive defeat
4. Chemical suffix
5. Loners
6. Vagrants
7. Lessens
8. Card game
9. Dangling jewels
10. Orchard fruits

11. Aristocrats
12. Baseball play
13. Italian family
18. Charged particles
23. Part of "BPOE"
24. Virginia cowslip
25. Movie: Spanish
26. Cain's brother
27. — out, distribute
28. *Les Etats* —, USA
29. Quaker colonist
30. Perfect model
31. Hostess Mesta
33. Pulls along
36. — Voyage!
37. Attack
39. Fish eggs
40. Go by
42. Daisy: Scottish
43. Wash cycle
44. — fide, authentic
45. Arab nation
46. Indian clerk
47. Mr. Karloff
49. Condemn
50. Less common
51. Actor Sharif
52. Defense pact: abbr.
53. Sufficient: arch.
58. Those who oppose
59. Ale ingredient
60. Apple variety
62. Colony insect
63. Hurt
64. Mistake
65. Florida crop
66. "— there?"
67. Feel unwell
69. Fay of films
70. Pear center
71. Charity donations
72. Fence stake
74. Believable
75. Light; breezy
78. — *Karenina*
79. Artfulness
81. Diner patrons
82. Tattletale: slang
84. Stallone hit
85. Sail support
86. District
87. Freshwater fish
88. Perform opera
89. Diminutive ending
90. African country
93. —Vegas
94. Angry

HARD

"GLAD YOU'RE THERE!"

ACROSS

1. Gala affair
5. Postponed sleep: 2 wds.
10. Character; nature
15. Roman court
19. Algerian port
20. City in Guam
21. Old-womanish
22. Cupid
23. Swimmers' protectors
25. Intersection policeman: 2 wds. (slang)
27. Takes away(from)
28. Cloys
30. Tatum and Ryan
31. Gaiety
32. Stirred
33. Calendar abbreviation
34. Dangers
37. Red cedar
38. Yearns after: 2 wds.
42. Medicinal plants
43. Flocks of mallards
44. Transmits
45. Genus of shrubs
46. Covers
47. Prowl-car driver
49. Northwest State: abbr.
50. One of the Three Stooges
51. Serbs and Poles
53. Unctuous
54. In that spot
55. Frontier fort
57. Pilfered
59. Manual arts
60. Doorbell sound
61. Aspect; stage
62. New Zealander
63. Respectful greeting
65. Unaccompanied
66. Retinues
69. Tiny particles
70. Flat-bottomed boat
71. Soup base
72. Title for a prince: abbr.
73. Cuts, as grass
74. AMA member
77. Remain
78. Massachusetts cape
79. Jackrabbits
81. Campus buildings, for short
82. The ones here
83. Changed the form of
85. Awaits decision
86. Generous one
87. Johnson of TV
88. Spars
89. New Guinea gulf
90. Ship's crew
93. Hostess, Perle —
94. Monkeypod: 2 wds.
98. Lifesaving ambulance riders
100. U.S. shore patrol: 2 wds.
102. Satanic
103. Inasmuch as
104. Chef's sample
105. Longest river
106. Marries
107. Smudge
108. Spirited mount
109. Secluded valley

DOWN

1. Pleat
2. Cleveland's lake
3. 27th U.S. President
4. Active powers
5. Béchamel and marinara
6. Marble
7. "Old salts"
8. German conjunction
9. Jewish holiday
10. Make plumper
11. "The Lady —," old song: 2 wds.
12. Prejudice
13. Sprite
14. Establish anew
15. School playtime
16. Whale: Latin
17. Implement
18. Venomous snakes
24. Vexes
26. Arrow poisons
29. Dispatch boat
32. Marshal Dillon and namesakes
33. Having a metallic sound
34. Hand centers
35. Poet, T. S. —
36. Safety men for broncobusters 2 wds.
37. Urbane
38. Dr. Norman Vincent —
39. Engine-house employee
40. Manifest
41. Shows fury
43. Garden utensil
44. Happy look
48. Unbound
49. Chicago airport
51. Revue scenes
52. Metallic cloth
54. Faithfulness: archaic
56. Pals
57. Displays
58. Yellowish-brown
59. Supermarket wagon

61. Deceptive maneuvers
62. Planet satellites
63. Philippine island
64. Make up (for)
65. Hurt
66. Stuffs
67. Obliterate
68. Less bold
70. Binge
71. Lark and jay
75. That is: 2 wds. (Latin)
76. Gets in touch with
77. Silken fabric
79. Wives' quarters
80. Fitness
82. Leather strap
84. Turkish porters
85. Quarterback, often
86. Was right for
88. Saudi Arabian city
89. Hurry
90. Gush forth
91. Roof part
92. Dry
93. Lode site
94. Destroy: British
95. Wading bird
96. — Stanley Gardner
97. Genesis garden
99. Poorly lit
101. Cereal grain

SPECIAL CHALLENGER CROSSWORD

"BRAND NAMES THAT BECAME WORDS"

Here is a real toughie for you. We have omitted giving you such helps as "2 wds.," "hyph. wd.," and "slang"; but, in the spirit of fair play, all abbreviations and foreign words are so indicated.

ACROSS

1. European capital
5. Decree
10. Hash-house sign
14. Nursery words
19. Irish Rose lover
20. Device for generating electromagnetic waves
21. Photo, of a sort
22. Icon
23. Kitchen wrapper
25. Morning meal
27. Suffix with "journal"
28. Italian city
29. Alaskan Indian
31. Modifies
32. Snoozer, for one
34. Spanish cellist
36. Eight, long ago and far away
37. City on the Oka
39. Hurl, as a shot
40. School: French
42. Chorus syllable
45. Ghana's capital
48. European peninsula
51. An astringent
52. Inexperienced; untrained
53. Avoid consistently
54. Entrap
55. Avenues: abbr.
57. Capture again
59. Baseball putout
60. Dreamy; listless
61. Alley goal
63. Iowa college town
64. Afore, to odists
65. Ailing
66. Unflustered
67. Insolence
68. Eglantines

70. Department-store feature
73. Flee to Gretna Green
76. Make lace
77. Calling for prolonged effort
78. Botanical suffix
80. Murphy's —
81. Operator, as of a computer
83. Blue-green hues
84. Assays
86. Suffix for "act" or "destruct"
87. Did a carpentry job
89. Highway: abbr.
90. Daughter of Leda
91. "Crackerjack"
92. Symbol of strength
93. Mediterranean resort
95. Visit, informally
97. Winter vehicles
98. Document certifiers: abbr.
99. Musical composition for a solo
101. "You — There"
102. — homo
104. Junket
105. Optometry items
108. Vernaculars
112. City on Lake Ontario
115. Metal-ammonia compound
116. Gumbo ingredient
118. Ad —, for this purpose: Latin
119. Morning meal
121. Duplicator
124. Richard D'Oyly —
125. Wayfarers' havens
126. In any way
127. Tonsorial chore

128. Precincts
129. Piquancy
130. Viper colonies
131. Maine city or river

DOWN

1. Coe or Bannister
2. Corpulent
3. Marathon measures
4. Legless critter
5. Roman or Ottoman
6. Telegraph symbols
7. Asimov or Hayes
8. Long time: abbr.
9. Rate highly
10. Surpass
11. Stir
12. Acidulous
13. Together: prefix
14. Egyptian money unit
15. Strings expert
16. Construct
17. Ripening agent
18. Court period: abbr.
24. "Aida," for one
26. "Bust"
30. Prefix meaning wide
33. Riven
35. Mimicry
36. Library unit: abbr.
38. Floor surfacing
41. "— Royale"
42. Acrobat's exerciser
43. Libertine
44. Daunts
45. Daisylike flower
46. Latin entertainer
47. Mainstays of many a square meal
49. Anathema

50. Starry
54. Sun: Spanish
56. Waste-allowance on goods
58. Follow (a suspect)
60. Cloud
61. Vends
62. Lamp fuel
66. Raised the canvas
67. Majors and Marvin
69. Be remunerated
71. Refrained (from)
72. Voucher
74. Covered (a road surface)
75. Pitchers

79. Fuji, for one: abbr.
81. After which
82. Smack
83. Regular issue
84. Plains quarters
85. Biblical priest
88. Abilities applied with determination
90. Equestrian
91. Couturier Cassini
94. Trophy
96. Author, Ayn __
97. Scrawny beast
100. Violinist Mischa and kin
103. Seasonal songs

104. Seed coat
106. Once, in Hamburg
107. Intoxicating plant juices
109. "Butterfield 8" novelist
110. Theme
111. "Jerk"
112. Killer whale
113. Moselle river
114. Telegram
115. English composer
117. Weakened salmon
120. Show —
122. Native: suffix
123. Prerogatives: abbr.

DIAGRAMLESS

MEDIUM

This Diagramless is 15 boxes wide by 15 boxes deep.

ACROSS

1. Plead
4. Drilled
6. One-fourth
8. Rudely brief
9. Stairway unit
11. Schemes
12. Harvest
14. Grizzlies
15. Sports arena
18. Slope
19. Stylish
20. Sketched
22. Cooking vessel
23. Bed linen
24. Caspian, for one
25. Border (on)
27. Boys
28. Sulks
30. City roads

32. Musical sounds
33. Rescue
34. Attempted
35. Household animals
37. Bleeds, as fabric dyes
38. Withdraw; disavow
40. Two, in cards
41. Golf peg

DOWN

1. Watercraft
2. Make a mistake
3. Receives
4. Scorches
5. Take away (from)
6. 2 pints
7. Marsh grass
8. Scottish "tribe"

10. Gave money for services
11. Georgia crop
13. Chased
14. Spills the beans
15. Outbuildings
16. Neckwear
17. Encounters
18. Health resort
19. Converse informally
21. Existed
23. Fell as frozen rain
26. Snare
28. Aim (at)
29. Single bills
31. Always
32. Armistice
34. Tiny amount
36. Editor's note
39. Regret

DIAGRAMLESS

MEDIUM

This Diagramless is 15 boxes wide by 15 boxes deep.
Starting box is on page 217

ACROSS

1. Find the sum of
4. Leaves
6. Plant fluid
9. Encountered
12. Egg-shaped
13. Before: poetic
14. Grow older
15. Get rid of
19. Sock tip
20. Walk back and forth
21. Venetian-blind part
23. Church seat
24. Aroma
27. "Ready, —, go!"
29. Great Lake
30. Picnic pest
33. Line of seats
35. Health resort
36. Challenge
38. Angry
40. Shadowboxes
42. Make stitches in

44. Flower with three petals
46. Cubs or Jets
48. 2,000 pounds
50. Distraction
54. Reverential fear
55. Feminist issue: abbr.
56. Twirl
58. Cherry's color
59. Lair
60. Rational
61. Allow

DOWN

1. In the past
2. Bird of peace
3. Do business (with)
5. Miss one's footing
6. The Mediterranean is one
7. Dance and sculpture
8. Rinds
9. Is of importance

10. Conceit
11. Golf peg
16. Atlas item
17. Frosts, as a cake
18. More modern
22. Highest card
25. Bite; pinch
26. Indian export
28. Male cat
30. Public notices, for short
31. Short sleep
32. Taught; coached
34. Squander
37. Make a mistake
39. Fawn or doe
41. Sympathized (with)
43. Used to be
45. Be the father of
47. Fail to hit
48. Put pitch upon
49. Be in debt
51. Mover's truck
52. October birthstone
53. Three trios
57. Gross minus expenses

DIAGRAMLESS

HARD

This Diagramless is 15 boxes wide by 15 boxes deep.
Starting box is on page 217

ACROSS

1. Poet

5. Out of town

6. Early draft group: abbr.

9. Sleep sound

10. Large parrot

11. Wasted time

13. Humorist Rogers

14. Arizona Indian

15. Taro root

16. Stratford's river

17. Explosive sound

18. Neutral shade

19. Remarkable thing: 2 wds. (slang)

26. Color

27. Make unreadable, in a way: 2 wds.

28. Set on fire

29. Mrs. Dithers

30. Many: 2 wds.

31. Summers: French

32. Coward: slang

36. Fondle

37. Scoundrel

38. Attempt

39. Cupid

40. Auger

DOWN

1. Musical group

2. Military miscreant: abbr.

3. Scarce

4. Tinted

6. "Twenty-three —!"

7. Not often

8. Biblical dancer

9. Ugly duckling, eventually

11. Sofa

12. Surrounded by

13. Networks

14. Like Job

20. Site of U.S. air base in Greenland

21. The "H" of "H.O.M.E.S."

22. Other than; but

23. Pillager

24. Guarantee

25. Greek letters

28. Use the oven

32. Dungeness, for one

33. — sapiens

34. Stravinsky

35. Heal

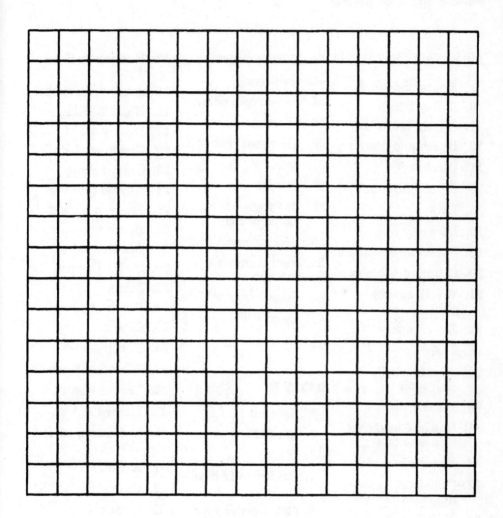

DIAGRAMLESS

EXPERT

**This Diagramless is 17 boxes wide by 17 boxes deep.
Starting box is on page 217**

ACROSS

1. Appraised amount
6. D-Day beach
7. City in Morocco
10. Harsh and piercing
11. Discharge
13. Brief delirium
14. Patsy
15. Daises
18. "Con game" : slang
20. Group of vehicles
21. WWII agency : abbr.
22. Zoo category
23. Jeté
27. "Gunsmoke" character
28. Disastrous
31. One of Chekhov's "Three Sisters"
32. Entertain
33. "100 Club" headquarters : 2 wds.
36. Noted contrapuntist
39. O'Casey or Connery
40. Standoffish
42. Eggs : Latin
43. Apt to snap

44. Tonic extract
46. Quipster
47. Iroquoian Indian
48. Shortage
50. Charisma, for one
51. Shadow
53. Uproar
57. One form of the name "Helen"
58. Kick up one's heels
59. Paul Bunyan's toothpick
60. Some almanac data
61. Cisco Kid's rope

DOWN

1. Sported
2. Muscat's land
3. Heckle
4. Bridge-tally heading
5. Chinese dynasty
7. Gratified
8. Ratite birds
9. Part of an address: 2 wds.
10. Jackanapes
12. Tempest container

13. Holiday in Honduras
15. Army rank : abbr.
16. Elgar's "King —"
17. Disengage
19. Ceremonial staff
23. Crazy : slang
24. Angled pipe
25. Eastern bigwig
26. Beach toy
29. Basilica area
30. Song : German
32. Stuns
34. Baseball putout
35. Cicada
36. Punch server
37. What SAC men do
38. "Bronx cheer"
41. Hazard at sea
45. Thesaurus entry : abbr.
47. Avast!
49. Codeword for "K"
52. Straggle
53. Vetch
54. Layer of the eye
55. Castle defense
56. She-bear : Latin
58. Assembly-line product

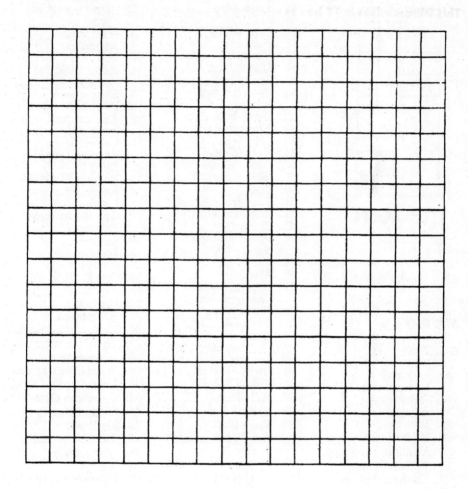

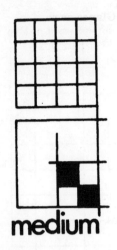

ACROSS

1. Busy place
5. Like Sue of song
10. Initiated
15. Decomposes
19. Individuals
20. Aspect
21. Venerate
22. Wickedness
23. Missing
24. "Waste"-maker
25. Chancy chances
26. Equal
27. Fully
29. Compass heading
31. Shadowed
33. Additional
34. Loses color
35. Not as much
36. Flee
39. Cart
40. Boxers
44. Give voice to
45. One who takes long
    walks

46. Like some trousers
47. Blame: slang
48. Several
49. Stationery
50. Spas
51. Talk wildly
52. Pub brew
53. Weary
54. Transplant
55. Out of bed
56. More lemony in
    color
58. Light-bulb data
59. Hinge (on)
60. Is in debt
61. Holy Writ
62. Coffeehouse
63. More poky
66. Cash
67. Gave in
71. Cantered slowly
72. Claret, etc.
73. Dumb blunder:
    slang
74. Mine find
75. Always
76. Leonine locks
77. Chesterfields
78. Fir feature
79. For each
80. Harasses
81. Dull sounds
82. Sturdy
83. Globe-trotter
85. Tête-à-têtes
86. Hair tints
87. Squeak cures
88. Flies aloft
89. Ash Wednesday
    begins it
90. Skimpy swimwear
93. Daring feat
94. Dieter's no-nos
98. Manipulated
99. Movie award
101. Avoid
103. Time of day
104. Make tracks
105. Approaches
106. Gamut
107. Albacore
108. Parry
109. Be aware of
110. Knight's mount
111. Footfall

DOWN

1. Predicament
2. Being a part of:
   2 wds.
3. Waistcoat
4. Appraise
5. Orb
6. Moby Dick, for
   example
7. Elementary
8. Founded: abbr.
9. Adolescent:
   hyph. wd.
10. Unfertile
11. Revises (copy)
12. Golly!
13. Retreat for Noah
14. Reserve funds:
    2 wds.
15. Oppose strongly
16. Ellipsoid
17. Tempo
18. Luge
28. Lariat
30. Scent
32. Pallid
34. Bluffed
35. Illuminant
36. Emersonian work
37. Shoulder wrap
38. Dromedary
39. Windshield adjunct
40. Lots
41. Clear the slate
42. Bird of poetry
43. Shell out
45. Swift mammals
46. Sew loosely
49. Might
50. "Breadbasket"
51. Reach fruition
53. Yielded (to)
54. Judicial wear
55. Apply (to)
57. Demean
58. Tendriled plants
59. Valleys
61. Crams (for an
    exam): slang
62. Pennies
63. Emulated Van
    Winkle
64. Romeo

65. Verdi work
66. Prospector
67. Thoroughfares
68. Dupes; stooges
69. Banks of baseball
70. Acts
72. Walks in water
73. Boxing matches
76. Lottery winnings, often

77. Hires
78. Capacities
80. Bridle
81. Word of comparison
82. Anger, envy, etc.
84. Canceled
85. Way; path
86. Plant again
88. "Top bananas"
89. Shelf

90. Polish
91. Capri or Wight
92. Sharp
93. Glance over
94. Copenhagen native
95. Defeat utterly
96. Musical sound
97. Easy task: slang
100. Get it?
102. Cask

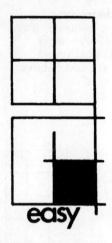

easy

ACROSS

1. Needy
5. Soreness
9. Trap, in a way
11. Lend an ear
13. Forward!
14. Prepare for print
16. Armored vehicle
17. You and I
18. Total (up)
20. Loam
22. Not genuine
23. Soup vegetable
24. Period in office
26. Run easily
28. Shoe bottom
29. Film players
30. Highway
32. Historical period
33. Golf mound
34. Short arrow
35. Baked desserts
37. Cuts into cubes
39. Take a chance
40. Require
42. Shallow
43. Nominate
44. Forgive
46. Excellent: 2 wds.
47. Sincere
49. Frolic
51. Anticipate
54. Baseball group
55. Pretend
56. Go by sea
58. Pull; haul
59. Takes the bait
61. Close at hand
63. Antlered animal
64. Youth
65. Pecan or almond
67. Stain
69. Window section
70. Blaze
71. Earth
73. Before long
75. Museum display
76. Lion's "neckwear"
77. British sailors
79. Boot part
80. At home
81. Track event
82. Boat dock
84. As far as
85. Dwell (at)
87. Girl
89. Rounded roof
90. Frog's cousin

DOWN

1. Think deeply
2. Rain — shine
3. Dollar bill
4. Warren Beatty movie
5. Long (for)
6. Inquire
7. That object
8. Latest
9. Paint layer
10. Wild protest
11. Huron or Erie
12. Tidy
15. Become weary
16. Story
19. Let fall
21. British title
22. Enemies
23. Recreation area
25. Principal; chief
27. Suit maker
28. Hearty dish
29. Lawsuit
31. Go off the — end
34. Piece of change
36. Mediterranean, for one
38. Join together
39. Sprinted
41. Nightmare
43. Short letters
45. Time division
46. Egyptian viper
48. Prolong
49. Juicy fruit
50. Fall behind
52. Metal container
53. Binds

54. Oak or maple
55. Military assistant
57. Circuits around the track
58. Fender nick
59. Unfurnished
60. Wardrobe item
62. Plant part

63. Mended
64. Fishing cord
66. Golf hazard
68. Blew a horn
69. Couple
70. Visage
72. Decorate, as a Christmas tree

74. Sign gas
76. Manufactured
78. Chair
81. Wheel's edge
83. River: Spanish
86. Thus
88. Elected prosecutor: abbr.

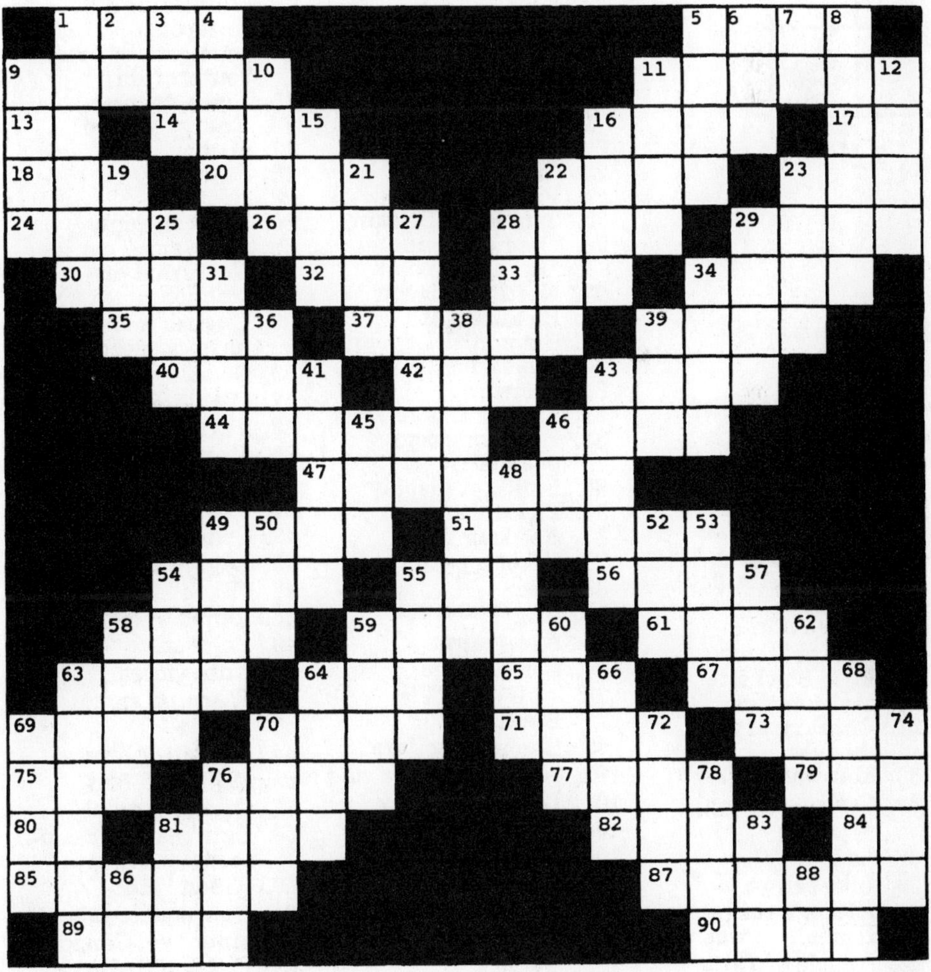

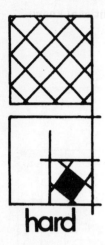

hard

ACROSS

1. Applaud
5. Sounds of relief
10. Out of kilter
15. Glaswegian
19. Unctuous
20. Angler's basket
21. French painter
22. Fizzy drink
23. General Bradley
24. Hair dye
25. Cite
26. Ark weather
27. Rose Bowl site
29. Make butter
31. Literary after-thought
33. Marceau, e.g.
34. Coil of yarn
35. ⅛ ounce
36. Long step
39. Like helium
40. Kicker's target, in football: 2 wds.
44. Article of faith
45. Inclined (to)
46. Ladder steps

47. De Oro or Grande
48. Muscovite: abbr.
49. Carnivals
50. Paris' river
51. Help in crime
52. "Exodus" hero
53. Furze
54. Abundant
55. Vibrant
56. Obelisk, for one
58. Cloth fold
59. Election rosters
60. Intrusive
61. Tennis exchange
62. Hideaway
63. Ice-hockey maneuver
66. Spartan serf
67. Arty
71. Tijuana fare
72. Sordid
73. City in Illinois
74. Pindaric poem
75. Symbol of Britain
76. "Beowulf" and "Paradise Lost"
77. Nestling pigeon
78. Be aware of
79. Columnist Landers
80. Gush (forth)
81. Scorn
82. Zuñi or Osage
83. Hormonic compounds
85. Brilliant display
86. Pick-me-up
87. Feedbag filler
88. Hiker's path
89. Ibex
90. Angel
93. Ascertain
94. Conjectured
98. — West, TV's Batman
99. Choirboy collars
101. Neither hot nor cold
103. Leak out slowly
104. Chablis or Chianti
105. Succinct
106. Chopin piece
107. Mrs. Nick Charles
108. Commotion
109. Bullock
110. Less abundant
111. Vega or Enif

DOWN

1. Poultry pen
2. Peruvian city
3. What a pity!
4. Structures at Giza
5. Intrigue
6. Nostalgic Broadway musical
7. Actress Rowlands
8. Female lobster
9. Relaxes
10. Exonerate
11. Grieve
12. Unyielding
13. Tosspot
14. Immigrants' area en route, often
15. Pinch pennies
16. Energy source
17. Medley
18. Piquancy
28. Antic
30. Roll-call reply
32. Huck and Tom
34. Nocturnal distraction
35. English metaphysical poet
36. Go away!
37. Cornwall city
38. Varnish base
39. March 17 celebrants
40. Culpability
41. Planet's path
42. Colander
43. Lugs
45. "Bash"
46. Reimburse
49. Palm off
50. Fuse (metal)
51. Warning signal
53. Luster
54. Pewter or bronze
55. 1979 sci-fi film
57. Gibson garnish
58. Chiromancer's concern
59. Hindu "sir"
61. Do a double-take
62. Mount —, Canada
63. U.S.A.F. ballistic missile
64. Canonized person

65. Tea cake
66. Legatees
67. Utter impulsively
68. Greek style of architecture
69. Sun-dried brick
70. More recent
72. Taters
73. Peer
76. Descriptive names
77. Sliver
78. GI emergency food fare: 2 wds.
80. Suds-maker
81. Isolated rock
82. British trolley
84. Itinerant
85. Bungler's aid
86. Frontier
88. Strained
89. Museum official
90. Proverbs
91. Revise (copy)
92. Bombay noblewoman
93. Traditional knowledge
94. Stimulate
95. Chimney grime
96. Hebrew prophet
97. Letter opener
100. Vietnamese holiday
102. Timetable abbreviation

SPECIAL CHALLENGER CROSSWORD

"PROS AND CONS"   by RUTH NALLS

Here is a real toughie for you. We have omitted giving you such helps as "2 wds.," "hyph. wd.," and "slang"; but in the spirit of fair play, all abbreviations and foreign words are so indicated.

ACROSS

1. Without briefing or prior knowledge
5. Plant fiber
9. Tip (one's hat)
13. Wolf's weapon
17. Curved molding
18. Archon, e.g.
19. In the van
21. Word with horse or curtain
22. Wildly extravagant
24. Accordion's kin
26. Plant's hair
27. Form of address
29. Protector, sometimes
30. Modern weapon, for short
31. WWII battle site
32. Jutlander
33. Train accommodations
36. Northwestern city
38. Mexican liquor
42. Body sac
43. Ceremonial staffs
44. Algonquian
47. A bit
48. Yoko's progenitors
49. Says in fun
50. Ancient battle site
51. Formerly named
52. Phony behavior
53. Emily and Wiley
54. Nickname for a big man
55. Certain chair maker
57. "They went —!"
59. Fine-arts school
61. Mew
62. Soft-drink nuts
63. King of the Huns
64. One who plays for pay
68. Role for Ava Gardner
72. Carries on
73. Dogpatch dweller
74. Cheaply showy
75. Fill in, for short
76. — Amin
77. Roman historian
78. Kin of "kinda"
79. An Arnaz
80. Throw wide, e.g.
82. Job for Philo Vance
83. Largest asteroid
84. L.A. athlete
85. Sligo staple
87. Persian king
89. Become furious
90. U.N. member: abbr.
92. Large containers
93. Scraps
94. Issues
98. Sumerian deity
99. Tourist site in Italy
103. Smuggler's haul
105. Dissemination of ideas to further a cause
107. Sharpen, tonsorially
108. Bits & skits show
109. Bottle size
110. Strikebreaker
111. Baltic Sea feeder
112. Certain swans
113. Czech river
114. Being: Latin

DOWN

1. Ancient Egyptian
2. Grim Grimm creature
3. Author Uris
4. Skill
5. Taps sounder
6. Wings
7. Defeat, at bridge
8. Sawhorses, e.g.
9. Fabric
10. "So *that's* it!"
11. Manage (for oneself)
12. Confronted
13. Jogger's goal
14. Lifeless
15. "And then there were —"
16. Growl
18. Haystacks
20. Malign
23. Petrarch's beloved
25. Frenchman's name
28. French atolls
31. Factions
33. WWII vessel
34. Quarrelsome puppet
35. Hero
36. Precipitate
37. Spanning
39. Expert in discrimination
40. Imam's associate
41. Suspicious; wary
43. Phoenix suburb
45. Picardy bloomer
46. Ogler
49. Dewlaps
50. Like Schoenberg's early work
53. Fence pickets
54. Food grinder
55. Spiteful
56. Tamarisk salt tree
58. Avian topknot
59. Pika

60. Orchid
62. Curving outward
64. Fuss about fixing oneself up
65. C.B., e.g.
66. *Hacienda* room
67. Wading bird
68. Worries
69. Scoreboard entry
70. Girl of song
71. In —, between two fires

74. Garment panels
78. Sixfold
79. Exhibition horse-manship
81. Stroll
82. Cheech, to Chong
83. Unpleasant fellow
84. Put a "rug" on
86. Autocrat
88. Sidesteps
89. — energy
91. Ancient instrument

93. Cowboy, at times
94. Yodeler's feedback
95. "— Indigo," song oldie
96. Mrs. Lindbergh
97. One of the Solomons
99. Ovine shelter
100. Biblical patriarch
101. Japanese plants
102. Rapunzel's pride
104. Point of a story
106. Equip (a ship)

DIAGRAMLESS

MEDIUM

This Diagramless is 15 boxes wide by 15 boxes deep.

ACROSS

1. Plaything
4. Carpenter's tool
7. Fruit drink
8. Color; shade
9. Knock sharply
12. Answer (to)
14. Eve's mate
16. Plot of ground
17. Heavenly streaker
19. Talking bird
23. Pool stick
25. In favor of; for
26. Concerning
27. Catholic service
28. Before: poetic
29. Spiders' traps
30. Word with "area" or "zip"
31. Weep
32. That thing
33. Thoroughfare: abbr.
34. Ma's mate
35. Sewing need
37. Worry
38. Spoken
41. Pale; ashen

42. Pesty plant
43. Look at fixedly
44. Also
45. Do sums
46. Abstained from food
47. Stalks
49. Be victorious
50. Chair, for one
51. Hand digits
55. Coloring agent
56. Large monkey
57. Not me
58. As — as a beet
59. — and flow

DOWN

1. Paving goo
2. Lyric poem
3. Affirmative
4. Fire (a gun)
5. Mother's sister
6. Marry
9. Speed contests
10. Commotion
11. Mollycoddle
13. Conspiracy
15. Gay; jolly

18. Foot digit
19. Dog's or cat's foot
20. Lincoln, to friends
21. Redbreast
22. Metal corrosion
23. West Pointer
24. Utilize
27. Changed residence
30. Was concerned
31. Gem weight
34. Cooking vessels
35. Trousers
36. Certainly
37. Gave meals to
39. Exist
40. Guided
41. Used to be
42. Squander
43. Warbled
46. Imposed a monetary penalty upon
48. "Merry" month
49. Dry the dishes
51. Distant
52. Visual organ
53. Steal
54. Underwater craft, for short

DIAGRAMLESS

MEDIUM

This Diagramless is 15 boxes wide by 15 boxes deep.
Starting box is on page 217

ACROSS

1. Wooden pin
4. Allow
7. Masculine
8. Boat paddles
10. Handbags
12. Denudes
14. It makes waste, sometimes
15. Spinning toy
17. Chairs
19. Picnic pests
20. Morse, and others
22. Fall in drops
23. Golf peg
24. Prison chiefs
26. Historic period
27. Lift
29. Was foolishly fond of
31. West Coast time abbreviation
32. Uncooked
33. Pares
35. Pigpens
37. Utilize
39. Come in again
41. Plaything
44. Nothing more than
46. Fathered
47. Well-cooked
48. Couples
50. Short sleep
51. Abates
52. Gloomy; sullen
54. Blackboards
56. — out, give sparingly
57. Lyric poems
58. Wield oars
59. Marry

DOWN

1. Portions
2. Otherwise
3. Golly!
4. Building site
5. Hearing organs
6. Attempted
7. Assemble, as troops
9. Was lenient
10. Window section
11. Market
12. Drive too fast
13. Mix
14. Sombrero, for one
16. Strange
18. Health resort
20. Regal residences
21. Snuffed noisily
24. More learned
25. Single step
28. Monkey
30. Female sheep
33. Sentence ender, usually
34. Paris' river
35. Paces
36. Rocks
37. Baseball official, for short
38. Sewing juncture
40. Anti gun-control group: abbr.
42. Small bills
43. Affirmative response
45. Mistake
47. Old-fashioned
49. Perform alone
51. Walk in water
53. Stitch
55. Depressed in spirits

DIAGRAMLESS

HARD

This Diagramless is 17 boxes wide by 17 boxes deep.
Starting box is on page 217

ACROSS

1. Drink daintily
4. Solving direction in this puzzle
7. Massachusetts Cape
10. Means of avoiding the law, as in contracts
14. Cry of surprise
15. Grain beard
16. — branch, symbol of peace
17. Toupees
19. Made (as fabric) on a loom
20. Frequently: poetic
21. Finale
22. Be mistaken
24. Patchwork bedcover
27. Require
29. Like a bright day
30. Charitable act
33. Heavenly body
34. Barge or ferry
35. V.I.P.
36. Individual
37. Favoring

38. Zig—, sharp angle
40. Rich veins (of ore)
43. At a distance
45. Got out of bed
46. FBI's kin: abbr.
49. Adam's mate
50. Agreed (with): 2 wds.
52. Marry
53. Become apparent
54. Kickoff gadget

DOWN

1. Coal-carrying boat
2. Mightiest of metals
3. Dad: slang
4. Southern State: abbr.
5. Display
6. Performance by one
7. Intimidate
8. "Beautiful" river of song
9. Tall, annual weed: 2 wds.

11. Animated
12. Milestone
13. Transmit
18. Thoroughfare
23. Boxing official: abbr.
24. More than several: 3 wds.
25. One: Italian
26. Country lodge
28. Apply, as rouge
29. Division of a song
30. Marsh
31. Ostrichlike bird
32. Dove's call
33. *Chicken — bleu,* restaurant offering
35. Mary Tyler —
37. Imperfection
39. Donated
41. Noble Italian family name
42. Juncture
44. Flushed
46. Innermost part
47. "Bus Stop" author
48. Lifetime
51. Permit

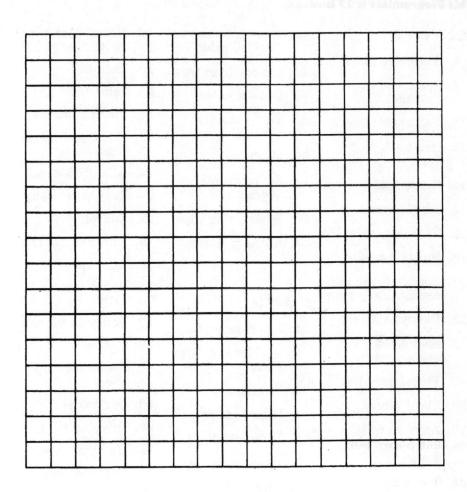

DIAGRAMLESS

EXPERT

**This Diagramless is 17 boxes wide by 17 boxes deep.
Starting box is on page 217**

ACROSS

1. Yuccalike plant
6. Spain and Portugal
8. Fall apart: 3 wds.
12. Great athlete, Jesse —
13. Cattle feed
14. Sir Guinness
15. Network: abbr.
18. Head: French
19. Good-hearted, dependable person
21. Danny or Marlo
25. Showed on TV again
26. Travel permits
28. Chess piece
29. Author of "Man and Superman": 3 wds.
35. Two-edged sword
36. Old World lizard
37. Bikini, for one
38. Periods added to harmonize the lunar and solar calendars
41. Wooded glens

42. Aga —, former Turkish ruler
44. Society-page word
45. Gdansk native
46. To —, exactly: 2 wds.
50. Machetes
51. Set up camp: 3 wds.
53. Restraining rope
54. Rhone tributary

DOWN

1. Small amounts
2. — -Wan, of "Star Wars"
3. Swarm
4. Whale genus
5. Is deceitful
7. Baseball-bat wood
8. Billy or nanny
9. Young "hooter"
10. Cogs
11. Appraising glance: hyph. wd.
15. Salad greens
16. Beginning

17. Milan opera house (with "La")
19. Thin nail
20. Sensed
22. Playing marble
23. Under sail, sometimes
24. Bilko, to his men
27. Easy task: slang
28. Oddball
29. Alumnus, for short
30. Ingested
31. Polish city on the Oder
32. Valley on the moon
33. "Takes"
34. Doctor's group: abbr.
39. Oar holder
40. Drawing room
43. Hatching post
46. Quick to learn
47. Part of man's wardrobe
48. Kett, of the comics
49. Acoustics problem
50. Unadorned
52. Clucker

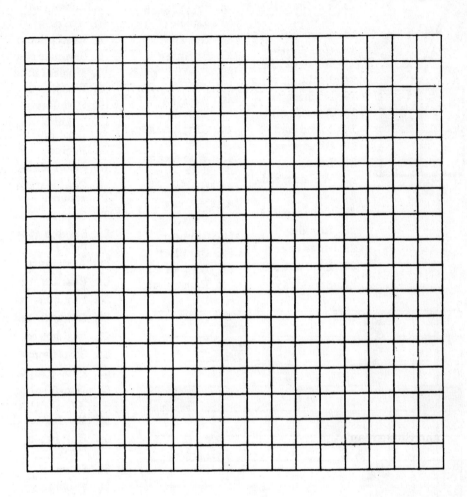

ACROSS

1. Cushion
4. Doc or Grumpy
9. Feathered scarf
12. Grow old
13. Competition for cowboys
14. Building wing
15. Highest part
16. Adam's mate
17. Fixed costs
19. Otherwise
21. Lease
22. Walking aids
24. Nuns
27. Take a cab
28. Rapidity
29. In or near
30. Paid notices
31. Small bays
32. Bakery item
33. Compass reading
34. Makes gentle
35. Workbench device
36. Got free
38. Sprinter
39. Crafts' "partner"
40. Breathe heavily
41. Christmas visitor
43. Was a candidate
44. Utilize
47. Not new
48. Frosting
50. Sunbeam
51. Cunning
52. Loop in a rope
53. Ram's mate

DOWN

1. Mr. Boone
2. In the past
3. Relies (on)
4. Attire
5. Used a loom
6. Summer cooler
7. Musical tone
8. Woodlands
9. Miss Davis
10. Spanish cheer
11. Hirt and Pacino
18. Poker stake
20. Confederate general
21. Gets up
22. Stretch (the neck)
23. Assistants
24. Rescued
25. Pay hike
26. Guide (a boat)
28. Residences
31. Ship's master
32. Photograph
34. Jam-filled pastry
35. Moving truck
37. Halloween treat
38. Stove
40. Cooking vessels
41. Distress call
42. Everyone
43. — Grande River
45. Cutting tool
46. Organ of sight
49. Business group: abbr.

Easy

154

ACROSS

1. Single bill
4. Takes part in a game
9. Cooking vessel
12. Angry
13. Up and about
14. Exist
15. While
16. Intentions
17. Lubricated
19. Actress Fleming
21. Painful
22. Cast a ballot
23. Delivers news
26. Magnitude
27. Safe harbor
28. Overhead train
29. *Corrida* cheer
30. Surfaced (a road)
31. Compass point: abbr.
32. Actor Pacino
33. Speedy car
34. Moore's role
35. Comments
37. Baseball team
38. Assists
39. Hate
41. Hi!
43. "Peace" bird
44. Yes: Spanish
45. Reverent wonder
46. Commotion
48. "Snaky" fish
49. Affirmative
50. Scoff
51. Encountered

DOWN

1. Actor Sharif
2. "Music City"
3. Actor Asner
4. Self-esteem
5. Capital of Peru
6. Donkey
7. "Seek and — shall find"
8. Was nosy
9. More ashen
10. Raw metal
11. Actor Knight
16. Poker stake
18. Press clothes
20. Seep
21. Cut off
23. Rants
24. Volunteer State
25. Luge, for one
26. Fly high
27. Chops
30. Excuses
31. Not any
33. Speak bitterly
34. Nip
36. Men
37. At no time
39. Medicine portion
40. Tip; slant
41. Horse feed
42. Ram's mate
43. Gambling "cube"
47. Atop
48. Printing measure

Medium

ACROSS

1. Nourished
4. Frustrate
8. Publicizes
12. Be in debt
13. Story start
14. Actual
15. Ring arbiters
17. — down, soften
18. Diner sign
19. Strikes (at)
21. Category
23. Dress in
24. Strong emotion
25. Hung around
29. Skilled pitcher
30. Jack rabbits
31. A Gabor
32. Cashed in, as trading stamps
34. Bucket
35. God of war
36. Wisconsin tree
37. Clergyman
40. Hornet
41. Door sign
42. Tornadoes
46. In addition
47. Compass heading
48. Trouble
49. One's equal
50. Henna, etc.
51. Rogers or Acuff

DOWN

1. Favoring
2. Flock member
3. Beat
4. Army posts
5. Wallet stuffers
6. Refrigerate
7. Abated
8. Apparel
9. Mighty metal
10. Tolled
11. Comprehends
16. Grace
20. Humorists
21. Scorch
22. Delicate trim
23. Telegraphs
25. Bewailed
26. Show up again
27. Maleficent
28. Valley
30. Deli sandwich
33. Event of April 7th
34. Gone by
36. Spars
37. Chirp
38. Wheel spindle
39. Start the day
40. Intelligent
43. Route
44. River: Spanish
45. Cunning

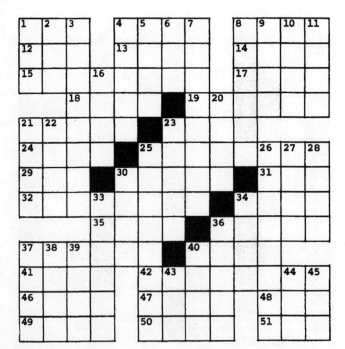

Hard

156

ACROSS

1. Theatre section
6. Cook (meat) in an oven
11. King's seat
13. Thwart; impede
14. Goal; purpose
15. Actor Niven
17. Before: poetic
18. MD's associate: abbr.
19. — rummy, card game
20. Richmond's State: abbr.
21. Conceit
23. Bluish-gray color
25. Actor Buttons
26. Pebble
28. Smudge
30. Tint
31. Crazy
32. Flower part
34. Middle Eastern country
36. Prohibit
37. For —, permanently
39. Lyric poem
41. Word of choice
42. Lawyer's charge
43. Pa's mate
44. Butterfly snare
46. Book of maps
48. Knight's title
49. Strength
51. Come back
53. Set forth in words
54. Do and re

DOWN

1. Look fixedly at
2. Items
3. Human limb
4. Move along
5. Stop; finish
6. Free (of)
7. Concerning
8. Summer drink
9. Waiter
10. Tire feature
12. U.S. national emblem
13. Indirect suggestions
16. By way of
22. The — day, recently
23. Lurk (about)
24. Certain entertainment awards
25. Disc jockey's industry
27. Not at home
29. Hearing organ
32. 43-Across, for one
33. "Southpaw": slang
34. Asparagus stalk
35. Have high regard for
36. Treats for Fido
38. Snakelike fish
40. Deserves
45. Pekoe, for one
46. Ripen
47. Word with "back" or "off"
48. Earth's star
50. Football position: abbr.
52. Toward

Medium

Easy

ACROSS

1. Comedian, Bob —
5. Mix
9. Walk the floor
13. Raise, as crops
17. Egg-shaped
18. Arrived
19. "Once — a time . . ."
20. Govern (over)
21. Allow
22. Finished
24. Jury group
25. Catch in a trap
27. Dines
28. Hand firearm
29. Grow old
30. Actress, — Tyler Moore
31. Assist
32. Steal: slang
35. Throw
36. Puts (money) in a bank
40. Jar tops
41. Misplace
42. Crawled
43. College cheer
44. Washington bill
45. Sulk
46. Happening every 24 hours
47. Lasso
48. Coffee's rival
49. Your and my
50. Jack rabbits
51. Subsided; ebbed
52. Coal scuttle
53. Small pies
54. Thick mist
55. Uncloudy, as skies
58. Shoe bottoms
59. Deface
60. Hooting bird
63. Wedding band
64. Desires
65. Fishing rod
66. Crusted dessert
67. Also
68. Rants
69. Raggedy Ann or Andy
70. Bay State: abbr.
71. Telegrams' contents
73. Roll-call reply
74. Bundles (of hay)
75. Frosted (a cake)
76. Final
77. Naughty
78. Prolonged looks
81. Valley
82. Chooses
86. Lemonlike fruits
87. Adorned
89. Ignited
90. Biblical garden
91. Texas, The — Star State
92. Jog
93. Hawaiian dance
94. Cozy rooms
95. Picnic pests
96. Stitches
97. Do as told

DOWN

1. Cavity
2. Baking chamber
3. Touches gently
4. — Paso, Texas
5. Tally
6. No longer wild
7. Devilish child
8. Set free
9. Sealing for windows
10. Large monkeys
11. Salty fish
12. 14th letter
13. Holds firmly
14. Undersized animal
15. Margarine
16. Water source
22. Zoo compartment
23. Corn spikes
24. Aviator
26. Short sleeps
28. Full of energy
30. Greatest amount
31. Bread ends
32. — machine, casino fixture
33. Brandy or champagne
34. Thought
35. Guided trip
36. Wipes, as dishes
37. Press (clothes)
38. Adhesive strip
39. Shack
41. Noisy
42. Shopping wagons
45. Needy
46. Ventures
47. Dust cloth
50. Stops, sentry style

51. Was clothed in
52. Witch
53. Musical qualities
54. Autumn
55. Stuff
56. Fishing cord
57. Odds and —
58. Rescued
59. Burrowing animal
60. October gem
61. Like the old owl
62. Not as much

64. Salary
65. Harbor
68. Runs (an engine) at high speed
69. Sahara and Mojave
70. Manufactured
72. Ambulance warning devices
73. Angelic arc
74. Hairless
76. Shoestrings
77. Red vegetables

78. Toboggan
79. Ocean current
80. Prayer ending
81. Fender mishap
82. Pack away
83. Night stick
84. Flooring square
85. Don't go!
87. Funnyman Rickles
88. Exist
91. Its capital is Baton Rouge: abbr.
93. Westward —!

ACROSS

1. Fodder for Dobbin
4. *Italia's* capital
8. Bedouin
12. Pub brew
13. Biblical husband
14. Go by bus
15. Bullfighter
17. Cone-shaped tent
18. Elevator cage
19. Walking stick
20. More rational
23. Type of novel
26. A long time
27. Jack rabbits
28. Mr. Pacino
29. Obtain
30. Shoestrings
31. Enjoy a winter sport
32. One
33. Talks wildly
34. Robert Frost, for one
35. Bell's clapper
37. Wash lightly
38. Smooth
39. Devotee
40. Window sections
42. Poisonous snake
46. Always
47. Step; stride
48. Miner's find
49. Handles roughly
50. Cast off
51. Roll of bills

DOWN

1. Incompetent actor: slang
2. Montgomery's State: abbr.
3. Up to now
4. Trooper's detection system
5. Smell
6. Deface
7. Exist
8. Boxing-match sites
9. Grow mellow
10. Fruit drink
11. Quilting event
16. Expert pilots
17. Domesticates
19. Apple centers
20. Heroic tales
21. 007, for one
22. Butterfly snare
23. Speedster, sometimes
24. Birthday items
25. Select group
27. Safe place
30. Erie and Huron
31. Junior, to dad
33. Large streams
34. Certain liquid measure
36. Begin again
37. Appraised
39. Clock feature
40. Liveliness
41. Actress Gardner
42. Word in a cheer
43. Depressed
44. Historic period
45. "Danger" color
47. Writer's afterthought: abbr.

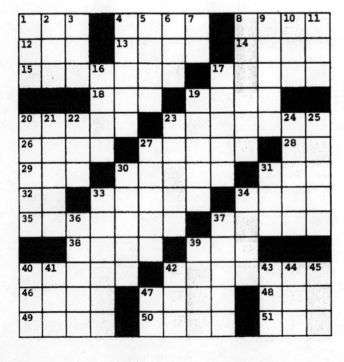

Medium

ACROSS

1. Comedian Conway
4. Stairway unit
8. Blossom or sprout
11. Commotion
12. Accept
13. Single
14. Fishing mesh
15. So be it!
16. Perform vocally
18. Glisten
20. Mode
22. Terminate
23. Paving goo
26. Prize
28. Cowboy Autry
29. Edge
32. Hawaii, for one
34. Great Lake
35. Boise's State
37. Precious stone
38. Distant
39. Sing, Swiss style
43. Call on
45. Budge
46. Celebrity
48. Pledge
50. By way of
51. Go by
52. Conceit
53. Mooselike deer
54. Aid in crime
55. Hurried

DOWN

1. Beige
2. The — of March
3. Parent
4. Get up
5. Domesticated
6. — out a living, earn a meager income
7. Writing tool
8. Employer
9. Single thing
10. Declare untrue
17. Forest clearing
19. Land of rajas
21. Female sheep
23. Oolong, for one
24. — Arbor, Michigan
25. Scarlet
27. Opera solos
28. Dreariness
29. Implore
30. Raw metal
31. Edge of a cup
33. Timid
36. Cabbie, for one
38. Earliest
40. "Peace" bird
41. Wicked
42. Seep
43. Flower holder
44. Roman robe
46. Health resort
47. Check; bill
49. Was victorious

Easy

Medium

ACROSS

1. One who has completed school
5. Commandments number
8. Room light
12. Soil
16. Ear feature
17. Cab fee
18. Brainstorm
19. Some male singers
21. Kiln
22. City home
24. Lease
25. You and I
26. Tide's partner
28. Geese formation
29. Eye part
31. Fuss
32. Asian staple
33. Marry
34. Flash
36. Pace
37. Pursue
39. Car fuel
40. Publish
41. Scoffs
42. Search (for)
43. Large
44. Actor Eastwood
45. Hive dweller
46. Hen product
47. Be victorious
48. Picture holder
49. Warm covering
53. Did garden work
55. Sea water
56. Fiber source
57. Creeping plant
58. That one
59. Stream
60. Limas
61. — and tuck
62. Flutter
65. Lucid
66. Sipped
67. Not busy
68. Fall behind
69. Dreary
70. Facial hair
71. Hirt or Pacino
72. Solitary
73. Heavy metal
74. Friars
75. Lone Ranger's horse
79. Cowboy movie
81. Elk relative
82. Wet earth
83. Adam's wife
84. Inquire
85. Abode
86. Ewe's mate
87. Bread end
88. Chefs
91. Perch
92. 8 ounces
93. Crooner Como
94. Entice
95. Uptight
96. Chewing goo
97. Precious stones
98. Ms. Landers
99. Helper
100. Forbid
101. Shut noisily
102. Sale notice
104. Scanty
106. Earth orbiter
110. Man or Capri
112. Hunting dog
113. Oak, for one
114. Level
115. Title
116. Plant's start
117. 12 months
118. Mondale, for one: abbr.
119. Happy

DOWN

1. Shine softly
2. Wander
3. Lincoln, to pals
4. Tooth man
5. Ribbon "record"
6. Period of note
7. Sensitive spots
8. Citrus fruit
9. Summer cooler
10. Males
11. Tolerant
12. Sandra and Ruby
13. Charming hotel
14. Turn; spin
15. Swapper
17. Renown
19. Clip; cut
20. Feeds pigs
23. Kennedy's nickname
27. Cold cubes
30. Rodent
32. Scope
33. Tail motion
34. Dirt
35. Fishing rope
36. Viewed
37. Masticate
38. Very large
39. Rummy variation
40. Board
41. Dungarees
43. Auction offer
44. Boo-hooer
45. Empty, as a page
47. Soaked; damp
48. Oddity
49. Steer marking
50. Sort; ilk
51. Wicked
52. Kind
54. Immerse
55. Sandwich need
56. Endures
59. Dirt-free
60. Car stopper
62. Stream; glide
63. Country road
64. Gets older
65. Office worker

162

66. Thick
67. Ailing
69. "God — America"
70. Help up
71. Assist
74. Mickey or Minnie
75. Total
76. Steers away
77. Always
78. Depend (on)
80. Accept
81. Cow calls

82. Atlas feature
85. Truthfulness
86. Sugar cane drink
87. Shortening a skirt
88. School group
89. There are 16 in a pound
90. Fancy
91. Crimson
92. Wavy
93. Pod vegetable
95. Row; layer

96. Girl
97. Valley
99. Shot a hole-in-one
100. Ale relative
101. Flower part
102. Ms. Gluck
103. Action
105. Highway: abbr.
107. Exist
108. Pekoe, for one
109. "— Got a Secret"
111. "My Gal —"

Easy

ACROSS

1. Distress signal
4. Stuffs; crowds
9. Marry
12. Exist
13. Mechanical man
14. Malt beverage
15. Pod vegetable
16. Large monkey
17. Elevate
19. Rescue
21. Quicker
22. Ill will; malice
24. Armored vehicles
25. Conceal
26. Airplane parts
27. Word of greeting
29. Single thing
30. Grazing land
31. Short-lived craze
32. You and I
33. Pennies
34. Satisfy, as a need
35. Adores
36. Sticky stuff
37. Uses a razor
39. Trail
40. Falk or Lawford
41. Bottle top
42. Ms. Lupino
45. Anger
46. Marinara, for one
48. Convent sister
49. "... a borrower, — a lender be"
50. Go in
51. Receive

DOWN

1. Tree fluid
2. Raw metal
3. Coast; shore
4. Long for; desire
5. Lasso
6. Mr. Lincoln, for short
7. Show-Me State: abbr.
8. Unusual
9. Lingers awhile
10. Otherwise
11. Antlered animal
18. Inquires
20. Dined
21. Snake's teeth
22. Exhibit
23. Fir tree
24. Dyes
26. Decreases in light power, as the moon
27. Stop!
28. Not busy
30. Driving gear
31. Angler's activity
33. Small bay
34. Plump
35. Tardier
36. Parchment or onionskin
37. Twirl
38. Brave man
39. Tempo; rhythm
41. Use scissors
43. Payable
44. Crawling insect
47. One

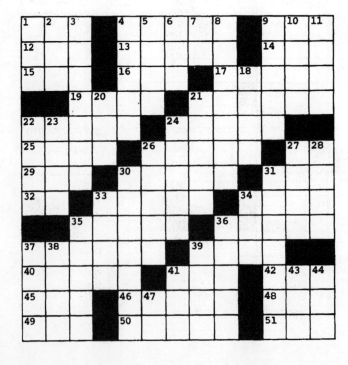

Hard

ACROSS

1. Placates
6. Executive's aides
11. Type of daisy
12. Wall decorations
14. Mont —, French peak
15. Part of a monogram
17. Withdrew (from a party)
19. Arafat's group: abbr.
20. Perpetually
21. Musical work
22. Wallpaper adhesive
25. Decorous
27. Miss Channing
28. UMW member
29. Western gully
31. Fourth-down kicks
32. Civil disturbance
33. Ski resort in Colorado
35. Recess game
36. Nitwit: 3 wds.
41. Daily chore, for some
43. Alpine region
44. Whine
45. Give the slip to
46. Poke fun at
47. Thickly populated

DOWN

1. Male swans
2. Wheel spindle
3. Vault
4. Talking bird
5. On the Q.T.
6. Hit hard: poetic
7. Piano adjusters
8. Like the Kara Kum
9. Taboo, to Jack Sprat
10. Saucy; impertinent
13. Greets, military style
16. Burgoyne at Saratoga
18. Hail!
21. Father of Thor
22. Social outcasts
23. Overbearing
24. Chimney buildup
26. Strove to equal
27. Peddlers' vehicles
30. Sheep
31. Metal casting
34. Viewpoint
36. Sutherland or Callas
37. In person, on TV
38. Teheran's country
39. Signals agreement
40. Holiday gaiety
42. Compete (for)

ACROSS

1. Tabby
4. That girl
7. Speed contests
9. Quiet
11. For each
13. Rough-voiced
14. Marry
15. Operatic solo
17. Require
18. Began
20. Walk through water
23. Looks at
24. Label
27. Revises a manuscript
29. Freedom from war
31. Four-poster
32. Pod vegetables
36. Cain's victim
37. Husband or wife
39. Perform alone
42. Quantity of paper
43. Sty's resident
46. Rubs out
48. Buccaneer
50. Abated; ebbed
51. Striped jungle-cat
52. Bandleader Brown
53. Jewel

DOWN

1. Garment for Batman
2. Sour; tart
3. Golf-ball holder
4. — by, support
5. Employ
6. Otherwise
7. Uncooked
8. Shoo!
9. Therefore
10. Guided
12. Epochs
13. Detest
16. Anger
18. Matching collection
19. The sixth sense, perhaps
20. Spider's home
21. Fruit drink
22. Performed (an action)
24. Bill
25. High card
26. Thicken
28. Health resort
30. Unit of corn
33. Makes a mistake
34. Consumed
35. Hard, thin cookie
37. Models for an artist
38. Send out; give forth
39. Stitch
40. Spoken
41. Narrow country road
43. Leaf (of a book)
44. Bit of news
45. Austria's language: abbr.
47. Ames or Asner
49. Tractor-trailer

Easy

Medium

ACROSS

1. Fibber
5. Wintry flakes
9. Part of mouth
12. Land measure
13. Miss Horne
14. Raw metal
15. Heavy string
16. Effort
18. Compass point
19. Wager
20. Country hotels
21. Strike with open hand
23. In favor of
25. Afterwards
27. Buccaneers
31. Region
32. Ventilate
33. "Gentle" bird
34. Marriage
36. Soft, French cap
37. Terminate
38. Have to
39. Prophet
42. Intention
43. Not on
46. Intrude
49. Power of the mind
50. Be sick
51. Revise
52. Largest continent
53. Affirmative
54. Bright and cheerful
55. 9th month: abbr.

DOWN

1. Shoestring
2. Sacred picture
3. Ran in
4. Bright color
5. Slumber
6. The following one
7. Smallest bill
8. Armed conflict
9. Cut of meat
10. Press
11. Writing tools
17. Scolding speeches
19. Legal profession
22. Conductors
23. Evergreen
24. And if not
25. Statute
26. Exist
27. Swine
28. Turtle's kin
29. Adam's mate
30. Gel
32. Also
35. At home
36. Hobo
38. Slightly foggy
39. Remain
40. Great Lake
41. Snaky fish
42. Sale phrase: 2 wds.
44. Toss, as a coin
45. Tire mishap
47. For each
48. Commotion
49. Used to be

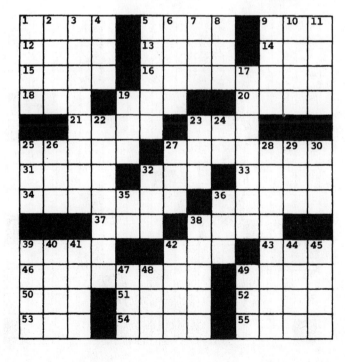

ACROSS

1. Promise; assurance
5. Party giver
9. Lion's home
12. Ended
13. Sedan or coupe
14. Grow old
15. Superman's girlfriend, Lois —
16. Sky "twinkler"
17. Use an oar
18. Raft
20. Demolish, destroy
22. Earn
24. Picnic pests
27. Dinner check
30. Cashew or pecan
31. Super!
32. Stop or check
34. Stalin's country
35. Depart
36. Actor's hint
37. "— as a fox"
38. Shoestring
39. Surmise; suppose
41. Come in
43. Main idea; topic
47. "Wise" bird
49. Cincinnati baseball team
51. Dry; desert-like
52. Female deer
53. — of Capri
54. Starchy grain
55. Speck
56. Encounter
57. Sharp

DOWN

1. Dog's "cousin"
2. Egg-shaped
3. Nevada city
4. Fantasy; vision
5. Possesses
6. Trick; baffle
7. Begin
8. Ripped
9. Gloominess
10. Conceit
11. Modern; recent
19. Nervous; edgy
21. Train parts
23. Groove
25. Puppy's "wagger"
26. Remain
27. High
28. Region
29. Jewelry item
31. Visitor
33. Equal
34. Regret
36. Turn sour, as milk
39. Ganders
40. "Star" of "Jaws" films
42. Decorate (the Christmas tree)
44. A Great Lake
45. Mickey and Minnie
46. Paradise
47. Peculiar
48. Court
50. Prepare (the table)

Easy

ACROSS

1. Sorrowful
4. Cut into two equal parts
9. Shade tree
12. Bullring cry: Spanish
13. City in New York
14. Ms. Arthur of "Maude"
15. Japanese warrior
17. Ducklike birds
19. Terminates
20. Type of bird
21. Swap
23. Distributed playing cards
24. Nevada city
25. Marie's brother
26. Nun: abbr.
28. Favored ones
29. Lump of turf
30. Command to a horse
31. High hill: abbr.
32. Indiana basketball player
33. Sphere; globe
34. Certain coins
35. Mass meeting
36. Tension
38. Part of 39-Across
39. Dwelling
40. Tiny Tim's creator
43. Omelet item
44. Unrestrained
46. Antique auto
47. German article
48. Diaphanous
49. Evergreen shrub

DOWN

1. Distress signal
2. Southern State: abbr.
3. Humbles; degrades
4. Wandering crowd
5. Woe is me!
6. Hawaiian wreath
7. Old Dominion: abbr.
8. Bewitch
9. Approximately
10. Theatrical backdrops
11. Chopped meat dish
16. Cancel; annul
18. — Field, Paris airport
20. Voice range
21. Neat; tidy
22. Tenant's payment
23. Peace birds
25. Cuts into small cubes
26. Vend
27. Depend (on)
29. Maidens: poetic
30. Museum display room
32. Pastries
33. Pitcher's mistake
34. Pharmacy items
35. Miler
36. Lean-to
37. Roman garment
38. Sage
40. Female rabbit
41. Born
42. Plant (seed)
45. Cry of wonder

medium

169

Hard

ACROSS

1. School subject
5. Burdened Titan
10. Jejune
14. Pack full
18. Shortening
19. Go very slowly
20. Ponders (over)
22. Tremendous
23. Number of Muses
24. Example: 3 wds.
26. Once more
27. Ring decision: abbr.
28. "Ties the knot"
29. Hits repeatedly
30. Declaims
32. Scarlett O'Hara, e.g.
34. Sheltered inlets
35. Rural estate
36. Make a choice
37. Relocates
38. Was curious to know
41. Configuration
44. More rational
45. Globule
46. Unity
47. Research centers
48. Daily delivery
49. Jungles
50. Essential thing
51. Malty brew
52. Future mare
53. Nob and Bunker
54. Mode
55. Favorite complaint: 2 wds.
57. Traffic sounds
58. Restrain
59. Pilaf ingredient
60. Lexicographer's concern
61. Jargon
62. Leatherneck
65. Robust
66. Disney specialties
70. Deputy
71. Sheriff's group
72. Maintains
73. Vietnamese city
74. Separate the coarse from the fine
75. Precipitancy
76. Inkberry
77. One of a nautical trio
78. Building wing
79. Poker stake
80. — Fe, New Mexico
81. Give a leg up
82. Votes into office again
85. Gala affairs
86. Mendacity
87. "— out," stalls
88. Categorizes
89. Agree (to)
93. Ornamental buttons
94. Olivier's milieu
95. Herringlike fish
96. Coal distillate
97. Principal
98. Outstanding athlete: hyph. wd.
101. Strong vapor
102. Eagerly expectant
103. Work (details) into a story
104. Came up
105. Notion
106. Sheet of stamps
107. Had creditors
108. — up, monopolized
109. Dry run

DOWN

1. One of twelve
2. Word for Tweedledum and Tweedledee
3. Pavarotti, e.g.
4. Weed chopper
5. Regional inflection
6. Player swap
7. Girl of Dundee
8. Veneration
9. Type of sweater
10. Oregon crop
11. Haley's best seller
12. Rainbow
13. Thieves' haunt
14. Opportunity
15. Rehearsal: hyph. wd.
16. Generations
17. Sea gull
21. Ocean shores
25. At no time
28. Dry off
31. Furthermore
33. Blunderer's exclamation
34. Rabbit fur
35. Thoroughfares
37. Sugar source
38. Founts
39. Follow
40. Dissuade
41. Rebuff
42. 1776 patriot
43. Aid feloniously
44. Healing ointment
45. Defrauds
48. Segment
49. Blustery
50. Guiding maxim
52. Boxing ploy
53. Crowd
54. Outlets
56. Lithograph
57. Palomino
58. Overdue
60. Dissipate
61. Showy lily

62. Microwave device
63. Nimble
64. Serious thought
65. TV emcees
66. Young zebras
67. La Salle's discovery
68. Carmelites
69. Membership
71. Trousers
72. Puts an edge on
75. Metal-cutting tool
76. North Carolina cape
77. Opposing votes
80. Suiting
81. Tie together
83. Backless sofa
84. Terminate
85. Frothed
86. Gave temporarily
88. Barrel slat
89. "Harvey" author
90. Chopin work
91. Designates
92. Unexpected pleasure
93. Heroic tale
94. Cabbage salad
95. Barge
97. Cartogram
99. A Zodiac sign
100. Dander
101. Appropriate

SPECIAL CHALLENGER CROSSWORD

"TITLE-ROLE ACTORS"   **by JOHN GREENMAN**

Here is a real toughie for you. We have omitted giving you such helps as "2 wds.," "hyph. wd.," and "slang"; but in the spirit of fair play, all abbreviations and foreign words are so indicated.

ACROSS

1. Boston area university
6. Junk jewelry
11. Angelico, et.al.
15. Formerly, once
19. Halt, to seamen
20. Novelist Shaw
21. Scottish isle
22. Jacob's wife
23. "Lawrence of Arabia"
25. "Merry Andrew"
27. Daisylike bloom
28. Half an umlaut
29. Garden area
30. Ill-fated
31. 25-Across is one
33. Staircase feature
35. Next of kin, perhaps
36. Málaga Mrs.: abbr.
37. One who disapproves
41. Accomplished
42. Nat and Natalie
44. Slice of history
45. Vagrants
47. "Dud"
49. Boutonniere's spot
53. Saucy, as a comment
55. Reminisce
57. Bureaucratic impediment
59. Nor'easter
60. Dimple: Brit.
61. Ulnas' neighbors
62. Ankle
64. Custom
65. Gould from Brooklyn
68. An Arab people
70. Sioux State: abbr.
71. Brown of "renown"
72. Church officer
73. Bombeck namesakes
75. Indian, e.g.
77. Location of the humerus
79. Corrida cheers
81. Anne Nichols hero
82. What many hobbyists do
85. Farm male
86. Amusement park offerings
88. Muse with a lyre
90. Small flycatcher
91. "Country" Slaughter
93. Hair style
94. Hose
96. 1400, in Latium
97. Ms. Moorehead
99. Facilitated
101. Acoustic
103. Succor
104. Neck tie
106. Cloudy
108. With gravity
110. Guidry of the mound
113. Like the proverbial hills
114. Strained
116. Trust (with "on")
117. Forward: Ital.
119. DeLuise
120. Sanction
122. Adenoidal
125. "Rabbit Run"
127. "Goodbye Mr. Chips"
130. Solar disk
131. Ireland
132. To the point: Latin
133. Straight: comb. form
134. Parched
135. Cutter, e.g.
136. A Cannon, et.al.
137. Becomes proximal

DOWN

1. Emulate Astaire
2. Iris layer
3. Domino of piano
4. African fly
5. Race-track section
6. Cherry stone
7. Sixth son of Gad
8. Unconsciousness
9. Askew
10. Compass point
11. First name in Cuba
12. Word before "block" or "bed"
13. — -Margret
14. Friar's footwear
15. Nevada city and county
16. Foolscap units
17. Word with "nay"
18. Bara of silents
24. William Jennings Bryan, e.g.
26. Alpine outburst
29. Eliot protagonist
32. "The Great Gatsby"
34. "The Life of Riley"
35. "The Buster Keaton Story"
37. "The Cloister and the Hearth" author
38. Swashbuckler Flynn
39. "Good Neighbor Sam"
40. Cape —, Portugal
42. Sir Arthur — Doyle
43. Droop
46. Streisand's "married lady"
48. Colorado time: abbr.
50. "Cool Hand Luke"
51. If not
52. Sides, at sea
54. Bonn salutation

56. Zodiacal sign
58. Snakebite antidote
63. Sheet metal for tubing
66. Emanation
67. Plant-spore producers
69. Milk-processing plant
74. Barkers, at sea
76. Rathskeller staple
77. Campground, e.g.
78. Echoed
80. Sans —

83. A. DeMille
84. Bear "type"
87. Phoebus
89. Emphatic adverbs
92. His or hers: Fr.
95. Wordless
98. Monarch Mary and poet Burns, e.g.
100. Dutch treat
102. Pale green
105. Cooper and Faye
107. Air
109. South India state

110. Punjab princes
111. Egg-shaped
112. Appointer
114. — down (subdued)
115. Actress Winger
118. Aloha State's avian
119. Challenge
121. High-schooler
123. Porch pier
124. "Wizard of Oz" star
126. Be indisposed
127. Energy unit
128. Boudoirs: abbr.
129. Prepositions

DIAGRAMLESS

MEDIUM

This Diagramless is 15 boxes wide by 15 boxes deep.

ACROSS

1. Affirmative reply
4. Encountered
7. Car for hire
8. Commotion
9. Leave out
10. Understand
13. — -size, small
15. Remainder
16. The "merry" month
17. Smoothly concise
19. Contributed
20. The Devil
22. Uncommon
23. Word with "boy" or "clip"
25. Nuisance
26. Goes to bed
28. Bambi, for one
30. French capital
32. Statutes
33. King with the golden touch
35. At any —, in any event
36. Lawful
38. Had dinner
39. Go by
42. Wicked
44. Marry
45. Headland
46. Small bill
47. Again, once more
48. Scarlet
49. For each

DOWN

1. Sweet potatoes
2. Depart
3. Command to a dog
4. Chart
5. Work on news-paper copy
6. Musical sounds
7. Boot tip
10. Intelligent
11. Roof edge
12. Organ of sight
14. Pitfall
15. Harvester
18. Looks fixedly at
19. Methane, for one
21. Gross, minus expenses
22. Live (at)
24. Actor Torn
25. Dangers
27. Male sheep
28. Old-fashioned
29. Mate to 27-Down
31. Stuffing seasoning
32. Tardy
34. Taste with relish
35. Uncooked
37. Border; boundary
39. Window section
40. Copycat
41. Embroider
43. Guided
45. Nurse's headgear

DIAGRAMLESS

MEDIUM

**This Diagramless is 15 boxes wide by 15 boxes deep.
Starting box is on page 217**

ACROSS

1. Speak imperfectly
5. Aroma
6. Health resorts
10. Commotion: hyph. wd.
11. Group of three
12. Drink like a cat
13. Swimming places
14. Griefs
16. Apron part
19. Ooze
20. Speed contest
21. Shriek
24. Was concerned
25. Challenge
26. Youth
28. Grew older
29. Resided
30. Tried out
32. Once again
33. Narrow bed
34. Marry
35. Not as long
38. Look at fixedly
39. Dog's foot
41. At this place
42. Cravats
44. Lambs' mothers
45. Capri, for one
46. Surrender formally

DOWN

1. Building site
2. Graven image
3. Soft drinks
4. Pop the question
6. Crouch
7. Bow of a ship
8. Troubles
9. Distress signal, asea
13. Happening before the usual time
15. Actual
16. Uncovered
17. Frosted, as a cake
18. Four-poster
20. Storm
21. Rescued
22. Team
23. Crimson
24. Feline
25. Eat
27. Fender mishap
29. Statute
31. Doubting Thomas
33. Dull persons
35. "Mulligan" dish
36. Rabbit
37. Lift
38. That woman
40. Fuse by heat
43. Observe

DIAGRAMLESS

HARD

This Diagramless is 17 boxes wide by 17 boxes deep.
Starting box is on page 217

ACROSS

1. Yemeni
5. Desert convoy
8. Military officer: 2 wds.
13. Slow, in music
14. Trevi Fountain locale
15. Brightest star in Cygnus
16. Subsided
17. Noted Virginian
18. Visibility reducer
19. Track and field event
21. Unadorned
22. Hemingway's nickname
26. Textile fiber
28. Seethes
29. Verve
30. Delight in
31. Fair-haired
32. Landed
33. In command of
34. Banquet
35. Volcanic peak
36. Bridge position
37. "The — Hurrah," movie
38. Jet personnel
40. Vaudeville segment

41. Congou or souchong
42. Marina space
45. Predilection
47. Mine entrance
48. Sell directly to the consumer
49. Be heeded by: 4 wds.
52. Roves in search of plunder
53. Apollo's instrument

DOWN

1. "You — There," TV show
2. "Made tracks"
3. Batters' statistics
4. Member of the peerage
5. Cheat on a test
6. In the past
7. Cognomen
8. Like Carroll's Hatter
9. An Astaire
10. Gaynor or Leigh
11. S-shaped molding
12. Set the pace

16. Universe
18. Indistinct
19. Constructs
20. Apply oneself energetically
21. Support enthusiastically
22. Nobel prize category
23. Give the green light to
24. Annoyance: slang
25. Kitty contribution
26. Stream forth
27. Kind of telecast
28. Explosion
31. Feature of Atlantic City
34. Blandishment
38. Composer Franck
39. Proportion
41. Cheerio!: hyph. wd.
42. Scrooge's word
43. Cheese-tray choice
44. Adversary
45. Golf-bag items
46. Folklore creature
48. Bureaucratic tape color
50. Viscous substance
51. Loud outcry or clamor

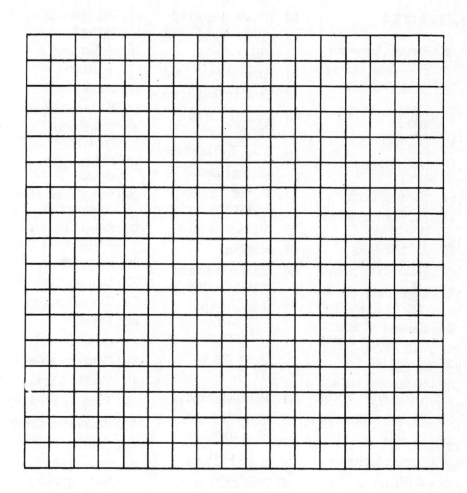

DIAGRAMLESS

EXPERT

**This Diagramless is 17 boxes wide by 17 boxes deep.
Starting box is on page 217**

ACROSS

1. Famous inventor
5. *Et* —, and others
6. Lombardy lake
10. Certain sports arenas
12. I agree!
13. Lox accompaniment
14. "City of Light"
16. Having an obligation to pay
19. Author Jong
20. Exemplary person
21. Legendary marksman and family
24. Release without punishing: 2 wds.
27. Essential
30. Nickname for a Texas city: 2 wds.
33. Without warning
36. Florida city
37. Arabic letter
38. National symbol
39. Dilemma
40. Suit
42. White's — Little
44. Move gradually
45. Additional

46. Wholly absorbed
48. Lively bout: hyph. wd.
51. Airport near 14-A
52. Tintinnabulations
55. Dodgers' Hall of Famer
57. Sing, Swiss style
58. Airport area
61. Bay of Fundy feature
62. Sight at Aspen
63. Noggin
64. Understanding words: 2 wds.
65. Gravitate

DOWN

1. Pointed remark
2. Charles Lamb
3. Parlance
4. Rapidly: 2 wds.
6. Ann or May
7. Bradley of the "brass"
8. Be in line for
9. In a state of readiness: 2 wds. (slang)

11. Playground apparatus
15. Volley
17. — *bene*
18. Maps
22. Pell-mell: hyph. wd.
23. Word with "by" or "pat"
25. College group, for short
26. Polyphonic music composition
28. Sleep like —: 2 wds.
29. Untimely
30. Innocent one
31. Type of holly
32. Freebies
34. Scheme
35. Consternation
41. Shabby: Brit.
43. Biblical weed
47. Earnest requests
49. Canine
50. From time past, as a song
53. Mother of Helen
54. Luge
56. Crumbling
59. Shop window sign
60. Exigency

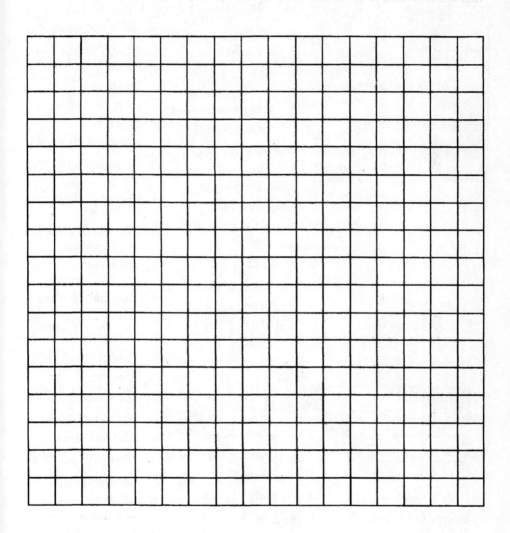

Easy

ACROSS

1. Singer Davis
4. Pests on Fido
9. Boxing punch
12. Big fuss
13. Oven-baked meat
14. Everything
15. "Sawbuck"
16. Your and my
17. Salary boost
19. Take care of
21. "Weeping" tree
22. Paid out (money)
24. Rouses from sleep
25. Magician's scepter
26. Zoo compartments
27. Mail depot: abbr.
29. Mr. Carney
30. Rescues
31. Adriatic, for one
32. Beatles tune, "Let It —"
33. Exceptionally fine
34. TV celebrity
35. Detroit baseballer
36. Lies in wait
37. Supports for broken arms
39. Window glass
40. Big
41. Massage
42. Behave
45. High card
46. Trap
48. Deface
49. Cot or crib
50. Drying cloth
51. Secret agent

DOWN

1. Gym pad
2. Fruit drink
3. Satisfied
4. Opposite of "back"
5. Noisy
6. Corn spike
7. While
8. 3 per baseball out
9. Prisons
10. In addition
11. Tooted (a horn)
18. Pub drinks
20. Conclude
21. Bet
22. Sailor's mop
23. Use a peeling gadget
24. Show indecision
26. Opera cloaks
27. Mountain top
28. Rowing blades
30. Hint
31. Small rivers
33. Warble
34. Source of solar energy
35. Exhausted
36. Tag
37. Thick slice (of bacon)
38. Hankie trim
39. Unpolluted
41. Not cooked
43. Tam or beanie
44. Attempt
47. Negative vote

ACROSS

1. Chess pieces
4. Petty quarrel
8. Musical symbol
12. Crude metal
13. Conceal
14. Rant
15. Unmarried man
17. Single thing
18. — over, fall over suddenly
19. Puzzling thing
21. Cut in half
23. Quote, as a passage
24. Pay attention to
25. Judge's garment
26. Dab of butter
29. Rainbow
30. Kingdom
31. Regret
32. Payable
33. Otherwise
34. Knowledge
35. Tidy
36. Heathen
37. Outcome
40. Couple
41. Sour; tart
42. Cone contents: 2 wds.
46. Coarse, long-napped carpet
47. Cast a ballot
48. Health resort
49. Where the heart is
50. Wide-mouthed pitcher
51. Matching collection

DOWN

1. Out-of-control crowd
2. Noteworthy period
3. String of pearls, for example
4. Word with "metal" or "music"
5. Unpleasant person: slang
6. Fuss; excitement
7. Very bad
8. Uncultured
9. Come ashore
10. Wicked
11. Gala entertainment
16. Will's beneficiary
20. Article
21. Food fish
22. Land of the Incas
23. Seashore
25. Aunt or cousin
26. Improvement
27. Distinctive air
28. Adolescent, for short
30. Fishing gear
34. Den
35. Push gently
36. Harness-racing horse
37. Reckless
38. Reverberated sound
39. Thailand, formerly
40. Singer Seeger
43. Farm animal
44. Mimic
45. Picture border

Medium

Hard

ACROSS

1. Chum
4. Log home
9. Grate against
12. The self
13. Very serious; crucial
14. Anger
15. Sovereignty
17. Cattle marking
19. Intentions
20. Befit
21. Untamed region
23. Wild duck
26. Poker stake
27. Sum
28. Otherwise
29. 24 hours
30. Ore deposits
31. Pool stick
32. Type measure
33. Dug for ore
34. Cooking vessels
35. Unit of loudness; power level
37. Sand hills
38. Singer, Ed —
39. Half a quart
40. Yellow-brown color
42. Model; plan
45. Scale tone
46. Concerning
48. That woman
49. Garden tool
50. Game of chance
51. Small child

DOWN

1. For each
2. In the past
3. Fidelity
4. Makes serene
5. Play sections
6. Purchase
7. That thing
8. Galaxies
9. Lariat
10. Coffee vessel
11. Four-poster, for one
16. Assistant
18. Small brook
20. Glutted
21. Walked in water
22. Silly
23. Ms. Tiegs, for one
24. Highway
25. Frock
27. Musical sounds
30. Generous
31. Competition
33. Marceau is one
34. Kind of football kick
36. Heavy wire rope
37. Likewise
39. Gasp
40. Hard wood
41. Cow sound
42. Kitten, for one
43. Greek letter
44. Fishing aid
47. Negative reply

ACROSS

1. Paper sack
4. Loafer or wing tip
8. Twirl
12. Woman's name
13. Tug
14. Walk the floor
15. Go down
17. Used a cassette
18. Acorn source
19. Lose color
20. "Jaws," for one
23. Baseball score: 2 wds.
26. Small nail
27. Peels
28. Not on your life!
29. President Lincoln's nickname
30. Toils
31. — as a fiddle
32. Smallest State: abbr.
33. Store events
34. Destiny
35. Hits
37. Is concerned
38. Malt drinks
39. Sunbather's reward
40. Caverns
42. Padded footstool
46. Ajar
47. Bottom of 4-Across
48. Payable
49. Fender mishap
50. Wise, old birds
51. Use a towel

DOWN

1. Evil
2. Fruit drink
3. Cooking fuel
4. Talk
5. Large piece
6. Ancient
7. Overhead railway
8. Small shovels
9. Writing sheet
10. Frozen water
11. Actor Beatty
16. Bottle stopper
17. Domesticates
19. Eating utensils
20. Sky twinklers
21. Custom
22. Highest card
23. Rabbits
24. Join together
25. Brief letters
27. Fishing rods
30. Gets up
31. Distant
33. Not speaking
34. Air coolers
36. Black bird
37. Packing boxes
39. High
40. Haddock's kin
41. Large monkey
42. In what way?
43. Strange
44. Mongrel dog
45. Lock opener
47. Very

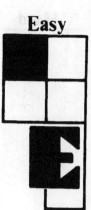

Easy

Medium

ACROSS

1. "— the season ..."
4. Eve's mate
8. Woody plants
13. Family group
17. Drama division
18. — slaw
19. Make cloth
20. Tramp
21. Peekaboo opening
23. Come in
24. Ailments
25. Wharf
26. Hues
28. Glen
30. Rotates
32. Subtle suggestions
33. Bucket
34. Camper's shelter
35. Amusing
36. Odd-jobs worker
40. Cereal grain
41. Loud noises

42. Squander
43. Raw mineral
44. Shields
46. Sections; pieces
47. Italian capital
48. Rodents
49. Groom's partner
50. Sprayed (down) with water
51. Emphasis; accent
54. Loot
55. Bob Hope's specialty
56. Have faith in
57. Hair-care tools
58. Assist
59. Ewes' mates
60. Indian group
61. Attractive
65. Commotion
66. Phone parts
67. Ilks
68. Moving truck
69. Acts
71. Turns towards
72. Look after; take care of
73. Pub brews
74. Blinks
75. Open wounds
76. Replace contents, as a prescription
79. Evergreens
80. Sect
81. Egg-shaped
82. Wed secretly
84. Newspaper caption
88. Broad
89. Bargain events
90. Rowing needs
91. Cut, as grass
92. Snow vehicle
93. Polo or golf
94. Victim
95. Before: poetic

DOWN

1. Spigot
2. Frost, as a cake
3. Enter: 2 wds.
4. Pains
5. Portal
6. Everything
7. Assemblies
8. "Double sawbuck"
9. Leases
10. Dines
11. Actress Arden
12. Household employees
13. Cool
14. Lounge around
15. Capable
16. Inquisitive
22. Half a quart
27. Charming hotels
29. Assistant
30. Halt!
31. Bosc, for one
32. Searches (for)
33. Gluelike stuff
35. Data
36. Robust
37. Elklike animal
38. Bearing weapons
39. Very poor
41. Wild animal
42. Lingers
45. Lock of hair
46. Investigate
47. Frolics
49. Complete flops: slang
50. Grasps
51. Leather fastener
52. Swap
53. Gossip's tale
54. Seethes
55. "Red" coins
57. Stuffs

58. Rabbits' kin
60. Indefatigable
61. Pawnbroker's office: 2 wds. (slang)
62. Beyond working hours
63. Lion's "collar"
64. Concludes

66. Toy baby
67. Rational
70. Was unsuccessful
71. The best
72. Highway fee
74. Windshield cleaner
75. Foamy
76. Arguments

77. Wicked
78. Slowly vanish
79. Horseback game
80. Concern
83. Racing circuit
85. Hearing organ
86. Neither
87. Ram's mate

Hard

ACROSS

1. Cult
5. Pledge
8. Karenina, of novel fame
12. Deceitful maneuver
13. Female sheep
14. Billiards
15. Moscow's country: abbr.
16. Standard for measuring altitude: 2 wds.
18. Witty reply
20. To wit
21. Alaskan city
23. Girl
24. Most inhuman
28. African river
31. Play on words
32. Ingress
34. Knight's title
35. Among
37. Truck driver, for one
39. Chew the —, ponder
41. Sake source
42. Refuge
45. Canal country
49. Muddles
51. Plod
52. Author, — Stanley Gardner
53. Petition
54. Aroma
55. Golf gadgets
56. Spread (grass) to dry
57. Pro —, proportionately

DOWN

1. Urge to action
2. Other
3. Price
4. Actor, Power
5. Papal robe
6. Be in debt
7. Baby: Scot.
8. Tarzan
9. Danielle Steel, e.g.
10. Christmas carol
11. Cohort
17. Fall behind
19. Actor's part
22. Organic compound
24. Auditor: abbr.
25. Eggnog ingredient
26. One-wheeled vehicle
27. Wandered
29. Untruth
30. Go astray
33. Youth organization: abbr.
36. D.C. airport
38. Detector
40. Pair
42. Aid's partner
43. Withered: poetic
44. New wine
46. He played Hawkeye
47. Debatable
48. Taj Mahal site
50. Suitable

ACROSS

1. Brooch
4. Cereal seed
9. Which person?
12. Top card
13. Bring up (children)
14. Concealed
15. Morning moisture
16. Plus; also
17. Similar
19. Jerk; pull
21. Ohio and Utah
22. Golf or tennis
24. Barnyard birds
25. Hog product
26. Explosion
27. — and fro
29. Pen filler
30. Constructed
31. At this moment
32. Football score: abbr.
33. Takes care of
34. Nothing other than
35. Car stopper
36. Planted seeds
37. Whale features
39. Faucets
40. Bath necessity
41. Chum
42. "Loony"
45. Tavern drink
46. Vote in
48. In the past
49. River bottom
50. Types; kinds
51. Mesh trap

DOWN

1. Cushion
2. Frozen water
3. "The Big Apple": 2 wds.
4. Ulysses S. —
5. Official grade
6. Help
7. Exists
8. Tidiest
9. Color of snow
10. Walk a trail
11. Lyric poems
18. Final
20. Noah's boat
21. Shuts tightly
22. Barbecue rod
23. Small lake
24. Move smoothly
26. Shelflike beds
27. Ripped
28. Was indebted to
30. Ringo's group
31. Reporter
33. Factual
34. Wipe up (a floor)
35. Bent low
36. Epsom —
37. Poke with a knife
38. Warsaw native
39. Diplomacy
41. For each
43. Ripen; mature
44. Tiny spot
47. Look!; see!

Easy

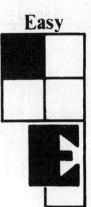

ACROSS

1. Nuisance
5. Noggin
9. Food fish
12. Above
13. "Born Free" lioness
14. Color
15. Roundabout ways
17. Toothed wheels
19. Spinning toys
20. Wise birds
21. Assists
23. Stock agents
26. Currier and —
27. Extinct birds
28. Mr. Jolson
29. Mom's mate
30. Dug for coal
31. River: Spanish
32. Actor Asner
33. Stove clock
34. Sunset direction
35. Tranquilizes
37. Goes white
38. Road grooves
39. Fit
40. Blackboard
42. Self-important person
45. Intention
46. Snout
48. Jacob's twin
49. Pekoe
50. Outbuilding
51. Lease

DOWN

1. Pea holder
2. Genesis woman
3. Made one's home
4. Soldiers
5. That woman's
6. City trains
7. While
8. Blondie's mate
9. Pursue
10. Belonging to us
11. — Moines, Iowa
16. Downs' opposites
18. Large deer
20. Command
21. Conceals
22. Elude
23. Skeletal parts
24. Pay hike
25. Vending machine features
27. Ten-cent pieces
30. Fingerless gloves
31. Let go
33. Tight
34. Actor Matthau
36. Play
37. "Masterpiece Theatre" network: abbr.
39. Mocked
40. Took a chair
41. Fib
42. Employ
43. Jogged
44. Egyptian king, for short
47. Exclamation of surprise

Medium

ANSWERS

PAGE 1

```
S E A   D R A W   N A P A
W A S   E A C H   E D E N
A S P   S W E E T C O R N
T E A S E   D R A T
    R A R E   E N A M E L
C L A T T E R   R U L E
R U G   S L O O P   S S E
A B U T   W R E C K E R
B E S I D E   T R A M
    R E L Y   U P E N D
L I M A B E A N S   L E E
E K E D   C L U E   O R E
G E N E   T E N D   N O D
```

PAGE 2

```
G O L F   P R E S   A P O
E V I L   L I L T   N O W
N E M O   E M B O L D E N
T R A U M A   A M O R
    R A S P   P R O P S
M O I S T U R E   E P E E
U R N   T R O L L   O S E
S A F E   E N D E A V O R
E L A T E   E O N S
    M A M A   R A S C A L
F L O T I L L A   E R I E
I O U   L A I D   N E R O
R N S   E N D O   T E E N
```

PAGE 3

```
L I D   T E N O R   T A P
O R E   A W O K E   I D A
G A S   M E W   M O L E S
    S E E S   L O W E S T
S P E A R   L I V E S
P O R T   C A N E S   H I
A N T   T A N K S   B A D
N E   W O R K S   C A L L
    P A R T Y   C A N O E
S T A I R S   T U B A
W A S T E   F O R   N O D
A P T   N O O S E   A I R
T E E   T R E S S   S L Y
```

PAGE 4

```
B R A D   C B S   M E L T
L I M E   H U T   A R E A
O D E S   A D E   S I N G
B E N I G N   A C C E S S
    G A G   M O O
B L E N D E R   O T H E R
A I R   D O G   A Y E
T E R R Y   D E B A T E D
    H O G   O A R
D E T O U R   L Y R I C S
A C I D   A G O   A D A M
W H E E   S A G   Y O K E
N O D S   S P Y   S L E W
```

PAGE 5

```
T O T   P A N T S   W E D
A I R   E B O N Y   O D E
C L U T T E R   M A R G E
    M E A L   A B I D E D
R E P E L   P L O D S
O V E N   T I T L E   T K
B I T   P A N E S   A H A
E L   P O S E R   S C A R
    D A R T S   C E C I L
P R I N C E   O L E O
L E A S H   A V E N U E S
E E L   E A G E R   N A P
A L S   S T O R K   T R Y
```

PAGE 6

```
S L O T   W A I T   L A W
T O N E   A T N O T I M E
A S E A   T O N   R A I D
B E   H E M   C A R D S
    T A P E R   R A P
T I G E R   B A T   E G G
A M E N   T A N   P L E A
B E D   F A R   L A S T S
    M A P   S I D E S
I D L E D   E N D   O N
N E A R   E V A   L O V E
T A K E O V E R   A D E S
O R E   H E R E   P E R T
```

PAGE 7

```
PIGS  PAR  GARB
LORE  ACE  AVER
ADIT  STAMPEDE
TINS  SIDE  NEE
END  MANY  AGED
RESTING  STEMS
    WET  TOO
STAIN  GERMANS
HINT  PLAT  LET
ARK  IRIS  SPAR
PALISADE  TIRE
EDEN  DER  ANEW
DESK  OSS  BEDS
```

PAGE 8

```
   TEACH  GRASS
  BALBOA  RIGUP
CONSENT  IMAGE
ROT  TETON  PAN
ATAP  SET  PERT
FERAL  RIME
TEABAG  CUSTOM
   LYRA  MOORE
ALSO  IRS  SELL
MOT  STRAW  HOE
INAPT  ABALONE
GENOA  YOKELS
ORDER  STEED
```

PAGE 9

```
AYE  MORE  PINS
VEX  OVAL  ROOK
ASP  NEW  CATTY
   EDEN  ARIA
ANNOY  BLOSSOM
LIST  CRANE  LO
ACE  GLORY  BID
ME  CREAM  SAVE
ORCHARD  HOTEL
   RANK  CANT
STAND  BAR  ERA
LONG  TOSS  RUN
YOKE  OATH  YET
```

PAGE 10

```
NET  ASSAY  SAW
ORE  LEASE  ALI
TRAILED  ATLAS
   DAM  GREASE
HOLLY  WANED
EPEE  SALEM  BE
RAG  OTTER  PAN
EL  SPIES  BEND
   STEER  RINGS
BATONS  FIR
ELOPE  SENDING
EEL  RAKES  DOE
FEE  STYLE  AWL
```

PAGE 11

```
GAP  STOOP  OFF
ALL  TIARA  LIE
SEAPORT  LODGE
   CONE  LADE
SCARE  RECORDS
PARK  DIVER  OH
END  HIDES  CUR
NO  TAKER  CASE
DESIRES  BORED
   HENS  PURR
AROSE  PADDOCK
DAN  SWING  TOE
APE  SENSE  SPY
```

PAGE 12

```
  MOVE  SPOT
DIVINE  SHARON
UNEVEN  HUDDLE
DIRE  TROT  ALE
END  FIAT  DIED
  GOVERN  WINDY
   ELECTOR
MABEL  HOOKUP
OVER  LETS  NUB
DEN  VAST  DONA
UNITED  ERUPTS
SUGARY  RUPEES
ENVY  MEND
```

PAGE 13

```
CLAP   SCREW
PRICE  TRADES
LANES  RAT  SAG
ATE   TWINE  TIE
NEST  APE  BELT
     RARE  PORES
  GRUNT  FOUND
CREST  BEET
HALT  ARE  SAWS
ADA  SLATS  BOO
PET  TON  AROMA
  REMIND  MOVER
   DARES  EDEN
```

PAGE 14

```
BAR  NEAT  SPAN
ICE  ABLE  PANE
DECEMBER  ISNT
  ONES  RINSES
CARDS  JANE
LIDS  TICKTOCK
ADE  LOVES  POI
PERFUMES  PENS
   ALAS  BARES
RESULT  HULA
ERIC  OVERSTEP
NINE  EARS  OWE
TEST  SLOT  REP
```

PAGE 15

```
PAR  PRONE  BAS
ALE  HONOR  ALL
LISSOME  RANEE
  PANE  MALTED
OZONE  BETSY
POND  RADIO  PA
END  LILAC  SUN
NE  GAVEL  PUNT
  BONES  SENSE
ELINOR  UTES
MOTEL  USELESS
UKE  IBSEN  TEE
SIS  NEARS  SAW
```

PAGE 16

```
APE  SPADE  ADD
BIN  WAGON  LAY
ENGRAVE  TWINE
  LANE  LEAK
SPATS  HARDEST
PINE  GATES  TO
END  HIRED  RAN
AT  COVER  HERE
ROTATES  PIPES
  ANTS  BONE
RINSE  POSTAGE
ARK  SKIRT  TEA
YES  TOTES  SET
```

PAGE 17

```
LIT  ALIBI  COG
IDA  TOTEM  LIE
FELLOWS  PSALM
TALONS  DUTY
  TOE  PILE  HE
CLAM  TEASPOON
AIL  IRENE  RED
KEEPSAKE  RIDS
EN  ALMS  WIG
  WRAP  POTION
ALIEN  ARRANGE
CAP  DAVID  ARE
EWE  SLAMS  LED
```

PAGE 18

```
SPITZ  ROMPS
FAERIE  AVAUNT
UNDOES  DELMAR
STAN  TSAR  PRO
SOL  AFAR  SKIP
   SLUG  CHINE
 SPOOL  CLING
GLACE  ROAN
RINK  FOND  WPA
AVA  WRIT  SHAM
SECURE  EMPIRE
PREFER  NOISES
 SAONE  DENTS
```

PAGE 19

```
W A R   H E L P   F E E T
A P E   O V E R   L E A R
S T A M P E D E   A L S O
    S E E N   S E N S E D
S H O E   T H O N G
T A N K S   O R D E R E D
A L E   H A S T E   E A R
R E D R A P E   D R I V E
      E R O D E   A N E W
G R A P E S   L A N D
R A V E   T R U C K E R S
A R E A   L O D E   E A T
B E R T   E Y E S   R Y E
```

PAGE 20

```
E A T   W A G E   T R E E
L I E   A H E M   H A N G
F R E E D O M   D I T T O
    P R E Y   S E N T
S T E A D   N I A G A R A
P R E S   H I L L   N I L
I E   E L E V A T E   N D
E A R   O R E S   W I S E
S T A T I O N   L I N E R
    B I R D   P U N T
R U B L E   D U N G E O N
I S L E   S U N G   R N A
D O E R   C O K E   N O B
```

PAGE 21

```
S P A C E   B O A S T
A L L A N   A G R E E D
P A I N T   C L E A N E D
S I N   H I K E S   S P A
  D E L U D E D   T I E R
      U S E R   C R O N E
C H O R E S   H O U N D S
R A P I D   P A L M
A V I D   B U L L P E N
F E N   M E R L E   V A T
T A I L O R S   C R A V E
  T O O T L E   T I D A L
  N O S E S   S P E L L
```

PAGE 22

```
T I N   S P A T S   A L P
I N A   C A R O L   V E E
E N G R A V E   A G E N T
    O R E   S P O R T S
S H E L F   D E P O T
W E L L   W A V E D   H O
A R K   F I R E D   N O W
N O   S I R E N   P U L L
    P A N E S   G A T E S
S L I N G S   G U N
H I N G E   P O E T E S S
I K E   R E I N S   L E E
N E D   S L E E T   F E W
```

PAGE 23

```
A R E   D A T A   S L A W
R O D   U N I T   H O L E
A B I L E N E   B I B L E
B E T A   O R D E R
      S L Y   R E T A R D
C E A S E   P A L   L I E
U P T O T H E M I N U T E
L E O   T A G   N A M E D
T E M P E R   G E T
      A R M O R   T R E E
A M A S S   H A L Y A R D
F O R T   A I D E   F I G
T O T E   H O E D   T E E
```

PAGE 24

```
L A S H   E S P   B O S S
O L L A   V I A   O V A L
S T A Y C A L M   P E R U
T O P   A D O P T   R I G
      L I E   E O N S
B E H I N D   R O O T E R
I V A N           M E R E
T A L E N T   S H A P E D
    F R E E   C A D
P A T   W A G O N   N O W
A L I T   C A R D G A M E
C O M A   U L E   A S E A
K E E P   P A D   B A N K
```

PAGE 25

```
R I D S   P E W   B E N D
A R I A   A D E   A R E A
P A C T   V I T A L I T Y
T N T   M E T   B L E S S
      A P E D   Y E S
T I T A N   P A L   D A M
I C O N   H I M   P E R U
P E R   B A G   D I C E D
      B A T   S E E R
S E A R S   S E W   E A T
P A R A S I T E   S A L E
A V I D   M A D   A S I A
R E D S   P R Y   P E T S
```

PAGE 26

```
C A T   B R A S S   R O B
O W E   R A D I O   I V E
T E R M I T E   L E V E L
      R O S E   A D V E N T
S T I N K   D R I E R
T R E K   B A R E R   N A
E A R   T U T O R   F I B
M Y   T H R E W   P I N E
      H O U N D   R U R A L
S P O O N S   P O R E
W O U L D   A L A R M E D
A L S   E R R O R   A G E
T E E   R E E D S   N O W
```

PAGE 27

```
P E T A R D   M A R C I A
R A I D E R   A B O A R D
O S   S N U G G L E   O H
U T E   D I A N E   O N E
S E P T   D R U   A M I R
T R I A D S   M A L I C E
      T H E   V I C
S P O O N S   L E G R O S
P O M E   T I U   N O N E
A R E   S A L T S   N A T
S T   A L I K H A N   G O
M I G N O N   E X I L E S
S A I N T S   R E T I R E
```

PAGE 28

```
          M O S T   A P E R
B E E   Y U L E   D I V E
U R N   S T O P   H E E D
T A S T E   W I P E
      E L F   D A R T E D
C A R E F U L   L E A V E
O R E   N O T   P E N
L E A S T   T O R M E N T
T A M P E R   T O E
      A N O N   S N A K E
S P U R   P E R T   N E W
E A S E   E R I E   D Y E
E Y E S   D O O R
```

PAGE 29

```
B U S   T H E Y   W A I T
E S P   H I D E   A U R A
D E A L I N G S   S T O P
      A N T E   P H O N E
S P R I G   D E E M
H O U R   B O U N D A R Y
O L D   R A I N S   T O E
E L I G I B L E   S O D A
      M U S E   T U N E R
G E E S E   D E E R
U R N S   H A R T F O R D
S I T E   A R N O   W O O
T E S T   T E E N   L E G
```

PAGE 30

```
A I M   E M B E R   W E T
C O O   Q U I T E   E L I
E N T R U S T   D R A K E
      H E A T   S T O P
S T E A L   S H A D O W S
H U R L   S L I P   N O T
A T   M A T I N E E   M E
R O B   M A C E   R E A P
P R E P A R E   W A R N S
      S I T E   V A S E
M A I N E   P O L E C A T
O L D   U N I T E   T W O
B E E   R O P E S   S E W
```

```
M A T   F L E A S   O D D
A D E   R I N S E   P A Y
C O M M A N D   T H E R E
    P I N E   S T O N E S
S P E C K   H O L E S
L O S E   M O L E S   B E
A N T   W A T E R   B A D
B Y   H I K E S   W A R D
    M O T E L   P A N S Y
C L O W N S   P A R D
L A D L E   F U R N I S H
A C E   S K I R T   T I E
D E L   S O R R Y   S P Y
```

```
A R C   S O W E D   H I T
S I R   T H E R E   A C E
S P E A R   T R A P P E D
      E W E S   S L A P
R E P E A T S   S L I C K
E M   S M E L L   M E A N
A B E   S W E E P   R U E
C E L L   S E A L S   S A
T R E E S   T R E A T E D
    C E N T   N A M E
D E T R O I T   S E A T S
E V E   O L I V E   C O O
W A D   P L E A D   H E N
```

```
P A C T   S L A M   V O W
E I R E   T A X I   E V E
A M E N D E D   R A G E D
    A D A M   H A V E N S
T I M E D   B E G E T
O D O R   P A L E   A G E
R E F   S L I P S   B O B
E A T   T A T S   S L A B
    O P E N S   D I E T S
H O M E R S   T I E S
E L A T E   M O N S O O N
L E T   O M E N   T U N E
M O O   S E W S   A P E D
```

```
L A D E   A M O S   R O B
I R O N   W I T H   E V E
M E L T   L A T E   S E A
B A L E S   E L   I N K
    R E S E R V E S
L E D   T E E   E A T E N
A R I A   E R E   R E N O
P A S S E   I R E   D D T
    S H I V E R E D
O D E   T O   L A M P S
K I N   H I S S   T O O T
R A T   E C H O   E L S E
A L S   R E E D   D E E P
```

```
B A L M   O F F   S T E M
I S E E   B O O   H I K E
T H E E V E R G L A D E S
      K E Y   A W A S H
S T I L T   F R I L L
W I R Y   P E E R S   P M
A R E   H E A L S   L I E
M E   W E A R Y   K I L N
    M A I L S   A I D E D
O D O R S   O L D
M O U N T M C K I N L E Y
I N R E   O U R   A O N E
T E N D   T E A   P O D S
```

```
S I Z E   A P T   A D M S
A V I S   N E E   R U I N
R A N K   T R A V E R S E
I N C I T E   R O T A T E
    M A L T   L E T
H U M O R O U S   S I L O
E T A   S P R E E   O A R
P E R U   E N T R A N C E
    A N D   S A I D
L A U D E D   B E A D L E
E L D O R A D O   G A I T
A D E N   L O U   I R A N
D A R E   Y E T   O K R A
```

PAGE 37

```
RAY   STEM  SLAY
ADE   TONE  CAPE
WALLETS   PANES
   LIES   SAND
STOOP   POSTERS
TOWN  CANT   DOE
OW   STAGGER  BE
PEW  ORES   OWED
SLANTED   GLASS
   READ   SEEN
CANAL   PLASTER
OVER  DEAR   ERA
BEDS  RAPS   DEN
```

PAGE 38

```
ALL   CART  BRAN
RUE   OLIO  RAFT
EAT   POP  FAITH
AUSTIN   WIND
   WEEKEND   TI
FLAIR   AND  RED
LAWN   PUT  MARE
ACE   VIA  COMMA
WE   CAPITOL
   HOSE  HUDDLE
FRAME   FIR  ROD
OOZE  BANS   ORE
BEET  EDGE   PEN
```

PAGE 39

```
RHODA   CLARA
POOLED  AUGERS
ROUGED  TRENTE
OKRA  RICK   TIE
PSI  LECH  CASK
   MASH  COLTS
 THEWS  CRASS
CHURN   BOAT
ROSE  NORM   CBS
OUT  LOOK  CHOP
AGLEAM  ELAINE
THELMA  RAINED
 TRIAD  SYNOD
```

PAGE 40

```
 SPOT   SWEEP
STONE   PADDLE
LAKES  ODE   AXE
AGE  TAKEN   SPA
PEST  WED  STAR
   OPEN  TEENS
 LANES  BOARD
CADET   SOOT
ODOR  SLY   SAGA
ALP  STASH   WAD
LET  EAT  ORATE
 SENATE  MARES
 DOMES   ENDS
```

PAGE 41

```
HEM   SALAD  PAW
IRA   ENEMY  ABE
PATIENT   NICER
   UNDO  TACKLE
CORNY   TIMES
AWES  HUMID   DC
FED  TONIC   GOO
ED  LINED  SLED
 LACES  CEASE
FRISKY   BLED
LEASE  LAUNDRY
EAR  THERE   EYE
ADS  SIGNS   NET
```

PAGE 42

```
PAN   BEAR  VAST
UDO   ERNE  ERIE
NOSEGAYS   LIZA
   ETES  ERODES
SADAT   ATTU
AVIS  INTERNAL
LIV  EMILS   ORE
EDENTATE   ASTA
   INGA  GHEES
BONSAI   ARAB
AREA  NOSEBAGS
LEON  EPEE   NAP
IONS  STAT   DRY
```

PAGE 43

```
R O B E   S O S   A D D S
O B E Y   N U T   S U I T
S O L E   A T E   S E M I
S E L L E R   R A I S E R
      I S L A N D S
D E E D S   P E S T E R S
O U R   H E R   N E T
C R A S H E R   D A D D Y
    W A R S H I P
S H E E T S   A P P E A R
E A R L   E A R   L A M E
E V I L   L I D   E V E N
P E N S   F L Y   S E N T
```

PAGE 44

```
L A N A   S P A   T I N S
O R E S   K I N   E M I T
F E A S T I N G   M I N I
T A T E R   T E M P T E R
      S O D   L O L A
P U R S U E S   T E T O N
U S A   S O U T H   E N E
B E T T E   P R E S S E D
    T A R T   I R K
V A L I S E S   L I F T S
A B E L   P L A Y R O O M
S L O E   E A R   T U T U
T E N D   E Y E   S L O T
```

PAGE 45

```
S I T E   S H E   S W A P
I R O N   C A N   T R I O
R E N T   O L D   R I D E
      I S L E   T E N E T
S C A R E D   D R A G
L A T E R   W E A K   M E
A G E   P R A W N   P A W
W E   T E A R   S U E D E
    D E N Y   W I N N E R
P L A N T   D A T E
L A N D   G A S   A S I A
O N C E   A R T   S E L L
D E E R   G E E   Y A L E
```

PAGE 46

```
P O D   S T A I R   H E M
A X E   T A S T E   A G E
C E N T E R   A S S I G N
E N T E R   A L T A R
      S L I M Y   G L O B
M A R T I N S   P A I N E
A L E   N C   M U   N E E
S T I N G   T A L L E S T
T O N E   V E R S E
    D A V I D   A N T E S
S T E R E O   A T T A C K
O R E   S L A T E   P H I
P A R   T A L E S   S O D
```

PAGE 47

```
C A S H   E G G   O S L O
A R E A   L O O   S L E W
D I A Z   S O L I T U D E
S A L A M I   D O L M A N
      R E N T   N E B
L A N D L O R D   R E T S
A L E   T R E E D   R I O
D I P S   E N D O R S E S
    A H A   T U L E
S P L A S H   C E L T I C
E L E P H A N T   A I D A
R O S E   S E E   T R O T
E W E S   T E D   E E L S
```

PAGE 48

```
R E D   S E A T S   S E E
I R E   C A R A T   H A M
O R C H E S T R A   A G E
      L A N E   R I D E R
A W A R E   L O T T E R Y
C A R P   W A D E S
E Y E   D O V E R   B A G
    T O N E S   C O L A
E F F E C T S   P O W E R
S L E E T   M A L L
S A T   O B J E C T I V E
A R E   R O U T E   N I L
Y E S   S A G E S   G E M
```

PAGE 49

P	A	T		S	W	A	M		S	L	A	B
A	D	A		W	I	R	E		T	A	L	E
L	O	N	G	E	S	T		D	A	R	E	D
			L	E	E		W	I	N	G		
C	H	E	A	T		W	A	N	D	E	R	S
H	O	L	D		C	A	G	E	S		O	H
A	R	K		S	A	V	E	S		B	A	A
I	S		P	A	V	E	S		H	U	S	K
R	E	L	A	T	E	D		P	A	S	T	E
		I	R	I	S		C	A	R			
W	A	K	E	N		C	A	N	D	L	E	S
O	P	E	N		T	A	P	S		O	A	K
W	E	S	T		O	B	E	Y		W	R	Y

PAGE 50

V	A	T		I	S	L	E		B	A	R	E
I	D	A		D	E	A	N		O	R	A	L
C	O	N	T	E	N	T	S		L	I	N	K
			E	A	S	E		P	E	S	T	S
T	A	M	A	L	E		S	O	R	T		
I	R	I	S		L	E	T	L	O	O	S	E
F	I	N		M	E	L	E	E		T	O	M
F	A	N	T	A	S	I	A		A	L	U	M
		E	R	I	S		L	O	V	E	L	Y
P	O	S	E	D		S	A	M	E			
A	T	O	M		P	O	W	E	R	F	U	L
T	O	T	O		E	L	A	N		A	T	E
H	E	A	R		T	O	Y	S		N	E	D

PAGE 51

R	O	T		M	A	R			H	E	R	
I	R	I	S		E	X	I	T		E	R	E
B	E	E	T		M	E	S	A		A	I	D
			A	W	E		E	L	O	P	E	
	S	A	T	A	N		S	E	W			
L	I	B	E	R	T	Y			E	L	S	E
A	L	E		P	O	E	T	S		O	I	L
G	O	L	D			S	A	I	L	O	R	S
		A	S	S		I	T	E	M	S		
	R	E	M	I	T		L	E	G			
R	I	D		D	O	D	O		A	D	A	M
A	P	E		E	V	E	R		L	A	C	E
P	E	N		E	N	S			Y	E	T	

PAGE 52

	C	R	I	M	P		S	C	E	N	T	
H	O	O	V	E	R		C	A	M	E	R	A
U	R	B	A	N	E		O	Y	S	T	E	R
L	O	O	N		M	O	O	S		T	A	R
A	T	T		F	I	A	T		V	I	S	A
			B	A	S	K		N	O	N	O	S
	S	C	A	R	E		D	E	I	G	N	
C	H	O	R	E		G	I	L	D			
L	I	M	B		F	O	A	L		H	O	W
E	R	R		P	R	A	M		B	E	T	A
A	R	A	B	I	A		O	B	E	R	O	N
T	E	D	I	U	M		N	A	B	B	E	D
	D	E	N	S	E		D	R	E	S	S	

PAGE 53

P	I	G		S	T	A	R		S	A	L	E
A	D	O		T	A	P	E		P	L	A	Y
D	O	G	T	I	R	E	D		R	I	C	E
			E	R	R	S		K	I	T	E	S
S	A	T	E	S		C	H	I	N			
C	I	T	E		R	O	O	S	T	E	R	S
A	D	E		R	A	V	E	S		L	I	E
T	E	R	M	I	T	E	S		L	E	S	T
			O	D	E	S		C	A	V	E	S
S	T	A	L	E			T	U	N	A		
C	A	R	E		N	A	R	R	A	T	E	S
A	L	E	S		E	V	I	L		O	R	E
N	E	A	T		T	A	P	S		R	A	W

PAGE 54

O	F	F		B	W	A	N	A		D	A	W
R	O	E		A	E	R	I	E		A	P	E
B	R	I	S	T	L	E		R	I	N	S	E
			G	O	O	D		L	O	O	T	E	D
C	A	N	O	N		C	A	S	T	E		
L	I	E	N		C	O	C	O	A		B	E
O	L	D		R	E	P	E	L		D	U	D
P	S		M	E	D	E	S		R	I	N	D
		S	O	D	A	S		M	E	S	S	Y
S	K	A	T	E	R		T	I	N	T		
L	A	T	H	E		D	U	G	O	U	T	S
A	T	E		M	O	U	T	H		R	O	T
T	E	D		S	H	O	U	T		B	O	Y

PAGE 55

```
TAP   SCRAP   ADD
EWE   LOOSE   LAY
ALREADY   PHONE
    ACE   SPAN
SPARK   TEETERS
WELL   BEARS   OH
ADA   FALLS   SUE
MA   WALLS   PAGE
PLEASES   WAGER
   ANTS   PIN
WASTE   FASTEST
ADE   NIECE   BEE
GOD   STEER   BEN
```

PAGE 56

```
CHOIR   UPPER
GREASE   REELED
REAR   SUGAR   VA
EAR   MISER   HER
AS   SIDES   LEAN
TEMPTED   SELLS
   EATS   DIAL
SEARS   MIRRORS
TALK   SEVEN   AT
ASS   SPAIN   VIE
IT   ROUND   ROSE
REWARD   EDITED
RENTS   DOMES
```

PAGE 57

```
BLANK   MARNE
CRAVEN   ALIENS
REMOTE   RIPPLE
EVEN   SPIT   TIE
WED   OSLO   CUSP
   WHEY   VENTS
SPRIT   LANES
FOLIO   BUST
ANAT   HINT   SPA
LAC   PINK   STAB
STAMEN   ENTAIL
EATING   REALLY
SEINE   SORES
```

PAGE 58

```
HALF   PEDAL
TOWER   OLIVES
ORATE   LOP   CAT
ASK   TRIPS   TIE
DEEP   ACE   RULE
   LACE   CARES
SLATE   BAKED
SHINE   CANE
TANK   PAN   DASH
APE   SLUGS   DIE
GEM   HAS   ADORN
SALUTE   SORES
NOTED   SEES
```

PAGE 59

```
TAR   FREE   WARM
ODE   LULL   ERIE
POSSIBLE   AIDA
   TONY   GOLDEN
SHRUG   WANT
PAIR   PENCHANT
ARC   TRACE   BAR
RETRIEVE   PUMA
   ELSE   HONEY
TANGLE   MOLD
AVER   NEAREAST
CORE   CARD   NEE
KNOT   ERSE   TAN
```

PAGE 60

```
LAD   SHY   FOG
ORAL   LEE   SAGE
BARE   ERA   TIRE
BEGIN   SHARE
   SOD   TAR
GEM   NEW   MERIT
OVER   ROD   DICE
DATES   NIP   PEN
WAN   SET
PLATE   CARTS
PAIR   VIA   ARID
AGED   ERR   POLE
LED   RED   TON
```

```
P R O           P E P
P I E R S     T A L E S
I N D E E D   P I R A T E
T E E   W O M E N   T A N
  S E T   N A G   G E L
    M O T O R   F A D
      T A R   S A P
      M A P   S I T E S
    P A L   S I N   S I T
N O R   H I R E R   N A P
O L I V E S   W I G G L E
D E N I M     B E L O W
  S E E           T E N
```

```
C A P   P R O U D   S P A
U G H   L A P S E   T I N
B O O   A C T   P L A N T
    E R N E   G O A T E E
C A N O E   M A S S E
A R I D   H A B I T   B E
S I X   F A U L T   P A D
H A   C U R V E   T A N G
    H O R D E   L O D G E
R E A L T Y   M I N D
E A R T H   B A G   O R B
E R R   E P O C H   C O O
F L Y   R I G H T   K E Y
```

```
R O O M E R   C R E D I T
E F F A C E   H A V A N A
A F   T R I B U T E   T N
D I S   U N I T E   B A D
E C H O   E N E   S A K E
R E A P E R   S A C H E M
    D E W     P E A
S T O N E S   C O N M A N
C O W S   H E R   T A M E
H I S   P A G E S   S U E
E L   B E M O A N S   S D
M E D U S A   M A R C E L
E D I S O N   S P O U S E
```

```
H U L A   F R E E   B R E W   S C O W
A T O M   L E A N   R A G E   P O N E
M A P   S E A R C H I N G   B R A C E
S H E L T E R   L O C K   W A I L E D
    O A T   D O C K   P O R T
S H R U G   D U S K   P I O N E E R S
L O A D   B A S E   H A N D S   V A T
A N T   S O F T   W A N T S   P I C A
B E E   L O T   C A R T S   M I L K Y
    F A T   P A G E S   L O P
B E R E T   W I R E S   L I D   A D A
L A U D   C A P E S   F A K E   N A G
U R N   R A K E S   D I M E   H E R E
E N G R A V E S   H E L P   R O W E D
    E V E N   C A F E   B O O
S L I C E S   W A N E   P O S T A G E
W I D E N   S I N G A P O R E   R O D
A M E N   M O L D   T I L E   K I N G
B E A T   A N D Y   S E E S   C A G E
```

```
F A R E   B L A S T   S H E L F   W H E N
A X E L   A U D I O   P U R E E   R I D E
R I N K   S C I N T I L L A T E   I D E A
C O D   B A I T   N I L   L A T E N T
E M E R A L D   W A F T S   N I L E
  Z E S T   T I M E S   C O N T R A S T
E L V E S   C U T E R   V I R G O   T K O
R O O F   C E L T S   C E N T S   L A W
I O U   S A L L Y   P O R C H   P L A T E
E N S E M B L E   T O U G H   D I E S E L
  P O L O   B R I N E   B O L E
A D V I C E   B R U N T   R E W O R D E D
T R A C K   T R A C T   G I A N T   O R E
T A N   C R A C K   S U N N Y   T U N A
I C E   M O I S T   S W I S S   L A B E L
C O S T U M E S   P O I S E   R O L L
  A L P S   G A U G E   M A R K E T S
P U E B L O   E S P   S O R E   P O T
A N I L   S A F E T Y V A L V E   O L E O
S I R E   E R O S E   O R I E L   L A I N
S T E T   R E B E L   W A D D Y   D Y N E
```

```
P E R   D R A W S   S P A
A R E   R E L E T   P E N
R A W H I D E   O C E A N
    O O P S   B R A N
W A R P S   D R A S T I C
I N K S   R O U G H   D O
S I S   C A R N E   H E R
E L   T A C I T   H E A D
R E S I D E S   S I L L S
    O N E S   G U L P
S I R E N   C A P L E S S
A C T   C O U P E   R O T
Y E S   E N T E R   S P Y
```

```
M A S T   P E P   L A T E
A L C O   O A R   A M E S
T U R N   D R E S S E R S
A M I G O S   V I E N N A
      M U G   H E R R
S U P E R M A N   S P A N
I T E   E A R T H   A R E
B E D S   R E S O U R C E
      P A L S   U N A
A T T U N E   A R I S E S
E A R R I N G S   T I R E
R I E N   E O S   E T O N
O L E S   S A T   R E S T
```

```
  P I P   H E M P   V A T
  L A N E   A V E R   I R E
  A I D E   D E L I C A T E
  D R I V E   T O O
    G E A R   R O S E S
  B I N   C O O P   O R E
  I D A   H O A R D   L I E
  D E N   T R I O   I N N
  S A T I N   M O S T
    C Y D   R E A C T
  N O V E L I S T   D I R E
  A D O   O N E S   A R E A
  P E W   N E A P   N E W
```

```
A S H   S P A R   C O R E
R U E   H O P E   A V I D
C E N T E R E D   M E N D
  H O L E   E N E R G Y
S H O A L   P E A R
L O U D   C O M P A C T S
A M S   F A K E S   H O E
T E E T E R E D   D E N T
  H E E D   R O S E S
T H R I L L   F A S T
R O A R   E L E M E N T S
I N K S   S E E P   U K E
M E E T   S I T S   T O W
```

```
      R I G H T
    D E T O U R S
    B E S S   R I O T
  T A C T   S O   D U B
P A R K   B U N   N E T
A N D   G U S   O H A R A
S T   C O M P A R E   N C
T R A C T   E R E   M A O
E U R   A C E   F I R S
  M A D   R T   S A N D
    B O O G   F U N D
    G A U G I N G
    F E A T S
```

```
  S P R E E   G R A I N
T E E O F F   L O I T E R
R A R E   F L O O R   V I
A S K   B E A S T   P A D
D O   D O C K S   J A D E
E N   R O T E   S U G A R
  L A S S   M O D E
C R A F T   T A N G   C B
H U N T   R A N G E   H I
O N E   H O R N S   P A R
I N   S A U T E   T O L D
R E T U R N   R A I S E S
  R O B E D   S H E E T
```

```
P A P A   W A S H
A L I V E   B A L L A D
L I N E R   A S P I R E
  T E N A N T   C E N
    U S E   T E E
A W E   S C A R   S A P
A D E S   T O T   R I D S
H O T   K E P T   E N D
    R O D   L E T
  A G E   R E V I S E
  P A R A D E   E R O D E
  E L A T E D   R E S E W
    A N E W   D O N E
```

```
VAT  MAST  TRAY
ICE  ALTO  HONE
ARE  REEL  ADDS
LEMON  PLUM
     NET  SPELLS
SEVERED  ISAAC
APO   NOT   STA
SEINE  CHARTER
SEDANS  ERA
     MELT  RHONE
ELBE  OISE  VIM
NEAR  ODES  ALI
DIGS  PEAT  LET
```

```
FLOP  PETS  SEA
LOVE  ORAL  TAP
ABEL  TALE  USE
TENTS  SLENDER
    SOME  TEE
ROD  LIDS  ANON
ARISES  TATTLE
MERE  TROD  SET
    END  OWES
FACTORS  SCOPE
ACT  METE  AVID
IRE  EDEN  RANG
LED  SORE  ELSE
```

```
ALP  DOLE  DIDO
RYE  URAL  IRON
END  PROLIXITY
AXIAL  SIN  SOX
    PER  SRO
ANNEXED  EXTRA
PRIX  XII  HEAD
TAXED  ADMIXED
    SAD  SID
AIX  ROI  NEXUS
STRONGBOX  EVA
TEAS  MEDE  REL
AMYS  AXES  OAK
```

```
ONCE  HILL  DOG
DORM  AREA  RTE
DRIBBLE  SKEIN
    EARL  DENISE
LORRE  DORIS
AP  KAREN  TENT
SAW  DECOR  ROY
SLED  GOREN  OK
    DELAY  BERNE
ORDAIN  NEVA
PAINT  TELAVIV
INN  HOAX  DESI
EGG  EXIT  ANTE
```

```
HAZE  RAP  ALMS
EDEN  ICE  TOOL
RAPT  SEASHORE
EMPIRE  HATED
 ERE  CLAN
BALE  SLAPDASH
ELI  GOOSE  MOO
GENEROUS  CEDE
    SEND  SIR
SUITE  FINISH
INDETAIL  ECHO
PILE  IDA  MAUL
STEM  MOW  ANNE
```

```
 TOAST    BURST
PONCHOS  SAGUARO
EATHIGHONTHEHOG
AMI  PARROTS  AWE
LAMP  SORRY  CREE
SNEAK  VIE  COALS
    RILES  HAL
  SCALA  MYSTICS
SHADOW  SIDE  NAT
COPE  GENE  MARE
ARTS  DOVE  BONER
TEA  LOBE  SALUTE
  IMAGINETHAT
SENATE  SLIT  SGT
ANKLE  PEAR  WHOA
WRIT  PLAN  HEAP
TOD  DUOS  ATOLLS
OLDHAND   COOLS
   IVY  STEEP
SMILE  HEE  SEPAL
CANT  HALED  DURO
ADS  BERATED  CIO
DROPINTHEBUCKET
SILENCE  RAPPELS
 DENSE    REARS
```

```
DESI  LIRAS  APISH  LAVA
OVEN  INEPT  DELTA  IDOL
PEACHSTATE  OCEANSTATE
ENTAILED  NANAS  DECREE
       DER    RIN   AMAH
SASHES  GONGS  PIANIST
PROAS  RADIO  SORDS  HUB
EDOM  GOLDENSTATE  MOLE
NON  SOULS  TICS  BOWIE
TRESPASS  COACH  PROMPT
    RAITT  CHINK  SUEDE
WASTES  HAILS  REPASSED
ALTOS  TERM  REPAD  TAR
ROAN  BEAVERSTATE  PATE
POT  NAPPE  OPERA  GATES
FEMALES  CRASS  FRYERS
    IDLE   ARE    RIO
PERSIA  BLIMP  PULSATED
ALOHASTATE  FIRSTSTATE
ULNA  TIBER  GOOSE  TUTU
LEAP  SEARS  SUPER  USES
```

```
    COB    SHIP
    ADA    HATES
    BEGGAR   TART
       PARE    VIA
       BITE   SHOOT
    GRAPE   SHORT
GLARE  OPAL   SHOP
OUT   TRADE    APE
DEED  RARE  RAVEN
    IRATE   HAVEN
    DRAPE   WIPE
    EGG    LIST
    NEED  INSULT
       DATED  ROE
       MOSS   EWE
```

```
        WEAR
        OGRE
      MRROGERS
    TRIAD  OKIE
ADA  IONS   TSAR
DUCKSOUP
DARE  FEB
  LEG  STEAD  SSE
       RTE  ACED
       ROSEMARY
LACE  INKY   RYE
AMOR  GEESE
COUNTESS
  RIOT
  TEES
```

```
          LUG
    SEA  VALERA
CAMELS  ANOINT
AGARIC   MTS
REPUTE   OAT
   MENTOR
     DISC
     NET
      DIG
       COP
       COIL
       IDEALS
     ERN  TEAPOT
     ACE  HAVANA
  SWIRLS  EVENED
  OODLES  RED
  BOO
```

```
  SCRIMP
  OLIVIA     GUARD
  BIGAMY     ELLIE
   SNIT    REMUDA
GAB   CHASE    MER
OLE    RIAS
LILAC  OSLO
DELTA  ULTRA
  NEAT  AGE  TIPS
   PARCH   EDITH
   LOUT    DANAE
   OATH     TIE
GAG  GREED   ADD
ALEUTS   NUMB
LINGO   OREADS
LATHE   SEINES
    ERNEST
```

```
ALPS  HOST   COT
COAT  ANTE   AHA
MACE  TEEN   RIP
ENTER  EN    ROE
   LUCIDITY
LOS  GAD  SWARM
ONUS  BAH  OLEO
BASIS  HIP  LON
   PROPOSAL
SHE   NO   DEPOT
WIN  ALIT  AURA
ADS  TARO  SLAB
TEE  AREA  ELLS
```

205

PAGE 93

```
DAG  SCAB ADES
AGA  TARA WERE
DESSERTS  ASIA
    TEES  FREER
ELDERS  PEER
KEEP  SERA  VAN
ESS  VISOR  IRE
SEC  ANTS  KNEE
   RING  ALEGAR
OPINE  DIOR
ALBA  DESERTED
TEEN  ALMS  AVE
SADE  MISS  MEW
```

PAGE 94

```
TAB  SPANK  TWO
ADA  WAGON  ROW
PERCALE  ONION
    APE  STUB
SHIPS  HOTTEST
CORE  TALES  HA
ORE  HIRED  DAM
US  PARES  TORE
RETIRES  DUNKS
   WEDS  WIN
ARISE  BANANAS
CAN  SHAKE  OIL
EYE  TIDES  WRY
```

PAGE 95

```
CREST  ABATE
SHEATH  MAXIMS
QUIT  OBESE  BI
URN  FRANK  FAD
AC  BLEND  CARE
WHEREAS  MOCKS
  BEAU  SOME
CROSS  SINATRA
HINT  FASTS  ER
ANY  LEFTY  ACE
RG  LEVEE  EDEN
DERIDE  ROWENA
DEBAR  SCENT
```

PAGE 96

```
ALFA  OAT  FATE
SEEN  NTH  ASIA
POETRY  RACKET
   HEX  IRE
ACTED  BLITHE
BRIM  SOLE  ORB
COT  WAXES  MAR
SOL  AVER  MESA
NECTAR  SIREN
  HEN  FUR
RETURN  ABROAD
IRON  AND  OHIO
BANK  HOE  ROME
```

PAGE 97

```
DATA  POKE  SAP
USES  EVIDENCE
STEP  RED  RARE
TO  FIR  TIGER
 NAVAL  FAN
FIXED  BOX  BIG
ISLE  WAX  LANA
THE  LAD  TASTY
  JOY  POWER
SHEET  DRY  IN
PAVE  FEE  RAGE
OVERSEAS  OPUS
TEN  OWNS  BEET
```

PAGE 98

```
TOR  SOBS  RAMP
APE  INEE  ETUI
ASPIRANT  POSE
   USES  THEMES
ROBIN  ELIA
ELLS  GREETING
ALI  WEIRS  DOE
MACHINES  DENT
   ORES  SINES
CRATER  STET
LOGE  APPETITE
ABEL  THUR  FOE
WEDS  EIRE  YES
```

```
NAP  BELT   SHOW
ORE  ARID   LONE
DEPOSIT   DATED
     VEE  DONE
PALES   BATTLER
ODOR  BORES  LA
ROW  LANES  BAG
ER  WATER  MATE
SENATOR  MANES
    EVEN  PAD
LEVER   CAREFOR
EVER  LACE  EWE
TARS  ODES  END
```

```
ASS   SLIP  SPAT
RAT   CODE  ERIE
ALA  AVOW  DOME
BEGONE    CAN
   GAS  SPONGES
EVER  BLOTS  DA
PAR  SEATS  RIG
IS  SWAPS  BETS
CELLARS   SAT
   EAT  STRIPS
SCAT  HAHA  RUT
PAVE  ODOR  ERE
APES  PETS  DEW
```

```
CODA   SPARED
LAPIN  PAROLED
ALIEN  ACADEMY
PLUTOCRAT   VON
PAM  YAKS  TATA
   WIGS  TOTEM
CANINE   TOLEDO
ALONG   BAWL
NAME  BERN  SSS
AMI  SLAPSTICK
DONATES  HANOI
ADAMANT  INERT
ELANDS   PAWN
```

```
GAP  TRAIL  EBB
APE  HORSE  WEE
STADIUM  TREAT
   ACT  STORKS
SHARK  NEEDS
HOSE  WEARS  SO
ALP  FISTS  PAD
DE  PANTS  RENO
  BARKS  TIGER
STORMS  SIN
TRADE  SAGGING
OUR  ROUGH  DUE
WED  SHEET  ANT
```

```
ADS   STAFF  RAH
LEE   CAMEL  AGE
PRESUME   OSCAR
   SALE  SUPERB
SNAIL   DINER
COWL  MINCE  MR
AMS  RANGE  DUE
ME  DESKS  PETE
   PASTA  LAPEL
STUMPS   BAIL
NISEI  REPROOF
ITS  TAILS  RUR
TOY  ENATE  ETA
```

```
SLOPE     AMISS
HOVER    LENTO
ARENAS  WINDOW
PERT  TRI  DINE
END  MOANS  EER
  OLEANDERS
   OL    AT
  CATTLEMEN
PTA  SOARS  ION
EIRE  AMI  DECA
RAPPED  ELECTS
CREES    SLEET
HATES    TESTY
```

207

PAGE 105

```
N I P . P L A T E . S C I
A R E . L A B O R . C O N
P A N C A K E . A P R O N
. . C O N E . A S E A . .
S L I D E . G L E A M E D
T A L E . P I E R S . N O
A M S . B E A R S . A D E
M E . S L A N T . E V E R
P R O T E C T . F E E D S
. . D A N E . K I L N . .
S W O R D . C O N S U M E
H E R . E L T O N . E A R
Y E S . R I S K S . S P A
```

PAGE 106

```
S E E D . C R A M . S L O T . S A F E
C A V E . L A C E . H I D E . T R A Y
A S I S . O V E R T A K E S . R A R E
R E L E A S E . M A R E . T R I B E S
. . R Y E . W A G E . S T E P . . .
G R O V E . T H I S . S T U D E N T S
R I P E . S A I D . S T A B S . E R A
I C E . C A M P . S H A K E . B E E S
P E N N A M E . S C A R E . C O D E S
. . O N E . S L A V E . S O N . . .
S H O T S . S H I N E . H A N D O F F
L I M E . B O A T S . S O L E . V I A
A V A . S L U M S . M A L T . P A S T
P E R S P I R E . B O L D . H A L T S
. . P A S S . T U N E . S I R . . .
C H E A T S . R I T A . A T T E M P T
R O A R . F A I R T R A D E . N E A R
E L S E . U R G E . C L A M . T R I O
W E T S . L E S S . H A M S . S E N T
```

PAGE 108

```
P O P U P . J E T E . F R A Y . E M P T Y
A R O S E . I N O N . L I M E . A U R A E
R O S E P E T A L S . Y O U N G S T E R S
O N T . O U N C E . M I S S T A T E S .
S O O T . T E T . K I N . E A T . S I P S
. F O R A Y . R I N G O . S E W . D I E
G U F F A W . D E T E C T S . D I R E C T
U N I F Y . E U P H R A T E S . T A N K S
N I C E . A X E S . R A M O N . S T U B
S T E E P L E S . L A P W I N G S . S P Y
. S R O . F O V E A . A U K . . .
P E W . O N T A R G E T . S A M P L I N G
A D A M . G A L E A . T A L I . I D O L
J U L I A . G L E N G A R R Y . I S E R E
A C T S U P . A L B O R A K . B A T A A N
M E D . F I B . Y E A T S . P A N E L
A S I A . C R O . R L S . B U D . R I F T
. S C H O O N E R S . T A N G S . S L Y
C I N C I N N A T I . W H I T E W A T E R
A V E R T . C I T E . H A Z E . A L I C E
M A Y A S . O R E S . O W E D . T A C K S
```

PAGE 110

```
T O D A Y . B R O T H . S L O T . S C A M
E R O D E . R A D I O . T I M E . P O L O
A D V A N C E M E N T . A M E N . O N E S
S E E M . R A P S . L E G E N D . U S E S
E R R . H U T S . P I L E . E A S E .
. M U S H . B U N K . C O N T E N T S
T H R U S T . H O L E . V O I C E . S E A
R E A C H . C O O L . T A L L Y . R U N G
A R C H . L O O M . L A S T S . P A S T A
D O E . M U R K . P I P E S . R O C
E N S N A R E . R A K E S . B O O K L E T
. I R E . B I N E S . C O A L . E R A
A D U L T . S E V E N . G O L D . D E A L
C O P E . S P I E L . P O R T . P U R S E
E S P . S C A N T . M I N D . P A S S E S
S E E T H I N G . S O N G . S O R T
. R A Y S . T U N E . T U S K . G O T
O A H U . S A L A M I . D I N S . N O S E
S C A N . O R E S . T O U R D E F O R C E
L I N T . R I F T . O L D E R . O R G A N
O D D S . S A T E . R E E D Y . E M E R Y
```

PAGE 112

```
H A R P O . U R S A . H A R E M . W H A T
A M O R A . N E E R . A L A M O . H A T E
S I D E S A D D L E . D A V E N P O R T S
P E E V E D . D A N A . I N G R A I N S
. E S A . H O R D E . D O E . . .
C H M N . G A B . T O A D Y . L E A S E S
R I O T . I S A R . A D I O S . N A T A L
E R R . B O S T O N R O C K E R . A U T O
S E R V E . T O D O . T U D O R . D E W
T R I A L S . N I N E S . M U T E . I R S
. S T I E S . N E I L S . M A C R O
S E C . E R A T . S N I T S . S A U C E R
I C H . D U P E S . N A I L . L E O N E
R O A N . M I L K I N G S T O O L . U N A
E L I O T . D E E R E . H E R R . S C U D
N E R V E S . G E A R S . D E I . P H I S
. T E T . T E T O N . O W L . . .
S T E E R E R S . S M E E . L I A N A S
T E T E A T E T E S . B U C K E T S E A T
A J A R . H Y D R O . E S C E . C H A R O
T O T O . E S S E N . R E E F . H Y P E S
```

PAGE 114

```
B E D . . . . . . .
A D A M . . . . A H A .
T I R E S . . A L E S .
T E N T . S C A N S . .
. . R A T E S . . P E W
. . R I T A . . T A X I
. M A K E S D O . A L I T
D O V E . H A R E . M E T
L O V E S . M A R R E D
A P E S . . . T I E S
W E D . . T R E E S .
. C A R E S . . T O S S
. A R I D . . S A L T S
. P E P . . . T A I L
. . . . . . . P R Y
```

PAGE 116

```
        A S K S
        S T O W
        P E R U
P E N S   P A N
O V A L S   S T U N G
S T E P I T   T A P
O P E N   D E F E R   M A E
A U N T   P U P   M O T E
T N T   T O R S O   I D O L
      Y O U   I N S T E P
    S L A N T   N E A R S
    H E N     S P E T
    R A K E
    E V E N
    D E E D
```

PAGE 118

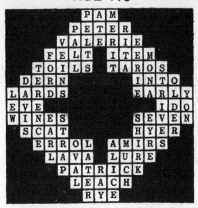

```
          P A M
        P E T E R
      V A L E R I E
      F E L T   I T E M
    T O I L S   T A R O S
    D E R N       I N T O
  L A R D S       E A R L Y
  E V E             I D O
  W I N E S       S E V E N
    S C A T       H Y E R
    E R R O L   A M I R S
      L A V A   L U R E
        P A T R I C K
          L E A C H
            R Y E
```

PAGE 120

```
            J O G
    L A M   A W A S H
    I S A A C N E W T O N
    D E L L A   K A U A I
    S A L O N   G R I N
      S U N G   I V E S
B I B   D E R M A   S E R A
A D A M   R O A D   T I C K
N E N E   Y O D E L   I N O N
G A I N   M A L I   A T L I
    S T A R   S T A V E   S O T
    H O N E   S E R B
    R I C H   S A L A D
    S T A I D   O T A R U
    A L F R E D N O B E L
      L I A N A   S A Y
        B E Y
```

PAGE 122

```
C L A M   S P U D   S H O E   S L A W
H O L E   C A R E   H O W L   T A M E
A V A   C A R N A T I O N   T O T E S
R E S T O R E   L I N K   S I L E N T
      A R E   R I C E   P U R E
S L I C K   W I N K   R E P E N T E D
L A R K   B A N G   D A T E S   R A Y
A D O   B A S K   H I K E R   W I S E
T E N   R I P   R I V E R   D O M E S
      M A T   L I N E S   F A N
F L O O D   H U N T S   B A R   A C E
L O A M   W A R D S   B A R E   T O N
E A R   H I R E S   P A G E   H O O D
A N S W E R E D   D O T S   R O M P S
      A L E S   L E S S   C O O
S T R I P S   D U E T   H O S T E S S
H A U L S   S E C R E T A R Y   D U E
E L S E   H U L K   R O L E   O G R E
D E E D   O N L Y   S E T S   F E E D
```

PAGE 124

```
T O R A H   H E L P   A B B E
A L O N E   O B O E   P L U S
B L U E R I B B O N   P U N T
S A T   M O O S   D E L E T E
      B I N S   C A L E B
A D U L T S   P I N K S L I P
B O N U S   T E N T S   O D E
E L I E   B O N E S   B O E R
L E S B R O W N   P E D A L
      E O N S   G R A S S L E
B I B L E   B O I S E
O R A L   B R O W N S T O N E
N A B   L A R A S   M A N
A Q U A M A R I N E   G A T O
      N A M E S   A R R O W
S E T T L E R   W A N E
T R A I T   W H I T E C A P
U R N S   C A R O L   N O L O
N O G   A R I A S   F I R M S
G R E E N E R Y   F I N E S T
      R A N D Y   R I N G
M A I T A I   C O N E   S E C
A R N E   B L A C K S M I T H
S E E R   L A R K   S A N T A
T A S S   E S P Y   E D G E D
```

PAGE 126

```
F E T E   S A T U P   F I B E R   R O T A
O R A N   A G A N A   A N I L E   E R O S
L I F E G U A R D S   T R A F F I C C O P
D E T R A C T S   S A T E S   O N E A L S
        G L E E   M O V E D   T U E S
P E R I L S   S A V I N   P I N E S F O R
A L O E S   S U T E S   S E N D S   I V A
L I D S   P A T R O L M A N   O R E G
M O E   S L A V S   O I L Y   T H E R E
S T O C K A D E   S T O L E   C R A F T S
    C H I M E   P H A S E   M A O R I
S A L U T E   A L O N E   C O R T E G E S
A T O M S   S C O W   B R O T H   H R H
M O W S   P H Y S I C I A N   S T A Y
A N N   H A R E S   D O R M S   T H E S E
R E S H A P E D   P E N D S   S H A R E R
    A R T E   M A S T S   H U O N
S E A M E N   M E S T A   R A I N T R E E
P A R A M E D I C S   C O A S T G U A R D
E V I L   S I N C E   T A S T E   N I L E
W E D S   S M E A R   S T E E D   G L E N
```

PAGE 128

```
ROME  EDICT  EATS  MAMAS
ABIE  MASER  XRAY  IMAGE
CELLOPHANE  CORNFLAKES
ESE  PISA  ALEUT  ALTERS
RESTER  CASALS  VIII
  OREL  PUT  ECOLE  TRA
ACCRA  IBERIA  ALUM  RAW
SHUN  SNARE  STS  RETAKE
TAB  MOONY  STRIKE  AMES
ERE  ILL  SERENE  LIP
ROSES  ESCALATOR  ELOPE
TAT  UPHILL  OME  LAW
USER  EMAILS  TESTS  IVE
PLANED  RTE  HELEN  ONER
OAK  NICE  DROPIN  SLEDS
NPS  ETUDE  ARE  ECCE
  TRIP  LENSES  ARGOTS
OSWEGO  AMIDE  OKRA  HOC
RAISINBRAN  MIMEOGRAPH
CARTE  INNS  ATALL  TRIM
AREAS  ZEST  NESTS  SACO
```

PAGE 130

```
        BEG
       BORED
      QUARTER
     CURT  STEP
    PLANS   REAP
   BEARS  STADIUM
  SLANT  CHIC  DREW
  PAN  SHEET  SEA
 ABUT  LADS  POUTS
  STREETS  TONES
   SAVE  TRIED
    PETS  RUNS
     RETRACT
      DEUCE
       TEE
```

PAGE 132

```
ADD
GOES      SAP  MET
OVAL      ERE  AGE
 ELIMINATE   TOE
   PACE  SLAT
    PEW  SCENT
    SET  ERIE
ANT  ROW  SPA
DARE  MAD
SPARS  SEW
 IRIS  TEAM
TON  DIVERSION
AWE  ERA  SPIN
RED  DEN  SANE
          LET
```

PAGE 134

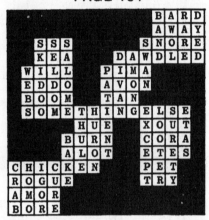

```
              BARD
              AWAY
  SSS        SNORE
  KEA      DAWDLED
WILL    PIMA
EDDO    AVON
BOOM    TAN
SOMETHINGELSE
     HUE   XOUT
    BURN   CORA
    ALOT   ETES
CHICKEN   PET
ROGUE     TRY
AMOR
BORE
```

PAGE 136

```
    WORTH
    OMAHA  FEZ
   BRAZEN  EMIT
   FRENZY  DUPE
PODIA      SCAM
FLEET      OPA
CATS   LEAP  DOC
 FATAL  OLGA  FETE
  CAPITOLHILL
BACH  SEAN  ALOOF
OVA   EDGY  COLA
WIT        HURON
LACK       ASSET
 TAIL   TUMULT
 ELLA  CAVORT
  LOG  AREAS
      REATA
```

PAGE 138

```
HIVE  SWEET  BEGAN  ROTS
ONES  PHASE  ADORE  EVIL
LOST  HASTE  RISKS  SAME
ENTIRELY  NORTH  TAILED
  MORE  FADES  LESS
ESCAPE  WAGON  FIGHTERS
STATE  HIKER  BAGGY  RAP
SOME  PAPER  BATHS  RAVE
ALE  BORED  RESET  RISEN
YELLOWER  VOLTS  DEPEND
  OWES  BIBLE  CAFE
SLOWER  MONEY  RELENTED
LOPED  WINES  BONER  ORE
EVER  MANES  COATS  CONE
PER  RIDES  THUDS  SOLID
TRAVELER  CHATS  RINSES
  OILS  SOARS  LENT
BIKINI  STUNT  DESSERTS
USED  OSCAR  EVADE  NOON
FLEE  NEARS  RANGE  TUNA
FEND  SENSE  STEED  STEP
```

```
POOR              PAIN
CORNER            LISTEN
ON  EDIT      TANK   WE
ADD  SOIL    FAKE  PEA
TERM  TROT  SOLE  CAST
ROAD  ERA  TEE  DART
  PIES  DICES  RISK
   NEED  LOW  NAME
   PARDON  AONE
      EARNEST
    PLAY  EXPECT
   TEAM  ACT  SAIL
  DRAG  BITES  NEAR
 DEER  LAD  NUT  SPOT
PANE  FIRE  DIRT  SOON
ART  MANE  TARS  TOE
IN  RACE  PIER  TO
RESIDE     MAIDEN
DOME         TOAD
```

```
CLAP  SIGHS  AMISS  SCOT
OILY  CREEL  COROT  COLA
OMAR  HENNA  QUOTE  RAIN
PASADENA  CHURN  EPILOG
   MIME  SKEIN  DRAM
STRIDE  INERT  GOALPOST
CREDO  PRONE  RUNGS  RIO
RUSS  FAIRS  SEINE  ABET
ARI  GORSE  AMPLE  ALIVE
MONOLITH  PLEAT  SLATES
   NOSY  RALLY  LAIR
ASSIST  HELOT  BOHEMIAN
TACOS  SEAMY  ELGIN  ODE
LION  EPICS  SQUAB  KNOW
ANN  SPURT  SPURN  TRIBE
STEROIDS  ECLAT  BRACER
   OATS  TRAIL  GOAT
SERAPH  LEARN  SURMISED
ADAM  ETONS  TEPID  OOZE
WINE  TERSE  ETUDE  NORA
STIR  STEER  RARER  STAR
```

```
COLD  BAST  DOFF  FANG
OGEE  RULER  AHEAD  IRON
PROFLIGATE  CONCERTINA
TENTACLE  SIR  DEFENDER
  NUKE  STLO  DANE
UPPERS  HELENA  MESCAL
BURSA  MACES  CREE  SOME
ONOS  JESTS  TROY  NEE
ACT  POSTS  MOOSE  CANER
THATAWAY  CONSERVATORY
  GULL  COLAS  ATLI
PROFESSIONAL  CONTESSA
RANTS  ABNER  GAUDY  SUB
IDI  LIVY  SORTA  DESI
MISS  CASE  CERES  BRUIN
POTATO  XERXES  SEERED
  USSR  VATS  ROWS
EMANATES  ABU  COLISEUM
CONTRABAND  PROPAGANDA
HONE  REVUE  LITER  GOON
ODER  COBS  EGER  ESSE
```

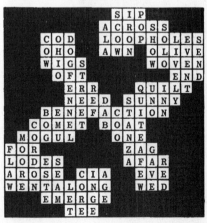

```
  TOY   SAW
  ADE   HUE    RAP
  RESPOND   ADAM
    LOT    COMET
 PARROT  CUE  PRO
 ABOUT  MASS  ERE
 WEBS  CODE  CRY
   IT  AVE  PA
 PIN  FRET  ORAL
WAN  WEED  STARE
AND  ADD  FASTED
STEMS   WIN
 SEAT  FINGERS
 DYE  APE  YOU
    RED  EBB
```

```
  PEG     LET
  MALE    OARS
 PURSES  STRIPS
HASTE  TOP  SEATS
ANTS  CODES  DRIP
TEE  WARDENS  ERA
  RAISE  DOTED
   PST    RAW
  PEELS  STIES
USE  REENTER  TOY
MERE  SIRED  DONE
PAIRS  NAP  WANES
 MOROSE  SLATES
  DOLE   ODES
  ROW    WED
```

```
          SIP
         ACROSS
COD    LOOPHOLES
OHO    AWN  OLIVE
WIGS        WOVEN
 OFT         END
   ERR    QUILT
   NEED  SUNNY
 BENEFACTION
 COMET  BOAT
MOGUL   ONE
FOR      ZAG
LODES    AFAR
AROSE  CIA  EVE
WENTALONG  WED
  EMERGE
   TEE
```

PAGE 152

```
        S O T O L
        I B E R I A
G O T O P I E C E S
O W E N S   M A S H
  A L E C           C B S
  T E T E           B R I C K
    T H O M A S     R E R A N
      V I S A S   C A S T L E
G E O R G E B E R N A R D S H A W
R A P I E R   A G A M A
A T O L L       E P A C T S
D E L L S         K H A N
  N E E           P O L E
      A T E C   B O L O S
      P I T C H A T E N T
        T E T H E R
        S A O N E
```

PAGE 154

```
P A D   D W A R F   B O A
A G E   R O D E O   E L L
T O P   E V E   R A T E S
      E L S E   R E N T
C A N E S   S I S T E R S
R I D E   H A S T E   A T
A D S   C O V E S   P I E
N E   T A M E S   V I S E
E S C A P E D   R A C E R
      A R T S   P A N T
S A N T A   R A N   U S E
O L D   I C I N G   R A Y
S L Y   N O O S E   E W E
```

PAGE 155

```
O N E   P L A Y S   P O T
M A D   R I S E N   A R E
A S   A I M S   O I L E D
R H O N D A   S O R E
  V O T E   R E P O R T S
S I Z E   H A V E N   E L
O L E   P A V E D   N N E
A L   R A C E R   B O N D
R E M A R K S   N I N E
    A I D S   D E T E S T
H E L L O   D O V E   S I
A W E   N O I S E   E E L
Y E S   S N E E R   M E T
```

PAGE 156

```
F E D   F O I L   A I R S
O W E   O N C E   T R U E
R E F E R E E S   T O N E
      E A T S   S W I N G S
C L A S S   W E A R
H A T E   L I N G E R E D
A C E   H A R E S   E V A
R E D E E M E D   P A I L
      A R E S   M A P L E
P A R S O N   W A S P
E X I T   T W I S T E R S
E L S E   E A S T   A I L
P E E R   D Y E S   R O Y
```

PAGE 157

```
S T A G E         R O A S T
T H R O N E   H I N D E R
A I M   D A V I D   E R E
R N     G I N       V A
E G O   S L A T E   R E D
  S T O N E   S M E A R
    H U E       M A D
    P E T A L   S Y R I A
B A R   K E E P S   O D E
O R     F E E       M A
N E T   A T L A S   S I R
E N E R G Y   R E T U R N
S T A T E       T O N E S
```

PAGE 158

```
H O P E   S T I R   P A C E   G R O W
O V A L   C A M E   U P O N   R U L E
L E T   C O M P L E T E D   P A N E L
E N S N A R E   E A T S   P I S T O L
      A G E   M A R Y   H E L P
S W I P E   T O S S   D E P O S I T S
L I D S   L O S E   C R E P T   R A H
O N E   P O U T   D A I L Y   R O P E
T E A   O U R   H A R E S   W A N E D
      H O D   T A R T S   F O G
C L E A R   S O L E S   M A R   O W L
R I N G   W A N T S   P O L E   P I E
A N D   R A V E S   D O L L   M A S S
M E S S A G E S   H E R E   B A L E S
      I C E D   L A S T   B A D
S T A R E S   D A L E   S E L E C T S
L I M E S   D E C O R A T E D   L I T
E D E N   L O N E   T R O T   H U L A
D E N S   A N T S   S E W S   O B E Y
```

PAGE 160

```
HAY   ROMA   ARAB
ALE   ADAM   RIDE
MATADOR   TEPEE
    CAR   CANE
SANER   ROMANCE
AGES   HARES   AL
GET   LACES   SKI
AN   RAVES   POET
STRIKER   RINSE
    EVEN   FAN
PANES   RATTLER
EVER   PACE   ORE
PAWS   SHED   WAD
```

PAGE 161

```
        TIM   STEP
BUD   ADO   TAKE
ONE   NET   AMEN
SING   SHINE
STYLE   END   TAR
    AWARD   GENE
BORDER   ISLAND
ERIE   IDAHO
GEM   FAR   YODEL
    VISIT   MOVE
STAR   VOW   VIA
PASS   EGO   ELK
ABET   RAN
```

PAGE 162

```
GRAD   TEN   LAMP   DIRT
LOBE   FARE   IDEA   TENORS
OVEN   APARTMENT   RENTAL
WE   TIME   VEE   IRIS   ADO
   RICE   WED   GLEAM   STEP
CHASE   GAS   PRINT   JEERS
HUNT   BIG   CLINT   BEE
EGG   WIN   FRAME   BLANKET
WEEDED   BRINE   BRAN   IVY
   IT   CREEK   BEANS   NIP
FLAP   CLEAR   DRANK   IDLE
LAG   BLEAK   BEARD   AL
ONE   LEAD   MONKS   SILVER
WESTERN   MOOSE   MUD   EVE
   ASK   HOUSE   RAM   HEEL
COOKS   ROOST   CUP   PERRY
LURE   TENSE   GUM   GEMS
ANN   AIDE   BAR   SLAM   AD
SCARCE   SATELLITE   ISLE
SETTER   TREE   EVEN   NAME
SEED   YEAR   DEM   GLAD
```

PAGE 164

```
SOS   CRAMS   WED
ARE   ROBOT   ALE
PEA   APE   RAISE
   SAVE   FASTER
SPITE   TANKS
HIDE   WINGS   HI
ONE   RANGE   FAD
WE   CENTS   FILL
   LOVES   PASTE
SHAVES   PATH
PETER   CAP   IDA
IRE   SAUCE   NUN
NOR   ENTER   GET
```

PAGE 165

```
CALMS   STAFF
OXEYE   MURALS
BLANC   INITIAL
SEPARATED   PLO
   EVER   OPUS
PASTE   SEDATE
CAROL   MINER
ARROYO   PUNTS
RIOT   VAIL
TAG   DINGALING
SHAVING   TIROL
SNIVEL   EVADE
TEASE   DENSE
```

PAGE 166

```
CAT       SHE
RACES     STILL
APIECE   HOARSE
WED   ARIA   NEED
   STARTED
WADE   SEES   TAG
EDITS   PEACE
BED   PEAS   ABEL
   PARTNER
SOLO   REAM   PIG
ERASES   PIRATE
WANED   TIGER
LES      GEM
```

PAGE 167

```
L I A R   S N O W   L I P
A C R E   L E N A   O R E
C O R D   E X E R T I O N
E N E   B E T     I N N S
    S L A P   F O R
L A T E R   P I R A T E S
A R E A   A I R   D O V E
W E D D I N G   B E R E T
    E N D   M U S T
S E E R     A I M   O F F
T R E S P A S S   W I L L
A I L   E D I T   A S I A
Y E S   R O S Y   S E P T
```

PAGE 168

```
W O R D   H O S T   D E N
O V E R   A U T O   A G E
L A N E   S T A R   R O W
F L O A T   W R E C K
    M E R I T   A N T S
T A B   N U T   G R E A T
A R R E S T   R U S S I A
L E A V E   C U E   S L Y
L A C E   G U E S S
    E N T E R   T H E M E
O W L   R E D S   A R I D
D O E   I S L E   R I C E
D O T   M E E T   K E E N
```

PAGE 169

```
S A D   H A L V E   A S H
O L E   O L E A N   B E A
S A M U R A I   C O O T S
    E N D S   T H R U S H
T R A D E   D E A L T
R E N O   D O N N Y   S R
I N S   D I V O T   G E E
M T   P A C E R   B A L L
    D I M E S   R A L L Y
S T R E S S   W A L L
H O U S E   D I C K E N S
E G G   L O O S E   R E O
D A S   S H E E R   Y E W
```

PAGE 170

```
M A T H   A T L A S   A R I D   C R A M
O L E O   C R A W L   P O R E S   H U G E
N I N E   C A S E I N P O I N T   A N E W
T K O   W E D S   P E L T S   R A N T S
H E R O I N E   C O V E S   R A N C H
    O P T   M O V E S   W O N D E R E D
S H A P E   S A N E R   B E A D   O N E
L A B S   P A P E R   W I L D S   M U S T
A L E   F I L L Y   H I L L S   V O G U E
P E T P E E V E   H O N K S   T E T H E R
    R I C E   W O R D S   C A N T
M A R I N E   H A R D Y   C A R T O O N S
A G E N T   P O S S E   H O L D S   H U E
S I F T   H A S T E   H O L L Y   N I N A
E L L   A N T E   S A N T A   B O O S T
R E E L E C T S   F E T E S   L I E
    C O N K S   S O R T S   C O N S E N T
S T U D S   S T A G E   S H A D   T A R
M A I N   A L L A M E R I C A N   F U M E
A G O G   W E A V E   A R O S E   I D E A
P A N E   O W E D   S E W E D   T E S T
```

PAGE 172

```
T U F T S   P A S T E   F R A S   E R S T
A V A S T   I R W I N   I O N A   L E A H
P E T E R O T O O L E   D A N N Y K A Y E
A S T E R   D O T   B E D   D O O M E D
    S T A R   N E W E L   D A D   S R A
R E J E C T O R   D I D   C O L E S
E R A   H O B O S   L E M O N   L A P E L
A R C H   R E C A L L   S N A G   G A L E
D O K E   R A D I I   T A L U S   U S E
E L L I O T T   I B A D   N D A K   L E S
    E L D E R   E R M A S   O C E A N
A R M   O L E S   A B I E   C O L L E C T
R A M   R I D E S   E R A T O   P E W E E
E N O S   A F R O   N Y L O N S   M C D
A G N E S   O I L E D   S O N I C   A I D
    S C A R F   D I M   S O L E M N L Y
R O N   O L D   T A X E D   R E L Y
A V A N T I   D O M   L E T   N A S A L
J A M E S C A A N   R O B E R T D O N A T
A T E N   E I R E   A D R E M   O R T H O
S E R E   S L E D   D Y A N S   N E A R S
```

PAGE 174

```
              Y E S
M E T   T A X I
A D O   O M I T     S E E
P I N T   R E S T   M A Y
  T E R S E       G A V E
  S A T A N     R A R E
      P A P E R   P E S T
        R E T I R E S
    D E E R   P A R I S
  L A W S     M I D A S
R A T E       L E G A L
A T E   P A S S   E V I L
W E D   C A P E     O N E
    A N E W     R E D
    P E R
```

214

PAGE 176

```
L I S P
O D O R       S P A S
T O D O       T R I O
  L A P     P O O L S
    S O R R O W S   B I B
      S E E P     R A C E
  S C R E A M   C A R E D
D A R E   L A D   A G E D
L I V E D   T E S T E D
A N E W   B U N K
W E D   S H O R T E R
    S T A R E   P A W
    H E R E     T I E S
    E W E S     I S L E
              C E D E
```

PAGE 178

```
            A R A B
          C A R A V A N
  M A J O R G E N E R A L
  A D A G I O     R O M E
  D E N E B     W A N E D
    L E E     F O G
  M E E T     B A R E   P A P A
F L A X       B O I L S   E L A N
L I K E       B L O N D   A L I T
O V E R   F E A S T     C O N E
W E S T   L A S T     C R E W
        A C T     T E A
  B E R T H     T A S T E
  A D I T     R E T A I L
  H A V E T H E E A R O F
  M A R A U D S
    L Y R E
```

PAGE 180

```
B E L L
A L I I         C O M O
R I N K S       A M E N
B A G E L       P A R I S
    O W I N G   E R I C A
    I D O L       T E L L S
    L E T O F F     V I T A L
B I G D   A B R U P T   O C A L A
A L I F     E A G L E   K N O T
B E F I T   S T U A R T   E D G E
E X T R A     E N R A P T
  S E T T O     O R L Y
    T O L L S   R E E S E
    Y O D E L     A P R O N
    T I D E       S L O P E
    H E A D         I S E E
                    T E N D
```

PAGE 182

```
M A C     F L E A S     J A B
A D O     R O A S T     A L L
T E N     O U R   R A I S E
    T E N D   W I L L O W
S P E N T   W A K E S
W A N D   C A G E S     P O
A R T   S A V E S     S E A
B E   S U P E R     S T A R
    T I G E R   L U R K S
S L I N G S   P A N E
L A R G E   R U B     A C T
A C E   S N A R E     M A R
B E D   T O W E L     S P Y
```

PAGE 183

```
M E N     S P A T     C L E F
O R E     H I D E     R A V E
B A C H E L O R     U N I T
    K E E L   R I D D L E
S P L I T   C I T E
H E A R   R O B E     P A T
A R C   R E A L M     R U E
D U E   E L S E     L O R E
    N E A T   P A G A N
R E S U L T   P A I R
A C I D   I C E C R E A M
S H A G   V O T E     S P A
H O M E   E W E R     S E T
```

PAGE 184

```
P A L     C A B I N     R U B
E G O     A C U T E     I R E
R O Y A L T Y     B R A N D
    A I M S     S U I T
W I L D S   M A L L A R D
A N T E   T O T A L     O R
D A Y   L O D E S     C U E
E N   M I N E D     P O T S
D E C I B E L     D U N E S
    A M E S   P I N T
A M B E R   P A T T E R N
S O L   A N E N T     S H E
H O E   L O T T O     T O T
```

PAGE 185

B	A	G		S	H	O	E		S	P	I	N
A	D	A		P	U	L	L		P	A	C	E
D	E	S	C	E	N	D		T	A	P	E	D
		O	A	K		F	A	D	E			
S	H	A	R	K		H	O	M	E	R	U	N
T	A	C	K		P	A	R	E	S		N	O
A	B	E		W	O	R	K	S		F	I	T
R	I		S	A	L	E	S		F	A	T	E
S	T	R	I	K	E	S		C	A	R	E	S
		A	L	E	S		T	A	N			
C	A	V	E	S		H	A	S	S	O	C	K
O	P	E	N		S	O	L	E		D	U	E
D	E	N	T		O	W	L	S		D	R	Y

PAGE 186

T	I	S		A	D	A	M		T	R	E	E	S		C	L	A	N
A	C	T		C	O	L	E		W	E	A	V	E		H	O	B	O
P	E	E	P	H	O	L	E		E	N	T	E	R		I	L	L	S
		P	I	E	R		T	I	N	T	S		V	A	L	L	E	Y
S	P	I	N	S		H	I	N	T	S		P	A	I	L			
T	E	N	T		F	U	N	N	Y		H	A	N	D	Y	M	A	N
O	A	T		B	A	N	G	S		W	A	S	T	E		O	R	E
P	R	O	T	E	C	T	S		P	A	R	T	S		R	O	M	E
			R	A	T	S		B	R	I	D	E		H	O	S	E	D
S	T	R	E	S	S		B	O	O	T	Y		C	O	M	E	D	Y
T	R	U	S	T		C	O	M	B	S		H	E	L	P			
R	A	M	S		T	R	I	B	E		H	A	N	D	S	O	M	E
A	D	O		D	I	A	L	S		S	O	R	T	S		V	A	N
P	E	R	F	O	R	M	S		F	A	C	E	S		T	E	N	D
			A	L	E	S		W	I	N	K	S		S	O	R	E	S
R	E	F	I	L	L		P	I	N	E	S		C	U	L	T		
O	V	A	L		E	L	O	P	E		H	E	A	D	L	I	N	E
W	I	D	E		S	A	L	E	S		O	A	R	S		M	O	W
S	L	E	D		S	P	O	R	T		P	R	E	Y		E	R	E

PAGE 188

S	E	C	T		V	O	W		A	N	N	A
P	L	O	Y		E	W	E		P	O	O	L
U	S	S	R		S	E	A	L	E	V	E	L
R	E	T	O	R	T		N	A	M	E	L	Y
			N	O	M	E		G	A	L		
C	R	U	E	L	E	S	T		N	I	L	E
P	U	N		E	N	T	R	Y		S	I	R
A	M	I	D		T	E	A	M	S	T	E	R
		C	U	D		R	I	C	E			
A	S	Y	L	U	M		P	A	N	A	M	A
B	E	C	L	O	U	D	S		S	L	O	G
E	R	L	E		S	U	E		O	D	O	R
T	E	E	S		T	E	D		R	A	T	A

PAGE 189

P	I	N		G	R	A	I	N		W	H	O
A	C	E		R	A	I	S	E		H	I	D
D	E	W		A	N	D		A	L	I	K	E
		Y	A	N	K		S	T	A	T	E	S
S	P	O	R	T		G	E	E	S	E		
P	O	R	K		B	L	A	S	T		T	O
I	N	K		B	U	I	L	T		N	O	W
T	D		T	E	N	D	S		M	E	R	E
		B	R	A	K	E		S	O	W	E	D
S	P	O	U	T	S		T	A	P	S		
T	O	W	E	L		P	A	L		M	A	D
A	L	E		E	L	E	C	T		A	G	O
B	E	D		S	O	R	T	S		N	E	T

PAGE 190

P	E	S	T		H	E	A	D		C	O	D
O	V	E	R		E	L	S	A		H	U	E
D	E	T	O	U	R	S		G	E	A	R	S
		T	O	P	S		O	W	L	S		
H	E	L	P	S		B	R	O	K	E	R	S
I	V	E	S		D	O	D	O	S		A	L
D	A	D		M	I	N	E	D		R	I	O
E	D		T	I	M	E	R		W	E	S	T
S	E	D	A	T	E	S		P	A	L	E	S
		R	U	T	S		A	B	L	E		
S	L	A	T	E		U	P	S	T	A	R	T
A	I	M		N	O	S	E		E	S	A	U
T	E	A		S	H	E	D		R	E	N	T

DIAGRAMLESS STARTING BOXES

Page 86 diagramless begins in the 9th box across.
Page 88 diagramless begins in the 11th box across.
Page 90 diagramless begins in the 4th box across.
Page 116 diagramless begins in the 10th box across.
Page 118 diagramless begins in the 7th box across.
Page 120 diagramless begins in the 8th box across.
Page 132 diagramless begins in the 1st box across.
Page 134 diagramless begins in the 12th box across.
Page 136 diagramless begins in the 7th box across.
Page 148 diagramless begins in the 4th box across.
Page 150 diagramless begins in the 10th box across.
Page 152 diagramless begins in the 7th box across.
Page 176 diagramless begins in the 3rd box across.
Page 178 diagramless begins in the 10th box across.
Page 180 diagramless begins in the 1st box across.